ALL
ELEVATIONS
UNKNOWN

ALL

ELEVATIONS

UNKNOWN

An Adventure in the Heart of Borneo

SAM LIGHTNER, JR.

BROADWAY BOOKS   NEW YORK

BROADWAY

Designed by Lisa Sloane
Maps designed by David Cain

The Library of Congress has cataloged the hardcover edition as follows:
Lightner, Sam, 1967–
All elevations unknown: an adventure in the heart of Borneo /
Sam Lightner, Jr.
p.   cm.
Includes bibliographical references.
1. Borneo—Description and travel. 2. World War, 1939–1945—Borneo.
3. Mountaineering—Borneo. I. Title.
DS646.312 .L54   2001
915.98'30439—dc21
00-069915

ISBN 0-7679-0775-2

This book is dedicated to
the men who fought World War II
on the island of Borneo.

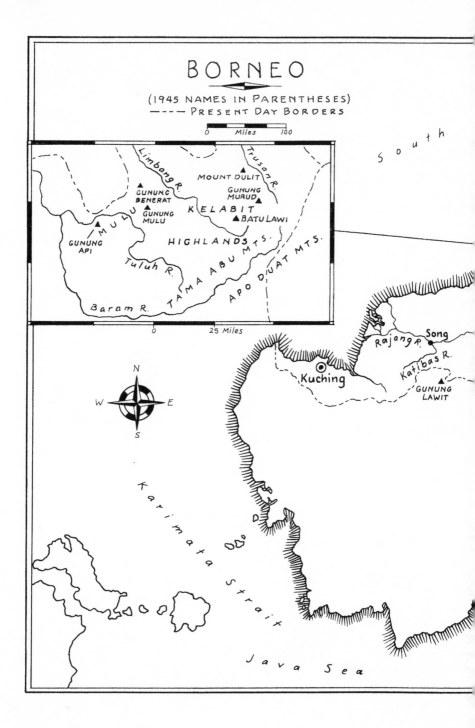

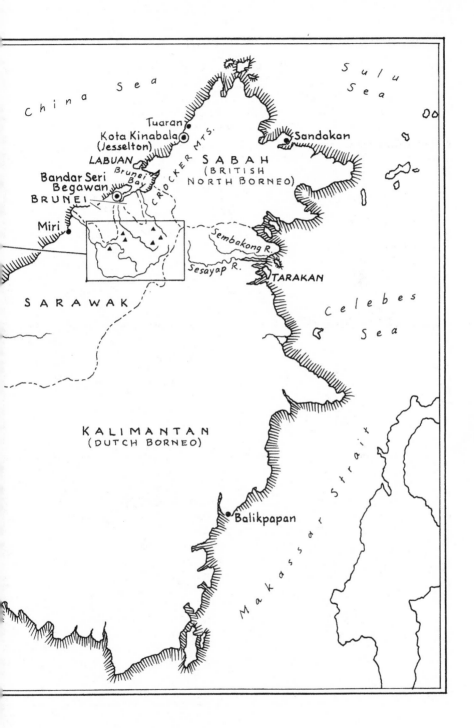

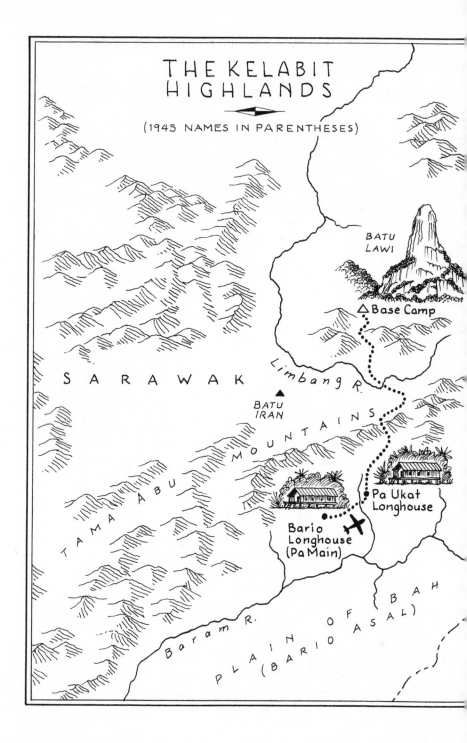

THE KELABIT HIGHLANDS

(1945 NAMES IN PARENTHESES)

BATU LAWI

△ Base Camp

SARAWAK

Limbang R.

BATU IRAN

TAMA ABU MOUNTAINS

Pa Ukat Longhouse

Bario Longhouse (Pa Main)

Baram R.

PLAIN OF BAH (BARIO ASAL)

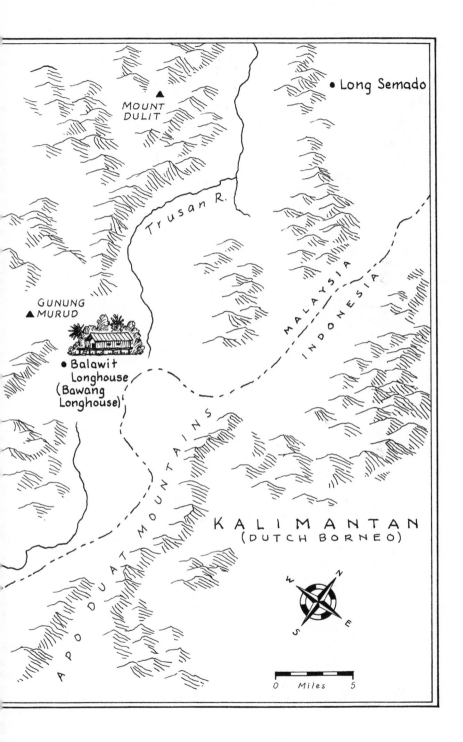

MOUNT
DULIT

Long Semado

Trusan R.

GUNUNG
MURUD

MALAYSIA

INDONESIA

Balawit
Longhouse
(Bawang
Longhouse)

KALIMANTAN
(DUTCH BORNEO)

APODUAT MOUNTAINS

0   Miles   5

Contents

Author's Note

THIS BOOK CAPTURES a number of the major splits in my personality. It is about a bunch of dirtbag climbers traveling through a remote and little understood land. It is also the story of one of the more colorful personalities to ever inhabit that land, and the people who welcomed him there. It is an adventure-travel story and a history book. However, true scholars and avid history buffs may be bothered with the way the history is told, and my approach to the subject deserves some attention.

My principal source of information on the Semut Campaign and the operations following Flight 200 was Tom Harrisson's biographical account of that time. His book, *World Within*, is a wonderful read for both historians and armchair travelers. I also used the memoirs of Sgt. Keith Barrie, who was one of the seven original men to drop into the Kelabit Highlands with Major Harrisson (at the time of this writing he was one of three men of the group still alive and the only one I managed to track down). Mr. Barrie was assigned to a post west of the Highlands and thus did not serve the entire campaign with Harrisson, so he gave a different perspective on the mission and a different window into Harrisson as a character. He had originally written his own memoirs for publication, but for reasons unbeknownst to me that has not happened. He passed them on without ever meeting me, and for that I am grateful. Just before I finished this manuscript, another book by Judith Heimann (see bibliography) came out, and it too served as a reference for much of the WWII information. Additional sources were the conversations I had with the Kelabit, Iban, Berewan, and other tribesmen who fought the war. When I first began speaking with them I did not intend to write a book on their experiences, so I never took down their names or made any notes. Much of the history that unfolds in *All Elevations Unknown* comes from their recollections and stories. To say the least, I owe a great deal to all of these men. The WWII history of Borneo is their story, not mine, and I appreciate their help. To them I say, I only wish I could give all of you the personal credit you deserve.

I was not there in 1945, but I have tried to recreate how it all took place by gathering together various pieces of military information, the locations of various battles, information on the soldiers fighting the battles, and the approach these countries took to the war. An absolutely perfect rendition of this history does not, as far as I know, exist. Nevertheless, I wrote this book from a very intimate perspective. After reading their accounts, talking with men who were there, and getting as much of a feel as I could for the personalities involved, I created dialogue. The dialogue is fictional. No one knows exactly what Harrisson said to the man working the radio on May 1, 1945, at 10:00 A.M., but based upon the way the war was fought, the way these men seemed to conduct themselves, and the way these events transpired, I have made an educated guess. And obviously, I have guessed at people's thoughts and motivations as well. Although it is not pure history, it comes close. Similarly, if I could have ascertained the details of who had done what, I would have given them credit by name. For the most part that particular information is lost in time. Nevertheless, the battles, the dates, and the major events that transpired are not made up. As best as I can figure, this is how it all happened, though the people involved might have talked of it differently or gone about it in a slightly different manner.

Finally, I should point out that I changed the names of a few people. Their real names aren't necessary and it may be that they would not want the fame that comes with being mentioned in a book.

ALL
ELEVATIONS
UNKNOWN

PROLOGUE

March 25, 1945

AMAT WAS RETRIEVING HIS BUFFALO from the paddy when he heard again, in the far distance, the sound. The sky was clearing for the first time in days, but Amat hadn't noticed until he'd looked to the sound. This same noise, a deep hum like the long bellow of a buffalo, had come from the clouds on many of the previous days, and numerous tribesmen had heard it, but no one in the longhouse could determine the source. Just as before, the sound was heard for a short while, then it disappeared. Amat shook his head at the strangeness of it, then went on about his work.

Amat's only buffalo had wallowed in the deepest part of the old and unused rice paddy, and as usual it had gotten stuck. The animal didn't need much of a tug to come free as it was capable of getting out of the mud on its own power, but without Amat's prodding it would sit there for no telling how long. For Amat the water buffalo was an integral part of life. When the buffalo wasn't pulling a plow, it tilled the soil, aerated the ground with its hooves, and of course spread around lots of fertilizer. Amat and the other members of his tribe, the Kelabit, could live without buffalo, but it would be a much harder life, with a lot more work and not nearly as much rice. The behavior of the buffalo, stupid and lazy, was a nuisance, but working with these animals was as necessary a part of life as planting and harvesting.

It had rained the previous night, and for many days before, so the paddy dikes were soggy and slippery. Amat balanced on a firm spot and pulled on the buffalo's leash, a thick rattan cord that ran across the muddy water and through the buffalo's nose, but the animal just craned its head a bit and let out a loud snort. Amat knew from experience that the buffalo didn't want to come all the way across the paddy, so he moved to the other side, closer to the animal and into the vines and bamboo that marked the edge of cultivated land and the beginning of the forest. He tugged again at the leash, its rough texture giving him a good grip despite the mud and slime. The buffalo let out a bellow, then made a few more grunts and took a few straining steps toward the edge of the paddy. Water and mud streamed off the animal's round gut, and Amat could see that a few leeches had found a nice breakfast on its neck. In a few more pulls the animal would be out of the paddy and they could get down to the planned task of the day.

At just over six feet tall, Amat was average sized for a Kelabit, and like the rest of his tribe a lifetime of hunting in the forest and working as a farmer had given him a powerful physique. His bronze skin sat tightly against a muscular frame as he tugged at the animal, and his toes dug into the paddy dike to keep him from tumbling into the muddy water.

For weeks Amat had been wanting to plant in the older paddy, but there just hadn't been time. He and his wife had been harvesting rice from their other two paddies and helping other families from the longhouse do the same. With that harvest complete, the time had come to close one of those paddies and start work in this one, but it would take a while to get it ready for planting.

Amat pulled the buffalo out of the water and then looked out over the paddy, contemplating where to begin. This paddy had produced rice before, but when the rice grew weak and produced a smaller yield, he had switched to the second paddy. Growing rice had always been done this way by the Kelabit. His father, his grandfather, and everyone before had moved from paddy to paddy, keeping the buffalo in the unused areas while letting freshwater from the mountains circulate through the mud. Somehow, in a way that Amat never truly understood, rotating the crops between paddies kept the rice yield high. If they didn't move from paddy to paddy, the rice would eventually cease growing altogether. His family was very fortunate as they had three paddies; he could keep two working and leave one for the buffalo, and always have a good supply of rice. It was a good system, and far more efficient than that of the other tribes who lived below the Kelabit Highlands. He had heard that each year they were forced to clear a new section of jungle to create a new paddy. That was an enormous amount of work, and none of the Kelabit envied their lives.

Amat was about to flick a leech from the stupid animal's neck when he heard the sound again. This was very odd. The Kelabit people had been hearing it for days, but never twice in one morning. Now, in just a short while, the sound had returned. It started out near Batu Lawi, the mountain that watched over all the Kelabit people and kept them safe from the fire god, Gunung Api, and the powerful lowland tribes like the Iban. Perhaps Batu Lawi was angry, or perhaps, being a sentinel for the Highlands, it was trying to warn the Kelabit of some impending danger. This strange sound had been the main topic of conversation during evening meals; the entire longhouse, the building that served as a home and gathering center for his tribe, had been chatting about it, and there was some concern as to what could make such a noise. The Tuai Rumah, the chief of all the longhouses, had been consulted on the matter. He too had heard it, but had no answers. To be on the safe side, the heavy mahogany log ladders into the longhouses had been pulled up in the evenings, and all the men had carried their blowguns and quivers of poison darts to work each day. There had been some discussion that the noise was coming from angry spirits, so each man also carried a piece of white cloth, as the pure color would tell the spirits that the tribe meant no harm. Now, for the fourth day, the noise had returned, and as on previous days it quickly grew louder. It was a deep droning, very low, like the bellow of a large male buffalo but with a rhythm like the hiss of cicadae. Amat turned toward the sound, toward the

rising sun and Gunung Murud, the largest mountain in the Highlands. The humming grew steadily louder, much louder than the
days before, but still he could see nothing but the silver and gray of
the morning clouds. Before, the loudest sound from the sky came
from the flapping wings of a hornbill, but that was nothing compared
to this hum. It overwhelmed all other noises.

Amat stared intently at the sky as the sound approached him,
moving over the ridge where the Ukat begins flowing, and toward Pa
Main, the largest longhouse on the Plain of Bah. It seemed to pass
right above him, louder than anything he'd ever heard, and then the
sound moved out toward the middle of the plain. Suddenly it was
there, emerging from a break in the clouds and plainly visible against
the pale blue sky—an enormous bird, much bigger than a great hornbill, flying very fast without flapping its wings. The bird made a big
arc, turned, changed direction, and flew straight back toward Amat.
He thought to run, but where could he go to get away from such a
beast? He stood his ground and watched closely, knowing he would
have to relate everything he saw to the people of the longhouse and
the *penghulu*. Then the bird dropped something. It fell rapidly but
suddenly grew very large, with a shape similar to that of the seed-
pods from the biggest trees, and slowed in its descent. Three more
objects quickly dropped and changed to a similar shape. The bird
then flew into the clouds as the seedlike things it had dropped slowly
descended to the ground.

Amat let go of the water buffalo's leash, picked up his blowgun,
and began trotting toward Pa Main. Not only was he eager to tell the
tribe that he had seen the source of the sound, but the dropped object could be very dangerous for his people. He ran fast along the
paddy dike, always watching a few feet in front to be sure no cobras
lay basking on the trail, but also feeling in his quiver bottle to make
sure that plenty of darts were available. Though he also carried a
white cloth to alert the spirits that he meant no harm, he wanted a
full supply of blowgun darts handy in case this thing didn't accept
the peace offering.

Amat arrived back at the longhouse to find the tribe gathering in front of the main door. The *penghulu* stood on the veranda and shouted down to Amat to stay at the longhouse and not return to the area where the objects had fallen. Three Kelabit men had already been sent and they would soon report back on what they had found.

It would be a long time before Amat planted rice in the old paddy again.

CHAPTER 1

Fall 1998

F OR SOME REASON which I will never bother to ascertain,
European phones make different noises when you call them
compared to American phones. I sat in my office and listened
as bleeps and honks came over the Atlantic in pairs, waiting for my
German friend Volker to pick up his end. It was seven o'clock in the
evening at my home in Wyoming, but some ungodly hour in
Germany, so Volk was taking a while to answer. I had important
news that couldn't wait, and since he is a doctor he would have to
answer the phone. For all he knew I might be a sick person needing
a bleeding or something. Suddenly the honks stopped.

"What?" He said in a startled tone.

"You can't answer the phone that way," I replied. "How do you
know I don't have a bratwurst stuck in my larynx or something?"

"I know because if this were a medical emergency, my handy
would be ringing." He paused long enough for me to remember that
a "handy" is what people in civilized countries call a cellular phone.
"Only you call me at three A.M. on this number."

"Well, you should be more polite," I responded. "Project Misty
Mountain has just cleared its biggest hurdle."

"You found *The Tower*?"

"Yes I did," I replied. "Now suck up to me for a bit or I won't
tell you where the thing is."

Volker Schoeffl and I had originally met while on independent climbing trips to the coastal rock spires of Pha Nga Bay in southern Thailand. Volker had been there a month before my climbing partner, Mark Newcomb, and I arrived. He had established a number of climbs on the steep limestone pinnacles with his brother Gerd and another German mountaineer named Frank Dicker, but had just sent Gerd home with a medical emergency. While they were climbing a three-hundred-foot vertical wall on a remote island, a small stalactite had detached seventy feet above Gerd and speared him through the kneecap. Volker was only in his first year of medical school, but even Germans have the education to realize that a twelve-pound chunk of limestone through the femur is a bit of a handicap, so he shipped Gerd off to be pieced back together, minus the extra geology, in Frankfurt. Mark and I stumbled onto him and Frank just days afterward, and we all wound up climbing together for the next few weeks. Meanwhile, orthopedic surgeons, clean linen, and probably a geologist helped Gerd to recover nicely, and I was later introduced to him while visiting Volk in Germany. The three of us have since traveled across the US and Europe, through South Africa, Zimbabwe, Laos, and the Philippines, all in a quest for good rock climbing in places that were exotic and unexplored by most of the world's climbers. Our shared passion for the sport of rock climbing, and the exploration of countries whose names we can't correctly spell, had made the late-night phone calls excusable, if not expected.

"So where is the mountain?" Volk was now decidedly more energetic. He went on, "Wait, are you still in Malaysia?"

"No, I'm back in Wyoming," I said. "Now go get a map." He dropped the phone and went off searching. I could hear this and that being thrown around as he cursed in German, and it occurred to me how amazing it was that Volker could slip back and forth between languages. He spoke English fluently, which was a good thing since my German was barely sufficient for ordering a beer. When we were off traveling together he made a constant game of correcting me in my mother tongue. It is embarrassing to have a foreigner correct you in your own language, but it was something I had to get used to when socializing with an overachieving German.

Volker had been somewhat of a child prodigy on the twelve-string guitar, and he and Gerd, who was a pianist, used to entertain at parties by playing their instruments in classical duets. They were eleven and nine years old at the time. Volker gave up the guitar but went on to medical school and got his degree, with honors, in the standard amount of time. The difference between him and his peers was that during his Western education he spent a year studying in Sri Lanka and China, surviving a nasty civil war and a bout with malaria and getting a degree in the Eastern art of acupuncture. He simultaneously received his doctorate in medicine in Germany, then went on to do an internship in an emergency room in Johannesburg, South Africa. These days he is a doctor at a sports-medicine clinic in Bavaria, nationally ranked in sport climbing, and an odd glint in many a beautiful woman's eye.

"I found a map of Malaysia and Borneo," he said when he returned to the phone, "but it's not very detailed."

"Then you won't find our mountain on there," I said. "To be honest, I haven't been able to locate it on any map yet, but I'm pretty sure I know where it is. Just look for Brunei, then look south to the Malaysian border. Right there is the Mulu region, where Gunung Benerat is. Just south of that, on the Indonesian border, are the Kelabit Highlands. The peak is one of the higher elevation points somewhere in there."

"How do you know?" he asked. "And how big is it?" He was mumbling in a way that told me he was actually focusing on the map.

"No two maps give the same altitude, but it's big enough that the Kelabit, the locals, have legends about it," I replied. We knew from experience that this was a good sign. Every major geologic anomaly, from Devils Tower in Wyoming to Mount Everest in Tibet, is the focus of legend by its local inhabitants. Volker and I had discussed this fact on numerous trips and eventually decided that there was a general mountaineering rule that could be applied: anything the locals have designated worthy of worship, a climber will, too (though services will generally be held in a different manner).

Volker and I, like so many of our peers, had been completely enamored with the sport of rock climbing since our first attempts at it in childhood. We had both grown up in the mountains and as a result had all the basics of the sport down by the time we were out of high school. As eighteen-year-olds, newly blessed with the freedom to decide what to do with our lives, we each made it a priority to visit all of the world's best and most popular climbing areas. Places like Yosemite, Canyonlands in southeastern Utah, southern France, and northern Greece had all been featured on our quests, and to date we had decided that the best climbing could be found in southern Thailand and central Germany. However, we had not seen everything. Not by a long shot. And so the search continued.

Though climbing has always been the guiding light on our excursions, the process of travel itself has become a strong rival. In an effort to alleviate the hateful spells of boredom that settled in on the days when we needed to rest from climbing, we began to travel to places where the culture, the history, and the natural beauty of an area were themselves our rest-day entertainment. Eventually this evolved into a kind of objective-oriented climbing trip. Reflecting on those trips, one might easily confuse our exploring with a masochistic desire to get lost, sick, or shot in the developing world. But those are the costs associated with exploring, just as tendinitis and fatigue are the costs of difficult climbing, and had we not endured those pains we would certainly not have seen so many of the world's wonders.

For example, if we wanted to see a city or place, such as the Forbidden City in China or the Kruger Game Preserve in South Africa, we'd page through geologic atlases and old travel guides in an effort to find photographs of interesting rock formations. In some cases, as with our trip to Cambodia, the idea that we just *might* go climbing drew us to the ruins of Angkor Wat, an eleven-hundred-year-old temple complex that is one of mankind's greatest architectural achievements. This approach to the sport of climbing had given us the opportunity to ride camels in the Sahara, trek the high plateaus of Xinjiang (Sinkiang) in western China, and even scuba dive deepwater reefs in the Indian Ocean. It had also opened our eyes to some of Earth's wildest geologic formations, the most striking being a phallic-shaped spire we had come across in an old French atlas. The caption beneath the black-and-white photo merely read "Mount Lawit, Borneo." Shrouded in wisps of water vapor, the sides of the spire were perfectly sheer, its summit barely piercing a ceiling of clouds. The mountain's height, location, rock type, and even the angle of the ridge that had faced the photographer could not be ascertained from the grainy photo, but it was a wild-looking peak that called to us like a Siren. With one glimpse, Volker and I decided that even though further research was called for, we would someday climb the shadowy tower. To keep it a secret from our climbing peers who might get their own ideas about the mountain should they hear us speak of it, we code-named our search Project Misty Mountain.

"As best as I can figure," I continued, "the peak is in the most remote part of the Kelabit Highlands. I don't think you could get any farther from civilization without working for NASA." I could hear him rummaging around, paging through a book, trying to find a map that would reveal the peak's location. At this point I had done far more research on the mountain than Volk and had all of the same maps, so I knew he wasn't going to find it. I could almost feel his frustration through the phone line. Finally I said, "You're gonna have to accept that it isn't on a map."

"Fine," Volker responded. "But is there something I can read about this mountain that will tell me what you seem to know? I'd love to talk about it all night, but I just got off a twenty-four-hour emergency room shift and I'm absolutely smashed."

"I've found only one book, but you're going to have a hard time locating it," I replied. "It's called *World Within*, and it's about this British guy named Tom Harrisson. The last printing was in 1958, as far as I can tell." I paused a moment to flip through a few of the first pages, dropping the phone in the process, then dropping the book and losing my page when I stooped to retrieve the phone. "Apparently, this guy Harrisson was dropped near the mountain during World War II. I've only just begun reading the book, but it appears that there are some large peaks in the Highlands."

"So why do you think we should assume the mountain is there?" Volker asked.

"Well," I began, "for a couple of reasons. The first is that we've looked everywhere else and there are no mountain ranges left in Borneo. The second is that there is a description of a peak in *World Within* that sounds similar to what we saw in that photo. I also remember just getting an impression from people, when I was in Malaysia, that the Kelabit Highlands was our place. I think this has to be it." There was a pause, and I could almost see the synapses firing in Volker's mind.

"I'm going to try to find some sources on these Kelabit Highlands in the morning. Let's talk in the afternoon," Volk said.

"Okay," I agreed, and hung up the phone.

I felt bad for Volker. I knew he wanted to learn every tidbit of information about the mountain, but there was no way I could go into all the details that made me realize we had found the peak. I had now made three trips to Borneo that involved climbing and general exploring, and on each of them I had asked people about the mysterious mountain. On the first trip I had wanted to explore a region where the peak Gunung Lawit, the name given to our spire in the old French atlas, was said to be. I had flown into the town of Kuching, then caught a boat up the Rajang River. The Rajang is enormous, big enough to let oceangoing container ships sail through its delta to gather millions of tons of hardwood timber. In places it is almost a mile wide. Twenty years ago the water flowed as clear as any mountain stream in Wyoming, but the rains that feed it are now washing away large amounts of soil as logging tears away the trees that hold the earth in place. I traveled up the Rajang as far as Song, a one-street town so small that a one-legged penguin could walk its perimeter in five minutes and see a few things twice. I spent a day there watching a wedding, then watching the bride and groom cruise back and forth on the town's hundred-yard-long street in a Daihatsu minicar. The next day I left with a guide, moving up the clear waters of the Katibas, a tributary of the Rajang that flowed out of the untrammeled slopes of the Malaysian/Indonesian border. It was there that Gunung Lawit lay, and I spent a week or so approaching its base only to discover once I got close that it was not our Misty Mountain. The French geographer had misnamed our spire in the atlas.

I returned to Borneo the following year with a friend, this time traveling in the northern province of Sabah. While there we climbed Gunung Kinabalu, a 13,450-foot peak that reaches its summit less than fifty miles from the island's north coast. Kinabalu is a relatively young granite mountain, perhaps only a few million years old, and though it rises steeply and has some enormous walls to its credit, it was not as stately or proud as the mist-shrouded spire in the photograph. A trail complete with ladders and marked signs runs all the way to its crest, and there are guest houses to stay in along the way. My friend and I spent a few days climbing near the summit, then retreated out of the intense tropical sun that frequently traded places with monsoon downpours and visited an orangutan rehabilitation center. We never found the spire.

I had all but given up, although the mountain remained in the back of my mind on my third trip when I went to Mulu National Park to investigate the climbing prospects of another mountain, Gunung Benerat. Benerat had never been climbed, and after numerous days in the jungle I found what I thought was its most promising line of ascent. Numerous parties had attempted to ascend the mountain by way of its lowest angle slopes, all failing miserably and running from Mulu's jungle in fear of snakes, disease, and horrible swarms of ground hornets. They most likely had good reason to run, but it sounded to me as if they had approached the mountain from the wrong direction. I reasoned that Volker and I would want to climb the mountain via its steepest possible line, avoiding the jungle and the karst limestone slots that crisscrossed the peak like crevasses in a Himalayan glacier. While I was there I described the Misty Mountain to my guide, Jacob, a local from a nearby village who had spent much of his life traipsing through the jungles of northern Borneo. He thought he knew what peak I was talking about and directed my search toward the Kelabit Highlands and a lone tower that stood above the headwaters of the Limbang River. He said that the locals called the mountain Batu Lawi, and that it held some religious significance for them. He, like just about everyone else, had never been there or seen it up close, but had heard descriptions of the mountain that were very similar to mine.

I trekked out of the Mulu region with a nasty intestinal parasite, a waistline that held nine fewer pounds than when I'd entered five days before, and possibly two mountains to climb in Borneo. Upon returning home I immediately began researching the Kelabit Highlands in an effort to find the "Misty Mountain," while at the same time jumping over the hurdles that lay between us and Gunung Benerat. Because Benerat was in a national park we would need special permission to climb it, and that meant writing to the Malaysian government. I sent in all the requests and filled out various forms, but was turned down with little or no explanation. Volker then tried to gain permission since we suspected that my American passport was the root of the problem. On this planet you either like Americans or you don't; there is no in-between. However, the German request was also denied, again with no explanation.

Just a few weeks prior to my call to Volker, the father of a friend of mine, who through a ranking position at Interpol had developed some interesting military connections, intervened and began working on obtaining permission for us to climb Benerat. I had been going about it all wrong, believing my eyes and ears when it came to the ways of the world. My friend's father explained to me that the people who claim authority by election, civil war, or bloodless coup don't ever really hold the real power in their country; generally speaking, in every nation from Indonesia to the United States, it is the lifelong bureaucrats and military generals who actually make the decisions that affect daily life. He knew many of those people, and with a week's time and the slipping of a few American dollars into the appropriate pockets, we had permission to climb Gunung

Benerat. Unfortunately, the buffoonish figureheads who appear to run things, such as the vice president of the United States, do have the ability to throw wrenches into the day-to-day business of your average nation. At a gala dinner in the Malaysian capital of Kuala Lumpur, held just a week after I was granted permission to climb Benerat, Al Gore insulted the prime minister of Malaysia on national TV in a way that would have made Don Rickles blush. With that, all "special favors" for Americans were rescinded, and the prime minister himself slammed the door on our climb.

During that time, however, I had continued my search for the Misty Mountain. As I did research in old atlases and travelogues, I began finding references to *World Within* and managed to track down a copy through my local used book store, whose owner is a wizard at finding rare and exotic books. Its brown-and-yellow pages contained numerous references to the Kelabit Highlands and the mountains around them. With a call to Jacob, my guide in Borneo on the Benerat trip, and a few referrals to travel guides and encyclopedias, I was fairly certain that no special permits were required for Volker and me to explore the region. That affirmed, I'd made the call to Volker to inform him that our next expedition would be spent searching for a virtually unknown jungle spire in a remote portion of the Kelabit Highlands in Sarawak, Malaysia, on the island of Borneo.

I got up and fixed myself a cup of tea, then settled onto the couch to peruse *World Within* and get a preemptive tour of the Highlands of Borneo. Just as I was getting comfortable the phone rang. I had no doubt as to who was pulling me off the couch just when I'd finally gotten the pillow perfectly situated under my neck.

"What?" I asked in a Teutonic tone.

"You can't answer the phone like that," Volker said matter-of-factly. "One thing you didn't tell me, and I doubt I'll sleep until I know it; when are we going?"

CHAPTER 2

1945

Borneo is the world's third-largest island. Its shores are formed by the South China, Celebes, Java, Sulu, and Flores Seas, and it rests on the Sunda Shelf, one of Asia's continental plates. Lying south of Vietnam and the Philippines and north of Australia and the Indonesian island of Java, the island is split in two by the equator. With roughly 287,000 square miles of land, you could fit France in the middle of Borneo and still have room for New England and Hawaii.

Despite its large size, no Westerner made mention of the island until around A.D. 160 when the Egyptian scientist Ptolemy noted it in his encyclopedia *Geographia*. How he learned about it is something of a mystery as the island is a good nine thousand miles from Alexandria, but Ptolemy knew lots of unusual facts, including the approximate size of our *round* planet and that Julius Caesar suffered from epilepsy. The Chinese discovered the island around A.D. 700, trading ornate porcelain jars with the local tribes for food items, supposed aphrodisiacs, and spices. In 1521, Antonio Pigafetta, the chronicler for Ferdinand Magellan's circumnavigation of the globe, made note of the island's dark forests and mysterious rivers in the ship's log. He also mentioned the unbelievable opulence and golden palace of the sultan of Brunei, an almost five-hundred-year-old observation that can still be made today.

The island is currently divided politically into three countries. Indonesia controls the southern two-thirds in a state they refer to as Kalimantan, though in the past, when the Dutch controlled much of Indonesia, this region was known as Dutch Borneo. The northern third of the island is controlled by Malaysia and a tiny but wealthy part, all but surrounded by Malaysian territory, is the Sultan State of Brunei. The Malaysian sector is divided into two states. The northernmost state, known in the nineteenth century as British North Borneo, is now taking the name Sabah. The other state, an area roughly the size of the state of New York, is Sarawak. Over the centuries Sarawak has been ruled by Buddhists from Sumatra, Hindus from Java, and the Moslem sultans from Brunei, all of whom barely knew of and never ventured into the island's dark interior. It is a region of high mountains, dense forests, and unyielding tribes of headhunters that epitomizes what we think of as the dark jungles of Borneo.

The most colorful period of Sarawak's history commenced in 1841 with the arrival of the Brit, James Brooke. Brooke, an adventurer who didn't fit in well with Victorian England, had been a mediocre military officer in India and then unable to find a decent job in London. Enamored with the idea of trading goods in the Far East, Brooke spent his inheritance outfitting a ship, then hired a small crew and set sail for Singapore. Intrigued by tales of wild adventures there, he was sidetracked to Sarawak, a place he had no intention of even stopping at when his voyage began. As luck would have it, James Brooke wound up taking control of the region during a tribal revolt through a perfect example of gunboat diplomacy. That is to say, he aimed his boat's guns at the capital building and ordered the sultan to hand the reins of the region over to him. He ruled Sarawak as its despotic king, or rajah, for twenty-five years. He made headhunting illegal, or at least a severely frowned upon activity, and all but ended centuries-old rivalries and warfare that split the interior tribes. Brooke and his native army also waged such successful campaigns against the coastal pirates that for the first time in history they began to steer clear of Sarawak's coast. Brooke's life was a near parallel to the main character's in Rudyard Kipling's famous novel *The Man Who Would Be King*, and he enjoyed great support from his subjects and considerable envy from neighboring nations and much of the English elite.

James Brooke's heirs, Charles and Vyner, governed Sarawak as the White Rajahs for two more generations. They successfully managed to enforce the first rajah's law against headhunting and helped the interior tribes to truly live in peace. Governing over the interior of Sarawak and enforcing this law was a tall order, but for the most part it was followed as most of the tribes could see the logic in it. Not having to post guards, always being on the defensive, or worrying about the women and children at the longhouse while the warriors were out hunting was a far more comfortable way to live than the terrifying days that had existed before the rajahs. This didn't mean that heads had stopped being taken. The act of headhunting was as much a religious practice as it was a sign of machismo, and it was a tradition that would not simply disappear immediately. A fight that ended in a death generally meant that the loser lost his head, and the occasional headless corpse could still be found in the jungle when a warrior from one tribe crossed the wrong territorial line. This was to be expected, if only barely tolerable. What did come to an end was the ancient practice of war parties from one tribe seeking the heads of a smaller tribe as trophies.

In all other ways, the Brookes' regimes kept the cultures of the interior in a safely protected enclave. To the White Rajahs, the *Orang Ulu*, or interior people, were special and their culture deserved special protection. The rajahs never kept the tribes from knowing about the outside world, but they refused to let its more pushy forces, such as missionaries, work their way through the interior. Even scientists, like Alfred Wallace, who by the late nineteenth century were becoming quite interested in Borneo, were often kept at bay and rarely given the right to enter. Sadly, this protection came to an end on Christmas Day, 1941.

Without doubt the ugliest part of Sarawak's history began that day in 1941 when the Japanese invaded. Ten years earlier, Japan had launched an aggressive campaign to assume control over many parts of Southeast Asia and began showing its cards when the Japanese Imperial Army occupied Manchuria. In 1936, Japan signed a pact with Germany that helped the two burgeoning world powers avoid confrontations, and by July 1937 the Japanese were invading China. The United States placed an embargo on steel to Japan in response, and thus became an enemy of the Imperial regime. In 1940, the Japanese signed the Tripartite Pact with Germany and Italy, a treaty that essentially decreed that if war broke out between any of these countries and the United States, the others would declare war on America as well. Thailand and Indochina (now Vietnam, Cambodia, and Laos) fell under Japan's dominance in 1941, and the United States, then the world's largest oil producer, responded by placing an embargo on oil. But the Japanese war machine, like all modern armies, needed oil to function in order to maintain its position in Southeast Asia. Borneo, with its rich oil fields, became their next target for conquest. The surprise attack by the Japanese on Pearl Harbor, Hawaii, on December 7 invoked the Tripartite Pact, bringing America into the war on both the European and Asian/Pacific fronts. Within days of that attack the Japanese Imperial Army invaded the Philippines, Malaysia, Java, and Borneo. Borneo's oil fields in Miri and Tarakan, the most prized real estate in the region, were quickly seized, and on Christmas Day Rajah Vyner Brooke was forced to vacate his throne.

The Imperial Army immediately forced much of the population into slave labor, stole food rations from longhouses, interned the entire Caucasian population, and killed and raped the natives at random. The Japanese enslaved "comfort women," native women forced to sleep with Japanese soldiers because it was thought to improve the troops' prowess in battle, in all occupied territories. Stories of women and children digging graves, then being forced to their knees and beheaded into the pits, were common. Near the town of Sandakan in British North Borneo, now known as Sabah, 2,740 Europeans were forced to build an airfield and then march 145 miles through the jungle to an internment camp. Twenty-eight survived. A rebellion in the towns of Jesselton (now Kota Kinabalu) and nearby Tuaran was put down with retaliatory bombing that leveled the cities, and untold hundreds were rounded up by the Japanese and then disappeared. People in the region who only had to give their food and livestock to the invading army got off lightly. Like all other Japanese-occupied areas, Borneo was ruled with an iron fist.

I knew very little about the operations on Borneo during WWII until I began reading *World Within*, which, in addition to providing an excellent portrait of the island and its cultures, chronicled the exploits and observations of Maj. Tom Harrisson of the British Special Air Service, or SAS. As I pressed on through its pages, searching for clues about our mysterious spire, I found myself irresistibly drawn into one of the most amazing stories I'd read in my ten years of world travel.

As the war unfolded, Allied Command in the Pacific and Indian Oceans—then comprised of American, British, Australian, and New Zealand troops—paid little attention to Borneo. It was known to be the source of most of Japan's oil, but our policy for defeating Japan did not include retaking Borneo. Japanese oil tankers could be stopped, it was felt, by an effective net of American submarines. The British, based in India, were fighting from the west, while the Americans were island-hopping in the Pacific to approach from the east. For a while, Borneo was between the two Allied theaters of operation, and as a result fell somewhat between the cracks. However, as a large Japanese enclave and source of fuel, the island could not be ignored forever. Since neither the British or Americans were focused on the island, the plan to invade was formulated by the Australians.

Now I like Australians. Some of my best friends are Australians. To meet an Aussie and give him a beer is to make a friend for life. They are the salt of the earth, those men from down under. Not only that, they are tough. Aussie men play football without pads and surf with great white sharks and saltwater crocodiles. Needless to say, if anyone can put up with the great hardships and obvious stresses that go with fighting a war in the jungle, it's an Australian. Unfortunately, to fight a war successfully you need plenty of knowledge about the area you are going to fight in, and the Australians didn't have that in Borneo.

At that point in the war there was virtually no contact with the island, and it was known that Europeans and Australians living there before the war had all been rounded up and put into camps, or worse. Numerous Allied pilots had been shot down over the jungle, but none of them were found or able to return to civilization. Virtually all of Borneo was covered by a two-hundred-foot-high canopy of trees and vines, making it all but impossible for a parachuting pilot to reach the ground safely. If he did reach the ground he had to deal with the Dayak,* the indigenous tribes of Borneo, whose headhunting activities were legendary. No one knew for sure, but it was strongly suspected that most of the downed pilots had lost their heads.

The Australians soon realized that they first needed someone to infiltrate the island and gather intelligence, and then if possible stop the flow of food supplies to the Japanese before the Allied invasion. That's what they wanted, but they knew next to nothing about how to pull it off. Trying to survive in the jungle for an unspecified amount of time, with the Japanese Army on one side and Dayak headhunters on the other, seemed a near suicidal mission. The only way it had a prayer of working was if they sent in a small commando force led by someone with experience in Borneo's interior. If possible, that man needed to speak one of its many languages. No one in the Australian Army, at least no one who they deemed qualified as a commander, fit that description. The military planners expanded the search, pulling personnel résumés from Allied forces all across the globe. Still, only a handful people fit the bill. Despite its size, the island of Borneo was just too obscure to have produced numerous— or any—foreign experts.

---

*The word *Dayak* is used like the word *Indian* in America. There are numerous tribes in Borneo such as the Kelabit, Kenyah, and Iban as there are numerous Indian tribes in America like Shoshoni, Arapaho, and Sioux. Dayak originally referred to just the seagoing Iban, but has been commonly used to encompass all tribes.

A number of men who seemed qualified, mostly British, were offered the mission, but knowing a little of what it would entail, they turned it down. Trying to survive the jungle, the Japanese, and the headhunters until the war's end, if that ever came, was absurd, and even the military considered the mission so risky that they refused to force anyone to undertake it. Then in 1944, having come to the end of the list of interviewees, the planners met Maj. Tom Harrisson. Born in 1911 in Buenos Aires, Argentina, Harrisson had attended Cambridge and was infamous for his drinking and brawling. Most who knew him recognized that he was very intelligent and had toughness and a headstrong approach to taking on any obstacle. He was a member of the SAS, the British equivalent to our Special Forces, and had actually been to Borneo thirteen years earlier. Harrisson had organized an Oxford University scientific expedition to Mount Dulit, west of the Kelabit Highlands, in 1932. He had spent six months in the jungle with his compatriots and Dayak guides and in the process had learned a bit of Malay, the coastal language of Sarawak. Amazingly, with full knowledge of what lay ahead, Harrisson accepted the task.

Allied Command had a number of possible ways to get him into Borneo, and these varied in concept from a submarine drop-off to a seaplane flight. It was thought that, for the most part, the Japanese controlled the coasts and spent little energy on the interior of the island. Like so many outsiders before them, the interior was probably seen as dangerous and being of little use from a military standpoint. The coastal oil fields were what mattered, and as the inland indigenous tribes were quite isolated they presented no immediate danger to the Japanese occupation. The drawbacks to the submarine plan were that the coasts were closely watched and so shallow that a sub would have to stop far out to sea, leaving the men exposed and easily detectable as they came ashore. The seaplane idea also proved unworkable when Harrisson pointed out that Borneo, despite being as big as Texas, has no large lakes. It was finally settled upon that the best method would be to drop Harrisson in by parachute, but this too was a very risky proposition. In 1945, Borneo, all 287,000 square miles of it, was almost completely covered by dense forest that would rip a parachute apart well before a man reached the ground safely. A few large clearings were near the coasts, but they would no doubt be patrolled and monitored by the Japanese. The interior held few clearings large enough for parachutists to aim for, and even if they found one there were other considerable dangers. Snakes, disease, and large animals were all major concerns, but they paled in comparison to the image of one's head roasting over a Dayak fire pit.

In the weeks that followed Harrisson's selection as expedition leader, photos and maps were studied and Harrisson himself made numerous reconnaissance flights, only to find that the only suitable terrain for a parachute drop was in an extremely remote region known as the Kelabit Highlands. At the center of the Highlands, a few hundred miles from the north coast and roughly four thousand feet above sea level, was an open plateau known as the Bario Asal. The local tribe, mistakenly named the Kelabit by a former governor of the region, grew rice in paddies and thus kept large areas cleared of trees. Information on the area was often conflicting, but it appeared to be secluded enough that the Japanese patrols might have passed it over.

Of course, the geographic location of the plateau created a problem in and of itself. As the highest region on the island, encircled by even higher peaks, the area often suffered the worst of Borneo's weather. Every morning the entire region was covered by a dense blanket of clouds and fog, making it impossible to see the ground and thus locate the forest clearing for the drop. Worse conditions came as the day progressed, when the sun heated the clouds, letting them break slightly, then reform into enormous thunderheads that could throw a plane around like a leaf. Most damning of this plan, possibly putting an end to the whole concept, was the fact that the incessant cloud cover meant that the plane's pilot would have no way to know exactly where he was over the island at any given time. Without knowing this, dropping Harrisson and his men in would be just a roll of badly weighted dice.

It was thus critical to locate a marker of some sort, and it was found on one of the first reconnaissance flights. Ten miles north of the plateau, a mountain unlike anything these men had ever seen spiked out of the jungle. Its name was unknown and its exact height was just as much of a mystery, as no one had ever climbed it and no Westerner had been to the mountain's base. But the shape of the peak from the air was unmistakable. It rose out of the forest like a spear, poking through the dense cloud cover at the blue sky above as if put there for this mission. If the flight could be timed just right with the weather, this mountain would be a visible beacon above the clouds and thus a locating device for the pilots. The peak, then given the code name Peak 200, derived from the mission's name of Flight 200, would serve as Tom Harrisson's natural lighthouse.

With the discovery of Peak 200, the mission, now known as the Semut Campaign, was now ready to begin. Seven other special forces members, four of which were in a second plane and would follow Harrisson's squad down if they survived their first encounter with the locals, joined the mission. A few weeks later, in March 1945, Flight 200 took off from a recently liberated airstrip in the Philippines. On the previous days, two passes over the Highlands had been made with Harrisson equipped and ready for the drop, but there had been too much cloud cover to see the ground or the spire. The military then decided the third try would be the last, as the big bomber had now spent thirty-two risky hours over Japanese-occupied territory. Fortunately for Harrisson and the Allies, three was the magic number as Peak 200 was spotted and a break in the clouds over the plateau was found. As he slid into the camera bay at the tail of the B-24, the mission's seemingly impossible agenda likely raised a sea of second thoughts. The plan was simple to lay out but hard to imagine being pulled off. Harrisson was supposed to:

1. Drop out of the plane at two hundred miles per hour over a land very much in the hands of the enemy. He and his three men, Sergeants Sanderson, Bower, and Barrie, would immediately establish contact with the inhabitants, and if they let them keep their heads he would fire a flare into the sky to let

the four men in the second plane know it had been a safe jump. This done, he would make friends with the locals to facilitate the rest of the mission.

2. The rest of the mission would be to find out where the Japanese were and set up an intelligence gathering facility so he could radio military info back to the Allies. Presumably he would be getting help from the local tribes to do this.

3. After convincing the locals that he was their friend and that they had an enemy they had never seen hundreds of miles away, he was to get them to stop supporting the enemy with food supplies. If any Allied pilots were shot down, the guerrillas were supposed to aid them and not take their heads.

4. If all that was completed and Tom was still alive, more members of Australia's Special Reconnaissance Detachment (SRD) would drop in to support him and do sabotage work behind the Jap defenses on invasion day. General Toby Carter, who outranked Tom, would eventually be brought in to command this sabotage and Tom would become one of three sectional leaders out in the field.

It all seemed rather unlikely, and one doubts whether the men who dreamed it up were willing to bet on its success. But while Maj. Tom Harrisson could have been assigned anywhere, something drew him back to the island of Borneo and the Kelabit Highlands of Sarawak. Perhaps he had fond memories of his moments of scientific and anthropological discovery from his first trip, or perhaps the thought of being so remote that he would be in complete control of his own destiny drew him there. Maybe it was what Robert Payne referred to in *The White Rajahs of Borneo* when he wrote: "To live among them [people of the Far East] is to know a contentment unknown in the West; and sometimes a wanderer in the East comes closer to Paradise than anywhere on Earth."

Whatever it was, Maj. Tom Harrisson had to be a man of considerable mettle. As he checked his parachute one last time, ignoring the roar of the plane as he went over his checklist and glancing down the chute toward the clouds and rice paddies of the Kelabit Highlands, he knew that many men below were probably watching him. None were Japanese, but they were warriors whose very name struck fear into all who knew of them. Isolated and fierce, these people had likely never seen a white face, or more specifically, a white head. Harrisson spoke a few words of Malay and one of his men, Sergeant Sanderson, spoke it well, but how far would that get them? Perhaps none of the Kelabit spoke the coastal Malay! Who was to say that even if they spoke the language, they wouldn't kill the commandos anyway? And what if they let him live, but the Allies did not manage to defeat the Japanese and liberate Borneo? Were he and his men about to jump out of an airplane and into a permanent and primitive life in the Stone Age? The entire mission was a long shot, but as Harrisson glanced back at the men in the cockpit, they gave him a few words of encouragement. It was the last time he would ever see them.

CHAPTER 3

Fall 1998 to March 1999

ONE DOESN'T PLAN on making a big climbing expedition to a place like Borneo without learning a bit about its history, but as I peered into the country's past, looking in every source I could get my hands on, I found almost no information on the island's interior. Borneo has always been a mysterious land to outsiders, and what little is known has not been inviting for anyone but the most adventurous. Its coasts have been threatened by pirates for all of recorded history, and to this day piracy is commonplace and a major problem for the governments that rule the island. But while sailing around the island can be dangerous, crossing Borneo is even worse. It wasn't until the late 1800s that a Westerner went into the island's interior, or at least went in and then came back out. Borneo's dark jungle, an inspiration to Joseph Conrad, was known to be inhabited by tribes of savage headhunters armed with poison darts and spears, men always looking for a trophy to put over the mantel.

The density of the island's forests are such that rivers have always been the principal paths of travel. Unfortunately, the rivers are home to some of the world's largest crocodiles and the infamous reticulated python, a snake as adept in the water as it is on land and high in the trees. Reticulated pythons can weigh over three hundred pounds and stretch longer than a city bus. To add to the aura of danger that big reptiles and fierce headhunters create, jungle flowers up to three feet in diameter give off the scent of rotting flesh, and some plants actually eat animals by trapping them and then dissolving their tissue in an acidic fluid. Up above, high in the canopy that blankets much of the island, birds with horns let out ghastly screams and strange primates howl like ghosts for much of the day.

Only a fool would want to venture into such a place. I'd been there three times. On each trip I'd contracted some sort of nasty disease or parasite. On the first trip, up the Rajang River to Gunung Lawit, I picked up Dengue Fever and was nursed back to life in a riverside longhouse by some Iban tribesmen. They were nice folk, but the fact that the men's fingers were tattooed, a symbol that denoted the taking of heads for each painted joint, did not escape me. I recovered, though I've since been warned against falling ill with Dengue Fever again unless I'm prepared for my immune system to send my temperature soaring up to over 108 degrees, which I'm not. My second trip went well, and I returned home seemingly unscathed, only to meet with a rude awakening one night as I brushed my teeth. Standing in front of the mirror, I noticed something fall from my nose. I picked it up, only to discover to my horror that it was a worm. I flipped out, as anyone would, and immediately took the worm to my local doctor, who always hates to see me coming because it means he is going to have to spend hours searching databases for things one might pick up in an inhospitable environment such as Borneo. I showed him the worm, he sent it off, then called me back a week later. It turned out to be a fly larva, or more commonly, a maggot. It also turned out that there is some sort of fly found in southern Asia that lays eggs in your sinuses so that the larvae have a food source—your brain. The doctors ran an MRI on my head and found no other parasites, but one small brain, which I am happy to still have. On my third trip I picked up an amoeba and lost a pound a day for over a week. Some people might want this sort of Jenny-Craig-on-steroids diet, but at five-foot-ten and 150 pounds, nine pounds is a lot of me, and a diet like that often means you lose parts you'd just as soon keep, like your muscles.

Volker knew about all of these little bugs and a whole bunch more. Through the planning of our trip we chatted on the phone at least once a week, and not one conversation passed in which he didn't tell me about yet another hideous illness that we could be exposed to. There were your common ones that most travelers have heard of, like malaria and encephalitis, and then there were a few that made me wish I'd never heard of Borneo, much less been there. Malaria, a name derived from the Latin words mal (bad) and air (air)—when people thought it came from bad air around swamps— is spread by mosquitoes and comes in a number of deadly designs. It kills roughly two and a half million people a year, usually by an uncontrollable fever, though kidney failure and the bursting of blood vessels in the brain are also common. Encephalitis, also spread by mosquitoes, is pandemic on Borneo and kills one in five people who get it. Since "encephalitis" translates to "a swelling of the brain," my guess is most of its victims die with a nasty headache.

The other more exotic diseases really get you going, like filariasis, otherwise known as river blindness. This one is also carried by mosquitoes and can cause such things as fever, sensitivity to light, eye lesions, and the swelling of one's scrotum with no female inducement. And schistosomiasis, a nasty bug that lives in freshwater and burrows through the skin, taking up residence in your gut and causing hives, diarrhea, and bloody urine. It weakens the immune system to the point that it's easy to pick up some hemorrhagic fever Western medicine has yet to see. Something like Ebola. Ebola, a filovirus first identified in central Africa in the '70s, is so nasty that its effects on the human body have given birth to entire horror movies. It's characterized by severe headache and muscle aches, followed by vomiting and diarrhea of blood, an inflamed throat, inflammation of the mucous membranes in the eyes, and the destruction of internal tissues. This last bit causes the neural connections to the muscles to fail, all but immobilizing the victim and leaving the muscles in the face mostly paralyzed. The "Ebola mask" is the drained look all victims have in their faces, both from the fact that they can't create a different expression and the knowledge that they have a 90 percent chance of dying through the next "bleeding out" stage. I won't go into that, but suffice to say that its side effects lack an upside like the "I lost ten pounds" bit that comes with amoebic dysentery. There are a number of hemorrhagic fevers like Ebola, and the fact that this disease was first seen in the tropical forests of Africa doesn't mean it doesn't exist elsewhere. The world's jungles seem to be full of nasty little bugs like Ebola, Marburg, and Lassa Lassa fever, and the outbreak of Ebola in a monkey farm in Reston, Virginia, is known to have started with monkeys from Southeast Asia.

Volker loves to see me squirm, but he has his pushable buttons as well. Volk really doesn't like snakes, and there isn't a place on the planet that has more deadly varieties of the little poison ropes than Borneo. I once saw a book that contained a map of the world that showed the number of types of deadly snakes in a given region denoted by color. Ireland was green, meaning there weren't any. The US was blue, which meant there were between something like ten and twenty. Australia, a country that prides itself on the number of poisonous animals it has and the speed at which they will kill you, was yellow, having something like forty to sixty deadly species. Central Africa, the region that sees the highest number of deaths in the world via snakebite, was orange, having like sixty to eighty kinds of deadly snakes. Only one spot on the globe was red, the eighty-plus color. As predicted, it was the island of Borneo.

In my trips there I'd seen a number of cobras, including one black spitting cobra while I was in Mulu. Spitting cobras, like other cobras, have a poison that is neurotoxic, meaning it affects the central nervous system. Over the millennia their fangs have adapted so the poison can be squirted forward up to ten feet. They generally aim for the eyes, and as one might expect from an animal that would go so far as to adapt such a weapon, they are pretty accurate with the stuff. The poison will blind a person in a matter of hours if not treated with an antitoxin eye rinse. A friend of mine from South Africa once had the misfortune of experiencing this, and though he still has his eyes, he said he'd rather have his girlfriend dump him a hundred times as a halftime show at the Super Bowl than go through it again. The poison was so intensely painful that he couldn't lift his eyelids. The hard thing was trying to figure out how to run from the snake over rough terrain with his eyes shut. That same squirtable toxin is deadly when injected, killing a man in as little as an hour, and the snake wouldn't have given the first treatment if he weren't ready to give the second. The eye squirt is little more than a warning compared to the bite. My friend escaped, but to this day he has eye problems.

The king cobra also makes Borneo its home. King cobras are the largest species of poisonous snakes, regularly reaching lengths of eighteen feet. Though their poison isn't the most deadly in the animal kingdom, they dose it out in such large quantities that being bitten by one is far less attractive than many things you would always want to avoid, like being mauled by a polar bear or run over by a Cadillac. They rear up off the ground as high as five feet and can strike at a distance two-thirds of their length. I'm not much for math, but two-thirds of eighteen feet is, well, pretty far, so you might not even see it coming. King cobras are so tough they eat other snakes, even deadly ones like kraits. As far as I'm concerned, if a banded krait, a snake whose bite can kill a man in less than twenty minutes, is afraid of a king cobra, Volker and I should be, too.

Cobras and kraits are by no means the only snakes to worry about on Borneo. There are Malaysian pit vipers, mangrove snakes, Popes vipers, and even Bamboo vipers, a variety nicknamed the Asian Two-Step by American soldiers during the Vietnam War who didn't get far after a bite. All the snake books that describe these animals go to great pains to tell you how very unlikely it is that you would ever be bitten by a snake, much less killed by one, and Volker didn't avoid research of the subject to the degree that he didn't note that fact. As the author's logic goes, most snakes live deep in the jungle where most snake-book readers are unlikely to go, so it's unlikely that those people would have to worry about an encounter. Some species, like the various green pit vipers that call Southeast Asia home, are very shy and live their lives high in the jungle canopy or on bushes that grow on mountain ledges. The books don't say that snakes rarely bite, they say that people are rarely bitten because we just don't find ourselves in the snakes' environment. I pointed this out to Volker whenever there was an opportunity, which was roughly every time we spoke. If I needed to know that there were worms that could crawl from my stomach to my lungs then into my heart, eating Swiss cheese tunnels in me like, well, burrowing worms, he needed to know that *we* were that rare exception for exposure to snakebites. We would be climbing a spire that projected through the jungle canopy, was covered in bushes and shrubs, and was in the most densely-populated-by-deadly-snakes region of the planet. Grabbing those bushes, crawling through the canopy, jabbing our hands into cracks in rocks and reaching up to ledges that we hadn't gotten a good look at were all no-no's, but they would all be necessary if we had a prayer of climbing the Batu Lawi.

Volker and I knew enough about climbing in the tropics to understand that this would be a major undertaking, both in time and money. For years we had been traveling to obscure climbing areas on a fairly limited budget, but the Kelabit Highlands were more remote than any other place we had been. To find the Misty Mountain and spend enough time at its base to successfully reach its summit, we would have to equip a full expedition. By that, I mean we would need to become self-supported. There would be no hotels to sleep in and restaurants to eat from along the way, so full camping equipment and three climber-size meals per day would have to be packed in. Since it might take a few weeks, we would need to bring in a lot more than the two of us could carry. The climbing equipment alone would be more than we could handle, and on top of that there would be tents, meals, rain gear, Volker's portable hospital that could stop deadly diseases, my snakebite kit and some form of antivenin, pots, pans, and more. To get it all there we would have to hire porters, and that would get costly.

We decided early on that our bank accounts could not handle the expedition. Some serious funding would need to be procured, and the best way to get that was by promising media exposure to CEOs and publishers who have bags of money lying around their offices. We had written magazine articles for years, but suspected that the magazines that had taken those articles might not be too interested in this sort of Indiana Jones climbing expedition. The climbing magazines had a limit to the obscurity of the climbs they would cover, and a mud-wallowing, infectious-disease-festering, snake-revel of a rock climb was not what they were likely to go for. And even if they did pay us, it wouldn't be enough to even get us to Borneo, much less to the mountain with three weeks' worth of food and climbing gear.

Numerous older climbers from my hometown, all of whom I held in great respect, or at least pretended to when they wanted to tell me something, had warned me not to let "the big corporate monster" into my world of climbing. They drew parallels between climbing and activities like painting or composing, where the participants are inspired to do something from inside. As one older mountain guide put it, "Painters can't explain 'why' they paint in a way so others can feel it any more than you or I could explain why it is we climb. Big media won't see what you see in a climb on Borneo." I guess I understood this. Volker and I had seen Batu Lawi in that old atlas years before, and just its shape, a lone spire above a dark forest, had compelled us to search it out and then plan to travel all the way around the world. If anyone were willing to listen, we could lay out the climbing prospects, like the steep cracks, overhanging arêtes, and the mystique of climbing in a jungle older than mankind. But no sponsor could feel what it was that drew us there. The old sages had told me that by having the media on the trip we'd lose control of what it was we wanted, or worse, lose sight of it. Perhaps, their argument goes, if one turns his passion into his work, then his passion becomes nothing more than a job.

I consoled myself with the knowledge that Borneo had seen a great deal of exploration via less than chivalrous support, and that our need for a little funding to help pay for a mountain climbing expedition probably wouldn't hurt anyone, except us. The tribal culture of Dutch Borneo, which was under different leadership than that of the rajahs of Sarawak, had been twisted and turned about for centuries by the one company that traded in men's souls: the church. Missionaries had been paid to convert its pagan tribes for hundreds of years, and the changes they had brought about had turned much of the region into something less Bornean and more Alabama Baptist. In the twentieth century, oil companies like Shell and British Petroleum had sent numerous expeditions to Borneo's remote regions with the hope they might find the world's most prized commodity. They had, but the men on those missions often died of malaria, or worse, during and after their quest. Then there were the armies. The Brookes had traversed much of the northern portion of the island in their effort to stop headhunting raids among the Dayak. Theirs had been a noble quest to save lives, but it had nevertheless been an outside influence on the culture.

The next army to explore Borneo, the Japanese Imperial Army, had intentionally caused a great deal of hardship. They were followed soon after by the Allies, in the form of Tom Harrisson. He had been to Borneo on a scientific expedition, but had returned as a soldier, shepherded to the island by the world's most lucrative sponsor, The Dogs of War. It seemed that sponsorship was as much a part of exploring Borneo as vipers and rain, so despite the advice of the old guys, I pushed on in my quest.

I decided to ask a friend of mine, Chris Noble, to join us on the trip. Chris had the right kind of contacts for this sort of funding. As one of the most respected photographers in the outdoor industry, Chris had covered expeditions for *Outside, National Geographic,* and *Men's Journal.* That kind of work makes retail marketers drool like a Saint Bernard in a meatpacking house. Drool money, that is. However, I didn't expect Chris to actually be interested in the trip. We had learned enough about the weather patterns of Borneo to know that our expedition would take place in February or March, the months that a photographer of Chris's stature would be preparing for some Himalayan nightmare-climb. Worse, Chris had been to Borneo before. He had a good idea of what the jungle would be like, and that was plenty of reason to say no. I gave him a call anyway.

"Hi Chris. Sam Lightner here."

"Hey Sam, what's up?" he said.

"Oh, not much," I said nonchalantly. His tone was pleasant, and I didn't want to be too pushy. Small talk was needed before I asked someone to join me on a three-week tour of the world's wettest mountain range. "I mowed the lawn this morning, wrote a few e-mails, and I'm going to climb a spire in a remote part of Borneo next spring—any interest in tagging along?"

"Sounds cool," he said. "I have a possible Everest expedition scheduled then, but I'm sure I can get out of it. What will it entail?"

I explained that I didn't have much information yet and that I was in the process of looking for sponsors. Chris reminded me that potential sponsors would want a formal-looking proposal complete with pictures and maybe even a bar graph or two. The North Face, the big cash cow for climbing expeditions, wouldn't get involved if they didn't see a lot of exposure through their participation. Chris gave me a few more pointers and let me know that "for some strange reason" he was interested. It was a start.

We talked more over the days that followed, and then we contacted The North Face, pointing out what we knew of the mountain and what a great way it would be for them to showcase their Gore-Tex products in a different environment from the classic snow and ice we are so used to seeing. They agreed, but then informed us that magazine stuff, unless it was a guaranteed feature in *National Geographic*, was no longer the venue of choice. For them to give us the big bucks we needed to get a video sponsor.

As luck would have it, another friend of mine, Rob Haggart, had done some video work for a company that had been making adventure-travel videos for years. Having a soft spot in his heart for my quest for a jungle-encrusted rock, he made a trip to Anywhere Adventure Pictures with me. They, as well as The North Face, were initially more interested in seeing us ascend an unclimbed mountain in the Mulu region. However, once I showed the producer my

picture of the phallic spike rising above the jungle, he was on board
for the climb. I pointed out that it would be difficult for us just to
make it to the mountain, but he recognized that the flora and fauna
of Borneo, not to mention its history, would enhance the story of our
climb.

Batu Lawi, an unheard-of spire in a remote part of a little-known
island, had just become a commodity. Our expedition would be paid
for by a combination of The North Face, who wanted people to see
their equipment being used in torrential downpours and in an environment no one in their right mind would ever use the stuff in, and
by Anywhere Adventure Pictures, who would be making a television
documentary about a rock climb in a very remote part of the world.
Chris and a cameraman would be there to document our efforts.
Now all we had to do was travel to Borneo, locate the mountain, and
climb.

Tom Harrisson's story in the *World Within* intrigued me the moment I began to read it, though my initial reason for finding the old
book was purely to research the Kelabit Highlands. Despite having
been written over fifty years ago, Harrisson's account of his time in
central Borneo provided the most reliable and current information I
would find on the area. Four weeks after our final conversation with
our sponsors I was in the unrelenting heat of the tropics, contemplating Harrisson's daunting mission and romantically trying to com-
pare it to my own. Leaning against a North Face backpack and a pile
of duffel bags, I stared out toward the pale-blue sky with its rapidly
building clouds. The concrete tarmac of the Miri airport, our entry
point into Sarawak, spread out before me like a wide tan beach, ra-
diating heat and blinding anyone not wearing sunglasses. Like a coconut palm, a forty-foot-tall aluminum hangar blocked the direct
rays of the sun, but the heat was still so intense that even without
moving I was sweating. The clouds were building all around the

airstrip at an alarming rate, and the thought of flying through them led me to question the sanity of this little expedition and contemplate the difficulties of the man who had, fifty-four years before, gone where I was about to go. Volker sat next to me, leaning against his own pack and staring through the rising heat waves toward the first nerve-racking portion of our little journey. His comments weren't helping me deal with the stress.

"That thing doesn't even look like an airplane," said Volker. "It looks like a shoe box with two tongue depressors taped to the top." I stared across the smooth concrete and pondered the twin-engine plane. It didn't really look like it could fly, having the aerodynamics of a coffin and the appropriate name of Skyvan. Sadly, it was a shoe box we would soon be climbing aboard for our flight to Bario. Even worse, we would already have been in the box on our way to Bario if thunderstorms hadn't socked in the airstrip and forced all flights to wait for a weather break. Getting on an odd-looking plane in the Third World was bad enough, but getting on one to fly into severe thunderstorms seemed as dangerous as falling asleep next to Jack Kevorkian. The pilot, standing near the hangar door, saw our long faces and tried to console us.

"It's the strangest damn thing," he said shaking his head. "The plane was delivered in a large box by a bunch of Frenchmen. They left the box and took the plane." He chuckled as we both turned to him and stared blankly. His white teeth stood out against his copper Malay skin and he carried himself with that high level of self-assurance you often see in pilots. He wore a spiffy blue uniform with one of those little pilot hats that have a small brim and only look right on older men. It was all nicely pressed, but a bit heavy for the 90 degrees and 95 percent humidity of coastal Borneo. I could see my own blank expression in his Raybans, and it was surprising that Volker, seeing that same expression, hadn't prescribed a few Valium. "C'mon," the pilot said quickly. "I thought you guys were supposed to be big, famous climbers who feared nothing. I know this plane like she's my wife, and she'll treat you well."

His demeanor was reassuring and it perked me up a bit. "I have some flying experience," I said, thinking he might let me ride up front in the thing. "I haven't gotten my license yet, but I'm pretty close. All of it is in single-engine Cessna, though."

"Oh, that's fine," he replied while walking out to see how the loading of our bags was going. "You're qualified to fly the Skyvan. Generally, we can only keep one engine running!" he yelled over his shoulder. Volker and I both nodded at his humor, thinking of the bits of abuse we had hurled at nervous novice climbers from time to time.

Thinking back over what I knew of the flight into the Kelabit Highlands, I was reminded that our position was fairly tame compared to what Tom Harrisson had gone through to arrive in Bario. His ride was a B-24, the plane that had arguably done more to win WWII than any other piece of machinery. Over the three days leading up to Harrisson's drop, the plane had spent thirty-two hours over Japanese territory. The clouds had been so thick and the storms so intense that even Peak 200, the mountain that stood so proudly above the forest, was lost in the tropical tempests. The Air Corps, knowing how much of a risk it was for a big bomber to be in enemy airspace for such a long time, had been ready to pull the plug on the entire operation. They allowed one last try, and on that effort the pilot had managed to spot the mountain poking through the blanket of clouds.

That was in March 1945, and our mission was a bit different now. It was March 1999, and Volker and I as well as a few additional members of our party had spent the last few days gathering supplies for our trek and climb. We had met in Miri, a concrete boomtown built from oil revenue on the north coast of Sarawak. Though few of us in the West have heard of it, Miri has its place in history. Near the turn of the century a small and newly formed company called Royal Dutch Shell discovered oil on a hill just a short distance from the center of town. Within a few years Miri was transformed from a small port trading ethnic goods to one of the largest oil exporting points in Southeast Asia. Its surrounding oil reserves helped make

Royal Dutch Shell one of the largest companies in the world, and later helped the Japanese war machine storm across the Pacific. Nowadays, Miri's oil is under the control of Petronas Group, the state oil company that is principally managed by the family of Malaysia's prime minister, Mahathir Mohamed.

Miri is now the largest city in Sarawak's Fourth Division, a political area equivalent to an American county. It is a collection of concrete buildings laid out in perfect squares and separated by well-maintained asphalt. A couple of high-rise hotels, like our Holiday Inn, poke above the otherwise three-story skyline, and its Malay and Chinese community drive around in Toyotas and Protons, not the rickshas one might expect in the Orient. For the most part Miri is rather dull to look at, having been completely rethought and then rebuilt since WWII in the cheapest and most efficient way possible. However, it had everything we needed to supply our trip, and as the largest settlement in this part of Borneo it was our obvious jumping-off point to the Kelabit Highlands and Bario.

The original plan was for our group—which, by getting the media involved, had grown a fair bit bigger than just Volker and me—to meet in Miri and begin gathering supplies. We would rendezvous with my former guide, Jacob Melai, and then fly to Bario, the only settlement with an airstrip in the Kelabit Highlands. Local porters, arranged far ahead of time by Jacob, were to meet us there. We would stay the night in their longhouse, then set out the next day for Batu Lawi.

There were now six of us, far more than Volk and I had anticipated when we first planned the climb, and we were no longer just a couple of buddies on a climbing trip. With a couple of sponsors paying for the whole adventure, it wasn't just a matter of making it or not making it, and Volker and I would have to deal with emotional fallout whatever the outcome. Failing is a part of climbing; it simply isn't a sport where you can always count on success. But failure is not part of a good business plan. Before I'd brought in the sponsors it hadn't occurred to me that they would actually expect us to reach the summit at all costs. But they had budgeted a large chunk of cash to see us stand majestically on a remote mountaintop with their gear on, talking about our great success on camera, and waxing poetically at the sense of accomplishment one gets from standing on a hard-to-earn summit. The pressure to be successful had increased with each dollar spent, and we had reacted by trying to come up with responses to all the worst-case scenarios.

One of the most likely parameters to hinder any climb in the tropics is to have one of the climbers, if not both, get sick. Free climbing, in order to be done quickly and efficiently, requires two people; one to climb and the other to hold the rope, or belay.* If either climber, in this case Volker or I, were to get sick with any one of the many diseases that Volker was so creatively reminding me of on a daily basis, neither of us could climb. One of us would spend the whole time sitting in the tent, listening to the other moan about diarrhea, or, according to Volker, watching him "cough up the larvae of echinococcus," a worm that can live in your lungs. We would do all we could to keep from having our bodies invaded by nasty little bugs like the latter, but just to be safe we decided to add a climber to the team.

Scott Morley, a strong kid from my hometown in Wyoming, was the perfect third person. He and I had established a number of new climbs together in Thailand, and though Scott lacked the jungle experience that Volker and I had, he was strong and very determined. Having been on the US Junior Biathlon team for some time as well as having been raised hiking and climbing in the Tetons of northwest Wyoming, Scott was fairly big for a rock climber. A little over six feet tall and perhaps 175 pounds with broad shoulders and a full-back's legs, Scott was well prepared for the hard work that would be a part of climbing Batu Lawi. If needed, he was strong enough to carry my backpack as well as his own, and he could come up with bizarre and original insults when Volker wasn't climbing well. He was

---

* Belay is the term used to describe the act of holding the rope to protect your fellow climber. If he falls, the belayer will catch him by holding the rope through a friction creating device. Belay can also be a noun, as in the place that the action of belaying will take place.

talented enough at our sport to be able to try most of what Volker and I could do and, as icing on the cake, he was eleven years younger than we were. If Volker or I were too scared to try something, or just didn't feel like putting forth the effort, Scott's youth and our maturity would allow us to easily con him into doing the task.

While Volker and I laid down on the bags of gear, comparing our flight to Tom Harrisson's and discussing the Skyvan's apparent lack of aerodynamics, Scott climbed the walls. Literally. Being young and full of energy, and knowing next to nothing about aeronautical engineering, Scott was bored and dealt with it by scaling the walls of the hangar. He did this with the full support of the other three members of the team. Chris was along, taking pictures of the Skyvan, the pile of gear, the mechanics working on the plane, and Scott as he clawed his way up the steel posts of the hangar. Then there were Ben Edison and David Mills, the cameramen sent by Anywhere Adventure Pictures, who were also filming Scott as he teetered along a beam thirty feet above the concrete.

Ben and Dave were both excellent climbers and had gotten the job with the production company because of it. I had pointed out that there might not be enough time for Volker, Scott, and I to guide a cameraman up the mountain while we climbed. Also, we didn't know how high Batu Lawi was, but there appeared to be at least 750 feet of vertical climbing, so anyone without climbing experience might be too scared to effectively film us. The company's response was to send Dave, a man with a fairly sizable reputation in the sport. After some thought, and just a few weeks before the trip began, they had added Ben, wanting to make sure that at least one man was able to film at any given time. Both Ben and Dave had climbed all over the world and were every bit as competent in the mountains as we were. Scott and I had spent the past week with them, having done a bit of climbing in Thailand before coming to Borneo, and so far we had gotten along okay. Dave was a quiet guy and very focused on his job, while Ben, who quickly let us know he "preferred to be called Eddy," seemed open and forthright about his feelings. I figured that we'd all get along just fine.

Our first day in Miri we met up with Jacob, who was to be our chief guide and porter liaison. Jacob had been raised at a longhouse named Terewan on the Tutoh River. The people there are members of the Berewan tribe, a group closely related to the Kelabit of the Highlands. As such he knew and understood the ways of the people who would help us find our mountain and get our equipment to its base. Having spent a week with Jacob in a remote part of the Mulu region, I knew him to be an intelligent but tough character who would quickly push his own limits to reach a goal. He had survived such exploits as breaking his ankle while guiding a couple on Gunung Mulu, and catching a spitting cobra with his bare hands, then carrying it for three days to the snake farm so he could gain free admission to the establishment. Jacob had spent much of the previous weeks on a radio, lining up our porters in Bario and gathering as much information as possible about the trek to our peak. With his help we had bought our food supplies at the local market, lined up the charter flight, and applied for official government permission to make our way into Bario and the Kelabit Highlands.

Getting permission to go into the Highlands was not as easy as had been anticipated. The Kelabit Highlands lie on the border with Kalimantan, Indonesia's state in Borneo. A border war between Malaysia and Indonesia had occurred after Sarawak became a part of Malaysia in 1963, but even though hostilities had ceased in 1965 there was still some resentment on both sides. This is what everyone is told when they ask why they have to apply for permission to go into the forest, or why they have to go through customs in Sarawak after going through it when entering Malaysia at the capital, Kuala Lumpur. In reality, "resentment" left over from the war is more or less an excuse to check up on everyone going into Borneo's interior. The new war in Malaysia, at least as far as the government is concerned, is with the environmentalists of the West. By having people check in at Sarawak and officially request permission to go into the forest, the government can make sure there aren't reporters who will point out what's going on. "What's going on" is that the rainforest is being cut down as fast as the timber companies can get to it, and the Malaysians, Indonesians, Brazilians, and just about everyone else in the tropics are getting a political whipping for it.

However, we must have looked okay because the district office granted us the necessary permission and gave us a few forms to prove it, but with the provision that we come out within twelve days. We had figured on four days in and four days out, plus at least a week or more to climb the mountain. The permit granted us only four days to find a good climbing route and then make it to the summit, plus film the whole thing. It didn't leave us much time to dilly-dally.

"I want you guys to go out and look around the plane," said Eddy, taking our minds off the sight of the fuel that had just spilled all over the wing. "Maybe talk a bit about where you're going and what the plan is."

Over the past few days the film guys had always been right there, running cameras and trying to "capture the essence of the climb" in every facet of our lives. It was annoying but a necessity to help pay for the trip.

"I don't mind doing this sort of stuff," Volker said quietly to me. "But a 'please,' or even a pleasant tone, would be nice."

"Uh huh," I agreed. "Maybe they'll lighten up as they get more footage."

One look inside the plane showed that the costs the production company and The North Face had been brought on board to help cover had stacked up quite tall. The tail of the Skyvan, a large door that swung in a vertical motion, was congested with a dozen giant duffels, each holding a couple weeks' worth of gear and food. We stood behind the plane with the cameras rolling, commenting on the equipment as it was loaded and occasionally joking with the captain, who was sitting in the front left seat making notes in one of the logs. Seven hundred dollars' worth of dried noodles, tomato sauce, dried beans, dried fruit, various dried drink mixes, and a lot of chocolate bars swelled the bags like puffer fish. We also had a few small stoves that could run on kerosene that Jacob and the porters would know how to use. To top everything of necessity off, we'd bought a couple bottles of scotch and vodka for celebratory purposes, and Jacob convinced us to purchase a few bags of tobacco as a topical repellent for leeches. All of this was added to the three thousand-plus feet of rope we'd brought plus pitons, rock wedges, camming devices, an electric hammer drill, and virtually every other bit of equipment a rock climber might need. It added up to somewhere near eight-hundred pounds, and I wondered if the captain was having to fudge the numbers a bit so that all of it could be loaded on the Skyvan.

Our personal clothing, toiletries, and rock climbing shoes and harnesses would be carried in our own backpacks, with the porters handling the food and most of the equipment. Each of us would carry a few extras to complement the necessities in a personal way. The film guys carried film and cameras. Scott, with the young metabolism, had a bag of energy bars. Volker carried a portable hospital. He was "prepared to remove an appendix, amputate a limb, and treat any known tropical infection" with his "little red box," though he quickly pointed out that there were plenty of things in Borneo's rainforest that modern medicine had never seen.

In the bottom of my pack, inside a garbage sack and a dry-bag under my extra pairs of socks and a picture of my home in Thailand were two books that would hopefully answer all of our questions about where we were. *Bario: The Kelabit Highlands of Sarawak* was a scientific journal produced by the University of Malaysia. It was brand-new and seemed to cover all aspects of flora and fauna of the Highlands, from life cycles of orchids and cicadas to the culture of the Kelabit people. Volk and I had gone through it the night before, noting that there were two different references to the type of rock Batu Lawi was formed of, and that the book even admitted that very little was known about the Kelabit Highlands. Still, it was the only scientific journal available, so it would have to suffice. Next to it was our bible, *World Within*. I had read it once when we'd first started planning, but the story was so compelling and full of observations on where we were headed that I had to bring it along.

Malaysian Air Lines, the national airline of Malaysia, sends a plane to Bario once a day except on Sundays. Rather, they *try* to send a plane. The weather is so bad in the Highlands that flights are often canceled, and the runway there is so short that the flights that do go in must follow strict weight restrictions. Our added team members, with all of their filming equipment and the added amount of climbing gear and food, made our pile of supplies far larger than anything Malaysian Air would let on one of their Twin Otters. Bribing airline officials to let us carry that much extra weight would have been very steep, so we ended up chartering the Layang Layang Air Services Skyvan. It was expensive, and the plane had seemed big for our little climbing trip until I saw all our gear piled up in the back.

"You'd think we were going someplace for half a year with all that," I said to Volker. "Not just two weeks." The pilot turned to us and smiled as he spoke to someone through a headset. The camera was running and he wanted to be on film. The copilot was there, too—trying to make himself look busy.

"It seems like a lot of weight," Volk replied. "But it's this little bit that upsets me the most." He slapped his hand on one of three pale-white plastic bottles, each filled with fifteen gallons of kerosene. They had been strapped down with thin brown twine in the very back of the plane, just where the door locks into place. The seats, arranged in four rows of four chairs, were a mere ten feet in front of it. "If we crash, at least it'll be spectacular," Volker added as he walked over to kick one of the plane's tires.

"Quit worrying about crashing," the pilot yelled back, his white teeth shining past the microphone of the headset. "I can crash better than anyone I know." He swiveled forward and mumbled something into the microphone, made a check in the manual, then swung back around and waved us in. "Bario is clear so get your friends. We must go now because it will cloud up any minute."

We rolled in over the gear, taking seats wherever there were no duffels. The film guys sat up front in the hope they might get a good shot out of the cockpit windshield. Scott, Volker, and I all dragged bags out of window seats and stacked them in the aisles, while Jacob just took whatever was left. He seemed to have no interest in looking out the windows, probably because he knew he would see nothing in the dense clouds—maybe he didn't want to see the ground rushing up at an unacceptable speed.

"For those who are wondering, this is a smoking flight," the pilot yelled back to us as he started the left engine. "Also, seat belts are optional."

"What about the kerosene?" Volker asked.

"No, no, no, don't smoke that. I lost a brother that way," he retorted.

Humor is generally a good thing for relieving stress, but it can only get you so far. It wasn't helping here. As the whine of the magnetos came on and the pilot flicked this switch and that, I snapped into the seat with a cord that vaguely resembled a seat belt. I quickly realized what a waste of time this was when I leaned back and the seat nearly tipped over. It was only pretending to be bolted to the floor. As the engines roared to a KISS concert level, Volker tapped me on the leg and pointed to the back of the plane. He made no effort to yell over the noise, but didn't need to as it was obvious he was pointing to the green liquid sloshing about in the clear containers. "I'm not that good with burns," he screamed.

The Skyvan was built for utility, not comfort, and the thin aluminum fuselage had nothing for insulation. It was deafeningly loud, and the whole plane twitched with the power of the spinning rotors. The engines revved higher and we pivoted around, taxiing toward the south end of the runway. Scott leaned forward to look out his window, his face pressed against the glass as if he were a dog trying to get out of a car on a hot summer day. Out his side I could see an MAL flight landing toward our end. It taxied away and we took the runway, but facing in the opposite direction.

"I know enough about flying to know that someone has just screwed up!" I yelled to Volker. "Either this plane ought to be taking off to the south, or the MAL flight landed in the wrong direction." He shrugged and pursed his lips as if to say, "In ten minutes, we won't care how we died."

The engines roared and the plane surged forward. I turned to look at the kerosene, the green liquid sloshing about but still seemingly contained in the plastic bottles. The plane shimmied a bit from side to side as it gathered speed, bumping hard on each swell in the runway and vibrating with the power of the engines. The bumps eased in their intensity, the shimmy slacked off a bit, and then everything was smooth. The Skyvan labored for altitude, and quickly I could see over the airport terminal and into Miri, then out to the South China Sea.

As I pulled out my camera for a shot of the coast, the plane swayed a bit to one side and much of the noise dropped off. I looked out immediately, fearing the worst, then seeing it. The right propeller, just outside my window, was sputtering to a stop. I glanced forward and saw the pilot and copilot throwing switches all over the dash and ceiling of the cockpit. The pilot turned to the copilot and said something, but it was his look that concerned me. Through every word he'd spoken before, a big grin with lots of white had shown, but now there was a very tight-lipped frown of intensity. A Waimea-size wave of sweat was forming on his brow, and the copilot looked like he might be crying.

"Volk, we lost the right engine," I said in a calm tone. Somehow, it occurred to me that we never know how we are going to react in such a situation, and though I was scared out of my mind, my response was a composed and unruffled manner that I could not duplicate. It then occurred to me that the uniqueness of my thought process was probably something that only comes once in a life—the serenity that Hemingway alluded to, that comes just before one suffers a horrible death.

Volker had been looking out the other window and hadn't noticed what was going on outside mine, so he was terrified but not over something he could actually look at.

"We're overloaded, going with the wind, and running on half power at best," I screamed—calmly.

Volker glanced out the window, then turned to look at the

kerosene as the plane slowly rolled into a left turn. "Should we pop the door and dump that shit out?" he yelled.

"I don't think we have time," I replied. "It'll take a minute to open the tailgate, and to be honest, I don't want to do it without being tied in. One way or another we will be on the ground in less than a minute."

"Why aren't we gaining altitude?" Scott yelled to me. He was sitting on the other side and also hadn't looked over to see the stopped propeller.

"We're on one engine right now. You're as close to a plane crash as you will ever be and still be breathing," I said. He leaned forward and glanced out my window, then slammed back into his seat, grabbing his hair. I could see his lips move but couldn't discern what was said. Another odd thought popped into my head, uninvited, as I sat looking at Scott. I'd always wondered what the passengers were reflecting upon when their 747 had just broken in two and was plunging earthward, and now I knew. They weren't really thinking of stuff like what their parents thought, lamenting the fact that they'd never learned to read Sanskrit, or whether or not they would be decapitated by the seat tray; they were thinking they had to take a piss.

The plane labored at a steep angle but seemed to hold its altitude. Small houses and banana groves lay no more than two hundred feet below and I could plainly see kids playing soccer in an open field. We leaned left again, the runway now behind the plane and off to that side. The Skyvan rotated around and then the good engine eased off.

I glanced out the window just as we passed over the end of the runway. Fifty feet, thirty, ten, *wham*. At 120 miles per hour the plane slammed onto the tarmac, the left side a bit forward of the right. The pilots reacted to the angle by overadjusting a bit and we heaved back with the right side too far forward. It surged back the other way so hard I thought the wingtip might bounce off the runway. The tires squealed as the nose was brought in line with our motion and we came to a stop within a few hundred feet.

We sat in the middle of the runway, the pilot leaning over the dash and wiping sweat off his face. His shirt, once light-blue, was now dark with sweat, and he had lost his hat on the landing, leaving wet messy hair behind. He took a deep breath, then revved up the engine, and we taxied over to the Layang Layang hangar. Numerous mechanics walked to us as the plane was brought to a sudden stop. I no longer had to piss.

———

It's funny how the level one commits to something can build on itself. For instance, one might begin doing the dishes just before the football game starts on TV, vowing not to miss the kickoff. As the game begins to come on, you find there are only a few dishes left . . . two plates and a dried-out glass of milk. You've been doing the dishes for five minutes, including a greasy pot that the game bratwurst had been prepped in, so a good effort has been put forth. You can clearly hear the national anthem coming to a close and the crowd beginning to roar, but rather than do the sane thing and watch the kickoff, you go ahead and finish the dishes. In doing so you have committed to doing something you said you would not when you started, mainly because after coming so far it makes little sense to stop. (Also, because your wife will never understand why the kickoff is so important when you try to explain the three remaining dishes to her.) This sort of thought process is basically what got us back on the Skyvan, the only difference being that at this point we had a bit more at stake than a football game kickoff.

The pilot, back to his bright, shiny smile, was quite sure the problem had been fixed. The throttle cable had been stuck, or the fuel line blocked, or a pterodactyl had flown into the engine, or something. A few squirts of WD40 and the plane was as good as new. There was some reluctance, and a few comments were thrown my way on how past adventures Volker had been conned into were already paling compared to this one. We'd come so far—to the other side of the world, with sponsors, cameramen, and a box of antivenin—that the silly flying logic of "the pilot wouldn't want to die" was brought up in a vain attempt to confirm that we would be safe on board the Skyvan. Of course, the thunderstorms had been given another couple of hours to build, but "that is a good thing," said the pilot. The storms were now higher, so he could "hopefully" get under them and see where he was going. Wind shear and lightning be damned; we got back on the plane.

It roared the same, it shimmied again, we lifted skyward, and this time both engines kept running. The plane gained altitude, lifting through some light clouds, then spun around heading almost due south. Within minutes we were away from the populated coast and over the jungle.

The forest spread under the plane like a carpet, with a kaleidoscope of green trees occasionally split by the twisting ribbon of brown water known as the Baram River. The Baram started in the pristine forests of the Highlands, but after hundreds of miles of untouched vegetation it began to drift through treeless, clear-cut sections, where rutted logging roads wound their way back from the coast and gave the rain something to grab before it entered the streambed. Though we were a few thousand feet above the ground, the depth and richness of the forest could plainly be seen when compared to the areas that had been logged. Without the trees one could make out the contour lines and see the roads hugging the edges of the hills where it was less steep, or the places where the earth had eroded away and sloughed off in a muddy avalanche. Opposite this were the treed areas, where the steepness of the terrain was completely obscured by the green carpet. The geology hadn't changed, only my view of it, and I knew that what looked to be a smooth landscape with little variety in elevation was actually a rugged, broken country of hills and cliffs smothered by a two-hundred-foot-high, verdant blanket.

Miri was at sea level while Bario at something like four thousand feet above sea level. As we flew inland the plane held its altitude, but the ground grew closer. As it did the clouds became thicker, the water vapor condensing with the cooling temperatures of the Kelabit Highlands. As my view grew more and more obscured by the cloud cover, our flight became more and more bumpy. Eventually the plane was being tossed around like a basketball—the pilots straining to gather control. Looking out the window, I could barely discern the tip of the wing and was occasionally blinded by a bright flash of lightning. Volker's fingertips were embedded in the sides of his seat, and Scott had his head resting on the palms of his hands, either praying to some unknown deity or fighting off the urge to vomit.

The camera guys had been adamant about getting aerial shots of our spire. We knew that the mountain lay between Bario and Miri, and the plane would fly somewhere near it, so despite the towering clouds they pressed the pilot to find the peak. How they would get the shots they wanted was beyond me, and more important, how the pilot would be able to see the mountain and thus avoid hitting it at 250 miles per hour was even more of a mystery. The photo of it in the atlas had shown that the mountain was probably sandstone or limestone, and thus its white color would completely camouflage it amongst the thick clouds. Tom Harrisson and Flight 200 had flown these same skies during the war, and clearly the weather patterns hadn't changed a bit. Harrisson had pointed out that the best time to reach the Highlands was early in the morning, partially because his plane could better avoid the Japanese fighter planes by approaching the island at night, but also because the early morning hours were the only time the Highland weather permitted a sight of Peak 200. Our pilot probably knew this as well, but under intense lobbying, he did what the film guys wanted.

We swerved and bounced around, the pilot staring intently at his instruments and occasionally glancing out the windows into the light-gray soup. At this point it reasoned that the use of certain instruments like the altimeter and gyro to keep the plane level must have been nothing more than a means of comforting himself. Eddy and Dave both stood up and tried to steady themselves as they pushed the cameras toward the windshield, but it was to no avail. The bouncing and swerving of the plane was so severe that it was all they could do to keep from tumbling around. The pilot made a sudden turn, and then out my window I caught a glimpse of the jungle.

Ten minutes before it had been a distant carpet, but now I saw individual trees less than a couple of hundred feet below the plane. The Skyvan went into a steep left turn, and out beyond the wing I could occasionally make out a steep incline in the canopy of green, then only briefly, a glimmer of white jutting from the dark forest. For just a moment I saw a blade of rock, like a headstone, rising from the jungle and into a ceiling of water vapor.

The pilot made one pass, then ignored the pleas of Eddy and Dave and began gaining altitude. He flew south for ten minutes then put the plane in a steep dive. I stared out my window in what I believed to be the direction of the ground. We had bounced around so much that by this time I wasn't sure which way was up, but trusted that the pilot had managed to keep the plane upright in the clouds and the ground under the wings. Suddenly we were in clear air. The clouds hung over us like a dense ceiling and rain could be seen falling as dark gray sheets off in the distance. The plane was rapidly descending into a deep valley surrounded by shadowy jungle and towering mountains. For the first time we were seeing the Bario Asal, the large valley of the Kelabit Highlands where Tom Harrisson had landed half a century before. The plane touched down and then braked, reversing the engines in a deafening wish to stop. I felt a sense of relief fill the plane, but noticed everyone staring, open-mouthed, out the windows at the otherworldly forest that enveloped the runway.

CHAPTER 4

March 25, 1945

S LIDING OUT THE TAIL OF THE PLANE, his first view of the jungle obscured by clouds, Tom Harrisson was knocked silly by
the 150-mile-per-hour slipstream of the big bomber. He
flipped over backward, horizontal to the ground, then instinctively
tried to right himself, only realizing the futility of the effort as the
chute opened above him. There was a brief moment of relief, his descent over the vast forest calm in comparison to the terrifying, blind
bouncing of the Liberator in the soup of clouds above the drop zone.
For just a second or two he felt the bliss of hanging in the harness as
the plane droned off to the east. Then came the jarring realization of
what he was dropping into.

Only a few hours earlier he had been lying in a field alongside
the airstrip in Mindoro with his friend, Graham Pockley, the captain
of the Liberator. With just hours until their departure, both men
were consumed by the mission that lay before them, grimly acknowledging to each other that Harrisson had perhaps no better than
a 50/50 chance of survival. He had found himself talking to Pockley
almost as if he were in a confessional, about some of the mistakes he
had made in his life: hearts he'd broken, the bullying of men who
didn't deserve it, and above all his efforts to make a name for himself. Years before, when studying the indigenous cultures of Papua
New Guinea, the actor Douglas Fairbanks had expressed an interest

in making a film about him and his adventures. Vanity had led him to court the idea despite the fact that he knew such a film would overshadow the true purpose of his work and abuse the trust he had built with the native tribes. Now, face to face with a mission that might very well prove to be his last, and in which he would again be called upon to earn the trust of an isolated people, he deeply regretted that he had let his own ambition undermine the integrity of his endeavors. It was the kind of conversation that occurs when men are faced with the dark realization of their own mortality, and he had vowed to Pockley that, should he survive the next twenty-four hours, he would permanently forgo such aspirations along with any thoughts of his own heroism. Fear had driven him to make such a promise, but it paled in comparison to the fear he felt now as he hung from a silk sheet over central Borneo.

"What are you getting yourself into now, Tom," he muttered aloud, noting that his London accent had been tinted by the months of training in Australia. As Tom glanced up to check on his companions he immediately found himself in a thick cloud, losing sight of both the big bomber and the approaching ground. He drifted for a minute or two, briefly getting a glimpse of Sergeant Barrie, one of the three other men in his initial penetration squad who had jumped from the plane behind him.

Allied Command had worked hard to assemble a team of men with the experience and training necessary to survive the inhospitable Bornean forests. Barrie was a tough guy from southeast Australia who had worked for Shell Petroleum in the jungles of New Guinea for a few years before the war. He knew how to navigate the jungle and would be an asset to the team because of it. Sergeant Bower, another Australian, was a radio operator who also had spent some time in the tropics. Perhaps the strongest of the group, however, was Sergeant Sanderson, a New Zealander with Asian ancestry and a very aggressive approach to fighting the war. Tom and Sandy, as he was called, had had their differences in training, but there was no question that the man knew what he was doing and would be critical to the mission's success.

Tom shifted his gaze downward, trying in vain to get his bearings in the milky, white soup. He stared at the white mist below him, hoping to see the ground before the collision and listening as the sound of his link to the outside world, the B-24, faded off into the distance. Without warning he slammed onto the ground and crumpled into the mud.

"Okay, okay. Nothing broken. Nothing broken," he said, hopping around in the mud in an effort to reassure himself that the various parts of his body still worked. If anything *had* been broken, he'd soon be dead.

"Bloody hell!" someone yelled. It was Sergeant Bower, his Victorian accent giving away his identity despite the thick mist. "I would have rather taken my chances with the bloody jungle." Tom heard more thuds as bodies slammed into the mud, then the light scratching of wet silk being dragged through the rice shoots and water. They had all landed in a swamp unscathed, but much of their equipment, dropped from the B-24 immediately after the men, was already coated in mud and soaked.

Though the men had expected to be wet from the moment they left the plane until the war was finished, they hadn't expected to be cool. They had touched down on a typical Kelabit Highlands day, and unlike the Philippines, Morotai, or coastal Borneo for that matter, the Highlands had a fairly constant weather pattern. Days were in the mid-seventies, nights in the low sixties. Mornings were foggy, followed by afternoons of broken clouds that gave way to violent thundershowers. The only change was the occasional lengthy storm, which brought constant rain. They'd be seeing plenty of those days, if they lived through this one.

"All right, everyone come to my voice," Tom yelled, "and keep your eyes open for the storepedoes. This is going to be a folly mission if we don't find the radio." The men themselves carried a few days' rations and weapons with ammunition, but the lion's share of equipment had come down in big aluminum tubes called storepedoes. One of these containers held the radio, which above all else was necessary to complete the mission. Within minutes of their

landing the fog lifted and the men were able to visually locate each
other. Their guns were drained of muddy water, then brought up and
cocked, just in case. Tom unclipped his chute, the green silk now
heavy with mud, and as he did so a flash of white in the jungle caught
his attention.

The outline of a man could be made out moving through the
dark undergrowth, then it disappeared. Tom instantly realized that
with the local tribesmen already aware of his presence, the mission,
not to mention the lives of his entire party, depended on how the
next few moments would go. The man appeared again at the perimeter of the forest with a look on his face as if he'd just seen a ghost.
He was an imposing fellow, perhaps six feet tall, with broad muscular shoulders and powerful legs. His black hair was thin and cut short
in a straight line around his head, and his earlobes had been
stretched long from the weight of brass rings and hung halfway down
his neck. He wore a breechcloth made from tree bark, a waist belt
of rattan fibers, and bead necklaces adorned with boars' tusks. He
was armed with a blowgun and a large knife, known locally as a
parang, but he carried a small piece of white cloth. From previous
experience Tom knew the blowgun to be as dangerous a weapon as
any a man could carry, and the parang was often used in the taking
of heads. The white cloth, however, was a mystery.

To Western eyes the cloth might have first been taken as a sign
of truce, which wasn't far from the truth, but to the Kelabit people
it meant much more. Kelabit stories, told over and over and passed
from generation to generation, were often centered around the spirits of dead tribesmen. The passing planes of the previous days had
been an unprecedented phenomenon, so it had been widely held
that the spirits were likely involved. The white cloth was only used
in religious ceremonies, but had been pulled out days before just in
case something strange were to happen with these giant flying birds.
Now four pale-skinned men with blue eyes, wearing green clothes,
and talking with odd lisps and whistle sounds had just dropped out
of the sky. For the man at the edge of the forest, something strange

had definitely happened, and he could only hope that carrying the cloth with him would appease the spirits.

Fortunately for Tom and his men, many of the old stories had predicted the return of ancestral spirits, all of whom would be friendly to the Kelabit. If the old tales hadn't been so pleasant, perhaps a number of poison blowgun darts would have already been fired and Tom and his men would have been writhing in the mud, dying in one of the most agonizing ways man has yet to conceive of. Tom turned to face the man in the trees.

"Selamat pagi. Nama saya Tom Harrisson," Tom ventured, hoping that his limited vocabulary of Malay would prove useful. Sergeant Sanderson, who'd worked in Malaysia before the war, glanced at Harrisson and nodded, letting him know he'd pronounced the Malay words correctly. With almost total silence two other men melted from the jungle and stood at the edge of the clearing. They were similarly armed and held serious but inquisitive looks on their faces.

Unfortunately, Tom Harrisson's efforts to find the right language went nowhere. He tried a few words of coastal Dayak, but they too received nothing more than blank looks from the two Kelabit men and panicked expressions from the three Australians who were counting on their leader to make a good impression. The Kelabit men were imposing fellows, and their tense faces were anything but reassuring to the newly arrived white folk.

"Major, tell me you can speak another language, please," said Sergeant Bower, knowing that Tom could not.

"Sorry, Sergeant," Tom responded quietly. "I'm fresh out. Sandy, would you like to say something to these gentlemen?"

"I'm sorry to say your pronunciation was perfect, Major." Sanderson replied. "I don't have much to add, I'm afraid."

The uncomfortable silence was broken only by the rumble of thunder over the mountains. With each passing moment the skies had grown darker, the air a bit heavier, and low rumbles could be heard in the mountains around the valley. Harrisson tried to ignore the intimidating weather, focusing his energies on making a good impression at this first meeting with the local inhabitants. Everyone was scared, but it was obvious they all wanted to communicate. Within minutes the newly arrived foreigners had settled on the one true international language, that of hand signs, wild arm gestures, and prancing about to get their point across. Harrisson would run in little circles, point at the sky, make threatening signs with his fists and point off toward the distant north coast, then smile intently at the Kelabit and think to himself, "God I must look like a fool." He wanted to explain why he'd come in as few gestures as possible, but the international chicken dance was no way to explain something as alien as strange-skinned men drifting from the sky in odd clothing just after a giant bird had flown over.

For their part the Kelabit men felt the same way, and said as much to each other as they intently watched the actions of the visitors. The men's demeanor was altogether unlike what the Kelabit expected from spirits, and they no longer seemed as intimidating as when first discovered. The first Kelabit man's name was Amat, and he was trying to tell these newcomers, spirits, or whatever they were, that his father-in-law was the *penghulu*, or headman, at a nearby longhouse. He had gotten to be the *penghulu* by knowing things other men in the tribe did not, including the language of the coastal people. If anyone could decipher the gibberish and stamping about of these unusual visitors, it was the *penghulu*.

"Major," commented Sergeant Bower in a low voice, "I think I could correctly say what I'm feeling right now if I stamped about with my hands folded under my arms, making squawking noises like a chicken." Everyone laughed, including the Kelabit, though it was obvious they didn't know why and were only trying to be a part of the joke.

Harrisson arched an eyebrow. "At least we're not dead yet."

After a few more minutes of Tom hopping about rather uselessly and everyone, Australian and Kelabit alike, chuckling at his forms of communication, Amat simply turned and walked away, beckoning the newcomers with his arms. Harrisson and his men gathered up their gear, the other Kelabit men helping by heaving a storepedo of equipment over their shoulders. Tom, Sergeant Barrie, and Sergeant Sanderson gathered their equipment and, even though it might upset their new companions, fired a shot in the air with the flare gun to let the other flight know they had landed safely. The Kelabit were startled by the flare and watched it in the sky for a few moments with anxious looks before continuing on. Tom and his men followed Amat out of the swamp, leaving Sergeant Bower and one of the other tribesmen behind to search for the missing radio.

The odd little group moved over dry rice paddies, past one-hundred-foot-tall stands of bamboo, and through clearings in the jungle where the grass was knee-deep. The clouds were rising quickly as they always did at midday, and the dark, vegetation-covered mountains around Bario were emerging from the vapor-heavy air.

"It's a beautiful place, eh, Major?" Sanderson said as they followed their new friends down a thin trail.

"Yes, it is," answered Tom, glancing about the far rims of the valley. "I'd almost forgotten how much I loved Borneo."

The lower slopes of the mountains around Bario quickly became clear of clouds as the mist lifted. To the south was the Apo Duat Range, the border between what had been Sarawak and Dutch Borneo before the Japanese invasion. To the north were the cliffs of the Tama Abu Range, shrouded in mist and obscuring their beacon, Peak 200. Somewhere out on the plain before them, flowing west, were the upper reaches of the Baram, one of Borneo's largest rivers, while off to the east stood Gunung Murud, Sarawak's highest peak.

They walked along the paddy dikes, past small grass huts built on stilts, and through thick stands of banana trees, but never through the dense jungle that surrounded the plain and helped to keep it isolated. Wider and wider trails eventually brought them to the longhouse, an imposing structure situated in a large clearing where everyone had gathered to see who, or what, had come to visit.

The word "longhouse" is as appropriate a term as any could be. Longhouses are designed to be the residence of many families, all living side by side in separate quarters off one main hall. A longhouse can hold a few families and be no more than a hundred feet long, or it might be the residence of an entire village and over half a mile in length. A long room running the full length of the building is used for cooking, communal dinners, and meetings. It serves as a central town square as well as a guest room, and being under a roof means it stays dry and warm in even the worst storms. Along an inside wall that splits the building lengthwise are doors leading into the semiprivate rooms of each family. Like most longhouses, this one at Bario was built on stilts and made entirely of tropical hardwood. The wall panels, each over an inch thick, were brown and gray with age and had all been cut by hand from the nearby forest. The front door, ornately carved from a single massive piece of hardwood, opened onto an elevated porch accessed by wooden steps. The elevation of the house kept its inhabitants off the damp ground and also worked as a defense measure, as the steps could easily be raised each evening.

The locals had gathered about in front of the longhouse and all along its large decks, chattering loudly about the newcomers. Amat led Tom up the steps to the deck and through the ornate door. Once inside the dimly lit interior, Tom could see that the ceiling was blackened and noted the distinct smell of wood smoke. The long room, which extended from one end of the building to the other, was filled with people. Women and children dressed in everything from naturally dyed, loose-fitting sarongs to nothing at all stared at the newcomers, asking each other questions about their skin, their dress, their hair, and their eyes. As his eyes adjusted to the weak light, Tom noticed, hanging in baskets and woven into rattan that hung from the ceiling, rows of human skulls. Many of the older folks seemed to be angry, and Tom couldn't help but discern their aggressive tones as they pointed at him and his men. It seemed that everyone in the room was talking of nothing but the four new heads that could be added to the trophy rack.

Near the middle of the long room, now completely surrounded by members of the tribe, Harrisson was presented to an older Kelabit man. The man wore a cloud leopard skin hat with long hornbill feathers, bracelets just below his knees, and heavy brass earrings. Most conspicuously, however, was his European-style, cotton khaki coat embroidered with gold, apparel quite alien to the Highlands. It set him apart, as did the dignified demeanor with which he presided over the crowd and the new arrivals. Tom again offered a few words of Malay, figuring it would get him nowhere but knowing it was far more appropriate than English.

"*Sila Masuk,*" replied the man, inviting the white men to gather around the longhouse fire pit. He spoke in Malay that was clear enough for even Tom to understand. The Kelabit man then continued by introducing himself: "*Nama saya Penghulu Lawai,*" he said with a smile. "My name is Chief Lawai." He welcomed Harrisson, and then went on to explain that what little Malay he spoke he had learned while working for a Brooke administrative officer on the lower portions of the Baram River.

Penghulu Lawai raised his hands and the crowd quieted. He said a few words which brought a brief murmur from the more angry-looking members of the tribe, and then the room was silent. A large vat of what looked to be old dishwater was brought out and hardwood cups of the liquid were passed around. It was *borak,* a liquor made from fermented fruit, and Tom remembered from his earlier trip that it was a sneaky drunk. The fluid was sweet and smelled a bit noxious, a combination that hid the fact that its alcohol content was quite high. Everyone followed the penghulu's lead and downed theirs quickly, then the cups were passed about for more and the mood of the group lifted a bit. There was a little talking between the Kelabit, and some seriously worried looks on the faces of Tom's men, but somehow Tom himself felt relaxed. The way the drinks were being passed around somehow reminded him of early evenings in his local pub when men received their first pint of beer.

The stifling tension was eased with the sweet borak, but many questions still needed to be answered. Both groups were concerned about the thoughts of the other, and the fact that the penghulu could speak Malay but had not bothered to since the beginning of the

meeting was disconcerting to Tom and his men. They were completely at the mercy of the Kelabit, divided, with minimal weapons,
in a hostile land, with no means of escape.

"We would like to know where you have come from," Penghulu
Lawai finally said in Malay. Tom explained, briefly, and Lawai seemed
to understand, though when he translated the answer to the Kelabit
there were some very puzzled looks from the men behind him. In
most cases the young Kelabit had never seen a white face. They certainly had never seen an airplane, or even conceived that such a thing
could exist. Tom was forced to back up his explanation a bit to assure the locals that he was indeed human, much like two other white
men who had passed through the Bario Asal on scientific studies
many years before. Tom had brought a few snapshots of himself with
other tribesmen that he'd been with on his previous trip, and as
these were passed around they were met with a lot of laughter.
Some of the older Kelabit actually recognized the men in the photos, and it was odd for them to see the faces printed on paper. The
giant, noisy bird that had dropped them was also of great interest,
and when Tom made a reference to the other white men, adminis-
trators from the highly held Brooke government, it was tentatively
accepted as a flying machine. The Brookes, after all, were capable of
anything it seemed, flying included.

The Kelabit men, through the penghulu, questioned all the
equipment and mannerisms of the newcomers for a very long time.
In the many holes that showed up in Tom's use of Malay, Sergeant
Sanderson translated. Tom and his men didn't know how long the in-
quisition had gone on, and after a few glasses of borak had forgotten
about their comrade Sergeant Bower, who was still out searching the
swamp for the missing radio. Somewhat reassuring was the fact that
the Kelabit men seemed to generally accept what Tom said, quickly
discussing the answer and then asking another question based on the
previous answer. It was all very trusting compared to how the British
might respond if strange, colored men dropped into Piccadilly
Circus wearing funny clothing and carrying odd instruments and
weapons.

"I'm still at a loss as to what their intentions are, Major," said Sanderson as his cup was filled with more borak. "Shouldn't we ask?"

"That would be quite rude if they intend us no harm," replied Tom. "And no matter their intentions with us, we have no control. We have to assume, as we decided months ago, that we are fine with them. There are bigger fish to fry."

Penghulu Lawai stopped his conversation with the other Kelabit and turned to Tom. "Many of my people think you are a bad omen and the best way to deal with you is to cut off your heads." He paused a moment, glancing around the room. "But I think it is too soon for that. We have not even heard why you are here."

"Penghulu, we need to know about the Japanese," Tom said. "They are men from a different land and have recently come to the coast of your island. Do you know much about them?"

Penghulu Lawai nodded and then translated the statements to the other men, not bothering to answer the question.

"Penghulu, we have many supplies that were dropped from the airplane," Tom continued in Malay. "And we must find them to survive." Penghulu Lawai barked out a few orders in Kelabit, then told Tom that his people would help find the equipment. A large contingent of those who'd been watching the discussion marched out the door with Sergeant Sanderson to assist in the storepedo search.

More borak was poured into coconut shell cups, and Penghulu Lawai explained everything he knew of the Japanese and his people's feelings about them. Rumors of their brutality had filtered from longhouse to longhouse, and many of the interior tribes feared them. The White Rajahs who had ruled before had, for the most part, kept to a hands-off policy and let the people of Sarawak live as they always had. The Japanese, however, had come in and immediately disrupted the old trading practices by taking goods from the longhouses on the rivers. Worse, Japanese brutality kept many people from traveling to areas known to have the ruthless soldiers. Food sources had been cut off and food stores had often been taken outright. When the Japanese had stormed the coast, many Dayak had been raped or killed and all the Europeans had either been shot, beheaded, or rounded up and put into camps. In one instance in the Dutch territory, two evangelical missionaries had been working with a longhouse for a couple of years. The Japanese had taken the missionaries out of the longhouse and killed them in front of the tribe.

The invincible presence the Brookes had sustained for a hundred years was destroyed in a matter of weeks by the Japanese. The Brookes had never been to the Highlands, Tom knew that, but they were well known and respected there, as they had brought security to many of the smaller tribes. But that security was now gone. The Imperial Army had spread word of its own invincibility by brutally putting down any who questioned its superiority.

As the borak continued to be passed around, Tom soon found he had the loose-lipped openness that comes with a good party. He and Lawai joked together, as best they could through Sanderson and in a language they barely shared, and the longhouse's higher-ranking men openly asked questions of the English newcomer. He'd been on Borneo less than two hours and already he was drunk and joking with the natives, but what that meant in the long term was still a big question. Tom had a mission to tend to, and it was hard to imagine that relations with his prospective allies could ever get any better. There was a lot of conversation going on around him that could not be understood, and the immediate hospitality seemed almost surreal. Maybe it was a front, or maybe, hopefully, he and his men were merely paranoid. In any event, they had been sent to Borneo with an overall goal of thwarting the Japanese, and so without further adieu he dropped a whole *new* mission in Lawai's lap.

"Penghulu, do you believe the Kelabit and other Dayak tribes would fight the Japanese if they were given support from other armies?" Tom asked in Malay, doing his best to piece together a coherent sentence through the cloud of borak. It was a big step from his initial mission of gathering intelligence and stopping food supplies, but the heads hanging around the room in twists of dried vines and thatch showed that these men knew how to fight. "I will be able to get some very good weapons for this, if you are interested."

Penghulu Lawai stared at him a moment, not bothering to translate what was said. He asked a few questions about the weapons, like whether or not the men would be allowed to keep them, then chatted with his associates in Kelabit. Guns were well-known and highly sought-after items in the jungles of Borneo, though very few Kelabit had them. They were valuable enough that a penghulu might try anything to get them for his men. Lawai talked with his men for just a moment, then nodded to Tom.

"I've never seen these Japanese," he said. "But I know that I don't like them. I will try to help you, but the penghulu of the entire Kelabit tribe in the other longhouses must know of this. I cannot speak for us all." Lawai called two younger boys over, telling them something in Kelabit and gesturing to the east with his hands. The boys listened intently, nodding their heads, then ran out the door. "In the morning the boys will return with a word on how this was received by the other Kelabit," said Lawai.

Tom nodded, then looked to Barrie with a shrug as if to say, "That's about as much as we can do."

Suddenly there was a commotion over near the door. With all the confusion and activity resulting from the initial parachute drop, Tom and his men had forgotten about the second group. A second B-24 had planned to drop another four men, including Tom's second in command, Eric Edmeades, if all went well with the first drop. Captain Edmeades, Sergeant Tredea, Sergeant Hallam, and Warrant Officer Cusack all had jungle experience similar to Tom, and it was an unexpected relief to Harrisson to see this group standing at the entrance to the longhouse accompanied by a group of Kelabit and all but one of the storepedoes. The radio had been found as had the other supplies and weapons. With most of the gear accounted for, all of the men alive and well, and what seemed to be friendly hosts with lots of alcohol at their disposal, the borak party was resumed.

They toasted each others' knowledge, then toasted each others' men, and even made a few toasts to the beauty of the women who were bringing in all the borak. It was a long day, and a lot of borak. Songs were sung by the Kelabit in honor of their new guests, with the newcomers returning the serenade with an inebriated rendition of the only songs all eight of the soldiers knew, "Three Blind Mice" and "She'll be Comin' 'Round the Mountain." Traditional dances were accompanied by Edmeades doing gymnastic moves among the rafters of the longhouse and various impromptu dance routines by all the men. They slept that night in the big hall of the longhouse, the calming effects of borak and the relaxed manner of the Kelabit off-setting the fear that the Japanese, having identified their plane, could burst through the door any moment. The constant noise of people walking about, chickens clucking under the building, and dogs howl-ing in the yard were noticed but hardly worth worrying over, and certainly not enough to keep Harrisson and his men from a much de-served night of sleep.

Tom woke the next morning with a hangover that could cripple a water buffalo. So did Lawai, Edmeades, Bower, Amat, and just about everyone else in the longhouse, but they all realized there was no time to sleep it off. Tom and Edmeades got up and rousted the rest of the men, though most of them were already awake from the clamor of dogs, chickens, crying babies, and Kelabit thundering about on the wood floor.

Still shaking the sleep from his body, Tom stepped outside to see something that no one, not even Lawai, would have expected to see. People stood everywhere, crouched in the cool gray mist that comes with Highland mornings, chatting as they faced the door. Dressed in animal skins, brass rings, long feathers, and colorful beads, they all were chiefs or ranking warriors, and none were from the main Bario longhouse.

"What is all of this, Major?" Edmeades said from behind.

Tom drew in a deep breath. "It's one of two things, Eric," Tom said as he stepped down from the veranda. "Either we are the focal point of a very big party, which we will not enjoy, or everyone has underestimated just how much these people love a good fight."

CHAPTER 5

March 3, 1999

MY MAPS SEEMED USELESS. Each one showed a peak where I felt the mountain lay, but none of them gave our objective a name. One map put the height at 6,650 feet, but couldn't define the river drainages that ran about its base. Another, produced by the University of Malaysia in Sarawak, showed it to be 5,703 feet high and to be a split in the highest reaches of the Limbang River. However, on careful inspection we noted differences in the topography that meant either the stated elevations of the Highlands were wrong, or the stated elevation of our mountain was way off the mark. Then there was the aeronautical map Layang Layang's pilots depended upon which showed the peak to be 6,703 feet high, but much of the area around it was tinted gray and labeled "All Elevations Unknown."

Vague references to Borneo have always been the norm, and making maps of the mountainous areas has never been a priority for the people who ventured into the island's interior. Men had sailed around the island for centuries, mapping the coast and noting prominent rivers. The Chinese had traded along the coast, as had the Dutch and Portuguese, but until the reign of the Brookes no one had made an effort to truly explore the interior with the intention of mapping. The Brookes set up government offices on the major waterways and kept complete maps of the rivers that could be used by

water traffic and transport. Occasionally, such as when an Iban rebellion against the new headhunting laws broke out, Charles Brooke
himself had trekked across portions of the interior, keeping detailed
maps of where he went. Naturalists like Sir Alfred Wallace, the man
who helped Charles Darwin formulate his theory of evolution, were
allowed to travel the island's waterways, but the mapping of those
areas had been done sporadically and with little accuracy. In spring
of 1999, when mankind had successfully mapped the surface of the
Moon, Venus, and Mars, there were still sections of Borneo that man
had nothing more to say about than "All Elevations Unknown."

"Getting back on that plane has to rank high on my list of
'Stupid things Sam and I did on vacation,'" said Volker as he
plopped down on a bagful of ropes. The duffels were spread across
the warm tarmac of the Bario airstrip like a patch of giant red and
yellow watermelons. They were filled with ropes, coats, and sleeping bags and served as nice beanbag-style chairs.

"According to Harrisson's book," I replied, not bothering to look
up from the map, "there are only two ways in or out of the Highlands. One is to fly, which takes roughly an hour, and the other is to
walk, which takes about five weeks. He did both, and when given the
choice, always flew, even though he had to *jump* out of the plane," I
said while grabbing a third and equally useless map from my bag. "I
think we made the right choice."

"Most people would say we were crazy for flying through *that* on
a plane with mechanical problems," he said, gesturing toward the
towering clouds while lying back on the largest yellow bag. The sky
above Bario Asal was threatening, and Volk was making note of it by
complaining about the flight. He wasn't any more bothered by the
plane ride than I was, but complaining about the fiascoes I'd conned
him into had become a mainstay of our friendship. "At least
Harrisson had the option of jumping out," Volker spouted.

After a few minutes of unloading the plane, lying about on the
tarmac, and getting our senses back from the nightmarishly bouncy
flight, we were met by our porters. Twenty men, all from Pa Ukat, a

Kelabit longhouse perhaps three miles from the main Bario settlement, came onto the tarmac and began shaking hands with each of us. Dave and Eddy darted around them in circles, filming all aspects of our greetings as I was introduced to Larry, a local guide with firsthand knowledge of the Highlands.

"Hello Sam, I am Larry," he said with a deep, rough voice. I shook his hand, noting that a man with forearms like Larry's might accidentally rip your arm off. "Jacob has called me many times about your trip."

"Larry knows the forest trails and river systems here far better than I," Jacob added, "and he is from Pa Ukat so he will be able to help us arrange the best possible deal with the porters."

"I thought you had already done that, Jacob," I said, wondering what had happened to our prearranged deal with the locals. He looked a bit sheepish, as though something was wrong.

"Yes," said Larry. He had a touch of a British accent and spoke very fast, though he held the S's a bit long, as if it were an effort to say them. "I just explained it to him. There is a bit of a problem with the compensation. You have a lot more gear than we expected and it is a very bad time for us as we are busy with a number of building projects. We will have a meeting tonight and get everything worked out." Jacob looked at me and shrugged his shoulders as if to say "I don't know what the problem is."

"I understand you want to climb Batu Lawi," Larry said with a wry smile that told me he presumed it to be an impossible task.

"Yeah, we've been calling it the Misty Mountain ever since we first saw pictures of it years ago. But I guess it's called Batu Lawi," I said. "We have been trying to find it for years, and only recently tracked it down through references in a book."

"Well, it is in a very remote place, and few people other than the Kelabit know of its existence," he said, glancing over to the mountains south of the airstrip. "It is a few days from here, through very tough terrain." He then looked back at the sky. "We should probably get your stuff and get going before it rains," Larry said as he tossed a seventy-five-pound duffel over his shoulder. The other Kelabit each grabbed a load and led us off the concrete slab and onto a red clay path that ran lengthwise through the valley.

Despite there being no roads to Bario, there is a road *in* Bario. It runs the length of the valley near the base of the mountains and is the modern replacement for a centuries-old jungle path. A small bulldozer, two Daihatsu mini-trucks, and a handful of 80cc motorcycles share the sandy path with the Plain of Bah's normal traffic of people, bicycles, and water buffalo. I was told that it is very rare for any two of these vehicles to be on the road at the same time and that our group of porters was a veritable rush hour for Bario. All the modern means of transportation had been flown in via the Skyvan on flights that most certainly pushed the little plane to its limit. Our North Face duffels were carried a short distance down the road, then loaded onto the motorcycles and trucks. Within minutes they'd disappeared down the clay path that wound through the jungle, leaving us to walk in the intense sun and, soon, rain.

"I hope you didn't have anything important in those bags," Larry joked as we watched them disappear down the road. "It only takes an hour or so to reach Pa Ukat, our longhouse, so it's better for us to walk and the bags to ride. We will work out the porters' fees and divide up the loads once we get to the longhouse."

As soon as the clouds blocked out the sun, the temperature was perfect for walking, perhaps seventy-two degrees, and depending on the whims of the building storms, a slight breeze blew. The views were impressive, with sweeping fields of grass broken by light-green paddies and groves of banana trees. The jungle surrounded the valley like a dark-green wall with somber gray clouds resting on it to form a solid ceiling. An untold number of insects buzzed, hissed, and chirped from the forest while thunder rumbled in the distance, reminding us that rain was always only a few minutes away. The Kelabit Highlands get around ten feet of precipitation a year, so rain is by far the most frequent visitor to the isolated community.

Lying perhaps three miles east of the main longhouse in Bario and at the base of a canyon that splits the rugged Tama Abu Range,

Pa Ukat was closer to Batu Lawi than any other settlement. Approaching it from the road, one comes down a steep hill that allows clear viewing across the canyon and all parts of this little village. It is a picturesque longhouse, nestled in a small hollow on the edge of the forest, with farm animals standing about in rice paddies of all shades of green. Ironwood timbers, perhaps a foot or more thick, brace the building six or eight feet off the ground. The wood has an aged look, cracked and gray, with black water streaks running down the least protected sections. Yellow lichen and dark moss grow in the cracks of the exposed timbers while the roof of the building, made of corrugated tin, is heather gray and rust brown. Banana leaves and various seeds are piled up in the gutters and fifty-gallon drums, copper-colored with oxidation, squat around its perimeter to collect rainwater. The whole place makes one question how important it is to paint a house, clear the gutters, and be concerned with the yard when a proper design and a few goats seem to handle the most extreme conditions.

A stream descending from high in the Tama Abu meanders through trees a hundred or so yards away from Pa Ukat. Water is channeled from the stream via bamboo aqueducts to keep the paddies green, and groves of bananas, pineapples, and other fruit grow in nearby clearings. Several buildings dotting the nearby paddies appeared to be simple homes and storage shacks for farm equipment.

When we approached Pa Ukat, each man and woman, ages six through sixty, came down the steps of the longhouse to shake hands with us. They wore Western-style clothing, the women in long skirts with cotton blouses and the men in shorts and polyester sweatshirts. Virtually everyone was shorter than us and stocky, although muscular and fit. The camera guys rushed to capture the unusual welcome, wheeling around the crowd, zooming in, mumbling to each other about lighting and sound as we walked along something akin to a wedding receiving line, shaking hands with each member of the tribe and thanking them for inviting us to their home.

"This is the penghulu," Larry said as I shook hands with one of the older men. "He is the elected leader and settles most of the disputes in the longhouse." The old man shook my hand and nodded, saying a few words in Kelabit to Larry.

The Highlands, despite being remote, have very good schools so many of the people speak English. I stood on the steps and explained to the crowd that we wished to climb Batu Lawi and that we were happy to be in Bario after so many months of preparation. Everyone seemed to listen politely, smiling at my words as Eddy and Dave filmed. I felt a bit self-conscious standing in front of an entire village with cameras rolling as I spoke for our group, but my words seemed well-received. After I spoke, the crowd broke up and went about their daily chores. Most of the bags were taken inside, and Larry had someone bring us some sliced pineapple. A few of the young men lingered and asked us questions about climbing, and a half dozen small children shyly stood off in the shadows of the longhouse, watching to see what the strangers might do next. I got out my maps and began asking Larry about the region.

"I don't know the exact height," Larry said as he took a deep drag off his cigarette, "but I know how to get to the base of it. It is right there," he said, pointing to the "6,703" on one of the maps. "I was there in 1994, and I can tell you that whether you climb the mountain or not, you will be eating a lot of wild boar." The guys around us seemed to speak English, but Larry relayed what he'd just said in Kelabit anyway. They nodded and smiled at each other with the mention of the wild boar. "The area is very rich in wildlife," he paused and took another drag on the cigarette as he looked up the canyon toward the Tama Abu cliffs, "but very rough." Larry continued to stare at the ridge for some time, mumbling something to the Kelabit men. They looked at our bags, then glanced up at the mountains and shook their heads.

I walked across the lawn to Volker and Scott to tell them what I'd learned from the maps, pondering the way Larry had said "rough." The words "rough" and "adventure" are often found near the word "Borneo," but we'd already nearly been in a plane crash that day and were far more interested in hearing words like "casual" and "hot tub."

"Look at Larry," said Volker. "He's built like a brick longhouse. Do we really want to go someplace that man calls 'rough'?"

"It's not that he said it was 'rough,' it's the way he said it," added Scott. "He gave the whole ridgeline the classic thousand-yard stare, as if we were going to war."

I nodded and glanced up at the dark mountains and clouds. Larry had been educated in the school at Bario and learned to hunt in the mountains of the Kelabit Highlands. All of us were quite fit, but probably not as prepared for the journey as he was, so his anxiety was a bit disconcerting. Despite prior planning, the difficulties of any journey are never fully accepted until they become reality, and at the moment those mountains looked very intimidating.

Without warning, other than the constant rumble of thunder in the distance which we had already begun to grow used to, the skies opened up. We each grabbed a bag as the men of the longhouse quickly came outside and hefted the remaining duffels over their shoulders, then wobbled up the steep wooden steps and into the dry building. As is the custom, and it only makes sense considering the various parasites that live in the dirt in Borneo, we removed our shoes before entering. Everything was stacked just inside the main door at the end of a long room that ran the length of the house.

With nothing else on the agenda and no place to go, we started sorting our stuff and preparing for dinner. It is customary for the longhouse to take in strangers, and they did provide us with rice. In most of the world meat is a luxury and is eaten far less frequently than in the West, so we politely turned down their offer to prepare some. Rice, however, is the grain of a grass that is indigenous to Southeast Asia. It is the principal food source for over half the world's population and has been cultivated in one form or another for over seven thousand years. The Kelabit are very proud of their rice; its fine grain and somewhat sweet flavor has given it a reputation as the best rice in all of Malaysia. Wealthy businessmen and politicians all over the country have created a demand for it, and the Kelabit produce enough to sell excesses as a cash crop. From time to time the sultan of Brunei, one of the world's richest men, sends a private plane into Bario just to buy the staple. Jacob made sure we had plenty, and that we understood just what a luxury it was for us to be getting this prized commodity. We went about boiling it and heating up a few cans of beans, then throwing in a bag of Mexican-style spices. Just as the meal was ready for eating, Larry came over and said something to Jacob, then ambled back down the hall.

"I think we should have the meeting," Jacob said. "Larry has gotten all the possible porters together and they want to talk to you."

"What's the problem, Jacob?" I asked in a low voice. "I thought you had the porters arranged via the radiophone."

"I did, but it seems they said 'yes' to my deal before actually talking it over," he replied as we walked through the smoky room where everyone had gathered. "I think Larry tried to call me back, but the radiophone up here doesn't work some days. Business deals are always a problem."

The men were sitting in a large half circle on straw mats and little wooden stools. A fire was burning in a large pit and the smoke billowed out the open windows and eaves of the longhouse. As I approached, Larry lit a kerosene lamp and sat it next to a couple of stools. Jacob and I took the seats and waited for someone to speak. Larry started off.

"Jacob had called many days ago. I told him I felt 5,400 ringgit was enough for these men and I to lead you to Batu Lawi, but there were some misunderstandings," he said. "We did not realize how much equipment you had, nor how heavy it was. We will need a lot more porters than originally were anticipated." Volker and the other guys came up behind me, standing about the fire pit and listening to what Larry had to say. "I'm afraid 5,400 ringgit will not be enough to cover all of our expenses."

Throughout the history of mountain climbing, mountaineers have hired porters to help get their equipment to the base of the mountain. In Pakistan, Nepal, Africa, South America, even Europe and the US, the need for porters has existed almost anytime a person has wanted to enter the mountain environment for an extended period. In most cases they are an absolute necessity. As such, they set the rules, and there is little that can be done about their demands other than accept them. Porter strikes have existed as long as porters have, but a strike and demand for higher wages is a bit stressful when it comes before anyone has even left home. However, the roughly $1,500 that 5,400 ringgit added up to was what we had budgeted for the trip, and any more would eat up the emergency reserve.

"Well," I asked, "how many more people will you need?" I heard Volker and Chris whisper something behind me and noticed the film guys scurrying about with their cameras. A boom microphone suddenly poked out of the darkness and hung over Larry.

The porters all mumbled to one another for a bit. Larry was leading the proceedings, but from the way they spoke it was obvious that each man had something to say in the matter. "They think you will need perhaps twenty porters, not fourteen, and the price for each is higher. It was thirty ringgit a day, but the penghulu of our tribe has said that all porters must be paid sixty-five ringgit. Also, Jacob had said that the porters should hike out once the equipment is there. This will not be possible, so they will need to be paid for each day."

"You must know," said one of the men near the fire. "We are building a new church right now so it is a very bad time for us to leave."

Discussions over how much should be paid, how many days were at full pay, how much each man would carry, who would pay for the porters' rice, when the church would be finished, and virtually every other aspect of our proposed trip were tossed around over the course of the evening. The fact that the video guys were there had been brought up, which let us know that the Kelabit were not so removed from the world that they didn't recognize the entertainment industry as a cash cow. They told me about every factor of life in the forest, how much work they would miss on their new church, and how difficult the trek was. I was overwhelmed by the details and couldn't focus on any given point.

At around 2 A.M. I called a halt to the meeting and agreed to meet again in the morning. The camera guys had long since hit the sack, accepting that the particulars of how many bags of rice each man would consume over ten, twelve, or fourteen days were probably not going to make interesting viewing for the home audience. Chris had gotten a few still shots and, having been through a number of porter strikes, stuck with the discussions while Volker and Scott stood by for moral support. With little discussion amongst ourselves, we wandered through the smoke to our sleeping bags and collapsed.

"At ten o'clock this morning, sitting in the middle of the runway, I thought we were never going to get to Bario," said Scott. "Now we're here, but it seems rather doubtful we're ever going to get to the mountain." Volker nodded in affirmation as he rolled his bag out on the hard mahogany floor.

"Harrisson said these people are very practical," I replied. "Maybe they don't need a lot of expensive items from the outside world, so they don't really care if we turn their offer down."

"Yeah. Usually porters need the work," added Volker, "but these guys have all the rice, fruit, and meat they could ever need just outside the door. You're right; they don't need our cash."

"He also said these guys throw big parties with lots of alcohol every time a visitor arrives, but that is not the way we were greeted," I continued. "Maybe things change."

With nothing else said, we drifted off. It was a restless night, however, as I woke every forty-five minutes or so, bruising on the hardwood floor and mulling over what we should do. The air was filled with smoke, which kept the mosquitoes at bay but burned my throat and nose. At each waking I'd take a slug of water from my Nalgene bottle, then step outside into a cold drizzle and get rid of the previous drink. The rain would thoroughly wake me, making sleep that much harder. At around 4 A.M. a dog began moaning under the longhouse, then at around five the roosters started crowing. Soon after that we heard a deep hum coming from the private rooms of the longhouse. We all sat up in our bags, trying to discern the low-toned humming. It went on for a few minutes, and only toward its end did we realize that the entire longhouse was praying. With the end of the prayers, everyone came out of their rooms and began the day's business. It was 5:15, and sleep time was over.

A faint light began to filter through the open windows and the smoke that filled the room. Dave and Eddy slid out of their bags and immediately started fiddling with camera gear while Volker, Chris, Scott, and I began rolling up our bags. The men of Pa Ukat had gathered around the fire pit outside the headman's room and Larry was leading them in a discussion. I called everyone together and we discussed the prospects of the coming meeting with the men who were now merely our *potential* porters.

"We really only have two choices: either we pay them what they want, or pack up our stuff and carry it ourselves to the airport and wait for a flight to come in," I said.

"They really have us over a barrel here," said Chris. "In Nepal there is a fixed price and you know it before you get there. We should have known it here, so I guess Jacob blew it."

"I think this was a surprise to Jacob, too," I replied. "He told me it's hard to get anything fixed in stone, and they had been trying to contact him via radio."

"Well, someone screwed up," he said, walking back to his bags.

I took a couple of deep breaths and turned to the others. "Dave, we can afford to pay them what they're asking but I won't have any money left if anything else comes up," I said to him as he adjusted a wire on one of the batteries. "Do you guys have some sort of contingency fund from Anywhere Adventure Pictures?"

"We do, but we're not supposed to use it except in an emergency," he said. "It seems like this should have been worked out ahead of time."

It was a jab at me, and I wasn't in the mood. "I'm going to agree to their terms," I said. "But let's keep in mind that the amount of climbing equipment has not increased over the last few months. There is, however, a lot more camera equipment and even one extra cameraman." He didn't look at me.

Volker, Scott, and Chris followed me through the long room to the fire pit. A couple of pots of rice were on the logs, one boiling over with white foam, the liquid hissing as it dripped onto the orange coals. Streams of sunlight filtered through the smoke-shrouded windows, creating a blinding white light for anyone attempting to look outside. The men of Pa Ukat had stopped talking and were sitting about, waiting for us to show up and for me to make the first move.

"Well," I said, looking to Larry, "we can afford to pay you a total of 14,000 ringgit. That has to get us from here to Batu Lawi base camp then back here plus back to the airport." I paused for a bit and looked around the room, trying to make eye contact for just a moment with everyone. With every culture I'd met in Asia, eye contact had been important in showing a serious commitment to what you said. "This is how much money we have. If it's not enough, then we will need help getting our stuff back to the airport today."

They spoke in low tones to each other, then one man said something to Larry in Kelabit. "They agree with your price and feel that you are being honest with them," Larry said. "We will leave in one hour." With that the men got up and came over to me, shaking hands just as they had the day before at our first greeting. Everyone was smiling, except those of us who had to pay the higher fee, and Larry seemed happy with his position as mediator. After they'd all gone off to their rooms he came over and patted me on the back.

"I think," he said, "by the end of the day you will understand why they wish to be paid so much for this trip. I hope you guys are as strong as Jacob says."

CHAPTER 6

March 26, 1945

L AWAI APPEARED ON THE LONGHOUSE VERANDA behind Tom, adjusted his coat so it hung straight, then went about introducing the major to the newly arrived warriors. Tom shook hands, looking each man in the eye as he did so and doing his best to memorize each man's name. The other men of the Special Recon Detachment kept busy cleaning the Sten machine guns, radio, and magazines of ammunition, and did what they could to explain how it all worked to the inquisitive Kelabit. All the while they were wondering what was going to unfold with the scores of approaching warriors. Most of the communication was done in the now familiar "chicken dance" manner, but both groups were beginning to pick up a few words of each other's language. As the morning passed, more warriors from the surrounding regions arrived, all wanting to meet the Europeans.

Penghulu Miri, chief of all the Kelabit tribes in Bario Asal, arrived with a small entourage late in the morning. Penghulu Miri was younger than Lawai but far more powerful and imposing as a leader. His physique was enough to startle the average man. Bracelets hung not just around his wrists but also his elbows and knees, held in place by the bulging muscles of his forearms and calves. His earlobes, like those of many Kelabit, hung low with large hoops of brass, and his formal attire included a belt of silver coins. Tom was introduced to

Miri and his ranking warriors, and he spoke to them as humbly as possible. He quickly learned that Miri understood the ways of the outsiders fairly well. Miri had made the thirty-day trek to the coast on numerous occasions during the rule of the White Rajahs and had learned to speak seven different languages, including Malay, Iban, and some English and Dutch as a result of his travels. The formal introductions with all the warriors were then halted so Tom and Penghulu Miri could speak.

"The foreign army you speak of has destroyed longhouses lower on the Baram River," Miri said solemnly in Malay. "They have taken the food reserves and the working buffalo from the longhouses, and we have heard that many of the women have been carried away for the enjoyment of the Japanese troops." Tom Harrisson nodded as Miri spoke, knowing that this is what the Imperial Army had done in Korea, Burma, China, the Philippines, and most of the South Pacific islands. Miri went on to explain that the Japanese had gone very far into the interior of Borneo, but the Tama Abu Range and jungle around it continued to be the impenetrable barrier it had been for all of Kelabit history. No Japanese troops had reached Bario, but it was only a matter of time before they did, and the Kelabit, who knew of the atrocities occurring elsewhere, were very afraid of the future.

"I have come here because I believe we can push these men back from your island," Tom said to him. "These things they have done to the people of Sarawak, they have also done to many other people, including mine, and we want to stop them."

Miri took a sip of water from a carved, wood cup, then looked off the high veranda across the throngs of people who'd gathered. The SRD men were spread about, some working on their equipment, a couple showing the locals how the snaps on a canvas backpack worked, and one fellow displaying the strength of parachute fabric to a few older women. Everyone seemed to be getting along, but would the harmony last?

"How are we to know that you are not the same as these men?" Miri asked gravely in Malay. His direct approach reminded Tom that despite the pleasantness of everyone they had met, their lives were still at the mercy and whims of the locals, and the locals had a fearsome reputation. "The Brookes never caused us any problem, but the Brookes and you are not the same. How do I know that you are not the enemy, just as these Japanese men are?"

"I can only give you my word. I do not have proof," Tom replied in Malay. "But I promise you I am here only to help, not to hurt the Kelabit."

Miri paused a moment more to think it over. It was a strong statement, and both men knew it.

"You say your people have been fighting these men in many places?" he asked.

"Yes, many places."

"How many have died?" Miri inquired quietly. Tom looked across the scene in front of the longhouse, then looked back at Miri with an expression that hardly needed words.

"Thousands."

"Thank you for telling me the truth," Miri said.

With that they separated and Tom went about meeting the other new arrivals. As Tom shook hands with each one, Penghulu Miri convened a meeting to discuss the newcomers, the Japanese, and the possibility of war. The meeting continued through the night, led on mostly by Penghulu Miri as he was the expert on white culture and politics. Tom and his men worked on cleaning their equipment and getting the radio working as the Kelabit leaders planned and conferred farther down the big hall.

"What do you think is happening, Major?" Edmeades asked as he pulled a boiling pot of rice off the fire pit. Tom had spoken with Miri and the other chiefs for much of the afternoon and got the general sense that they liked him and did not like the Japanese, but no formal statement to that effect had been made. Miri's questions had been direct, and the answers to them were uncomfortable to say. Tom knew they still couldn't be sure if they were being treated well because the Kelabit wanted them for their fighting abilities, or for the novelty of their white heads.

"I'd like to think we will be safe with these men," Tom replied. "But I don't know whether they want to take on the Japanese. The war hasn't really come to them yet, and maybe the best course of action from their standpoint is to just be rid of us."

Throughout the day Edmeades, Bower, and the other men had divided up their tasks and learned what they could of the area. As far as they could tell they had made friends with the local men and were becoming familiar with the language. "No matter what their intentions with us are, I have to say they are rather amazing people, Major," said Edmeades. "They seem to have put their own chores behind to begin helping us with ours."

"Yes, sir," said Bower. "While we were setting up the radio there were a number of men around us. We could see that they were quite interested in our equipment, but they were never so rude as to reach out and touch it, or even ask to for that matter."

"They are very interesting people," said Tom. "They seem very genuine. My biggest concern right now is not whether they will kill us to be rid of us or not . . . that seems unlikely and there's not much we can do about it anyway. We need to be thinking progressively, so let's start by deciding where we will make our headquarters, which is of utmost importance. Is this the spot?" he asked the men as they finished the first bowls of rice.

"The open plains are obviously the best for airdrops," Edmeades volunteered. "And if we ever get around to setting up an airstrip, it would have to be here."

"Yes, but it is quite open," said Tom. "You don't have anyplace to run to if the Japs show up. Also, Penghulu Miri told me a few things about his longhouse at Bawang that made it sound appealing. It is a bit northeast of here and offers easy access into the Trusan, one of the big rivers that drains into Brunei Bay."

"Have the Japanese been there?" Sanderson asked.

"Yes, but not recently, and I'm sure that if these people want to help us, they will be able to provide a very good warning if they were to return," Tom replied. "Apparently the Japs have not treated the people along the Trusan very well." He paused a moment, scraping up the last of his rice. "I think we have no choice. This is the best site for a runway and airdrops, but it's not the best place to run the battles from." Everyone nodded rather than speak. They were all exhausted.

"Should we contact HQ in Darwin yet?" asked Bower. He had the radio working but had not bothered to make contact with the base in Australia.

"Let's wait until morning and see what happens," Tom advised. He stared down the hall to the next open fire pit, watching the gray smoke drift up between the men as the orange flames danced around their feet and knees. He could clearly hear what the Kelabit were saying but remained in the dark as to its meaning.

"Think about what's going on here, from another perspective if you can," Tom said to Bower. "Those men down there are listening to us rattle on in some sort of gibberish we call English. We showed up here with weapons and immediately started speaking of starting a war, while they wanted nothing more than pleasant introductions and a party." Tom sighed and glanced at Bower, who was nodding as he ate his rice. "War is something to be avoided at all costs," he continued, "and it would take a very special people to see that we are telling the truth." Tom watched the fire intently as the men served him more rice, then they all fell asleep to the sounds of crickets, crackling coals, and the distant discussion of their fate. As he drifted off, Tom Harrisson acknowledged to himself what a peaceful place they had dropped into, and that in the end it might be better if the Kelabit didn't listen to him.

A few hours later Harrisson sat up and rubbed the sleep from his eyes. His nose and throat burned from the smoke of the fire pit that had filled the longhouse all night. Although the smoke was bad on the lungs and eyes, it kept the mosquitoes at bay, thus providing the longhouse residents with a bit of prophylactic protection from the horrors of malaria. The roosters, crowing in the predawn darkness two and three at a time, had by now been drowned out by the sounds of activity in the longhouse. People were moving back and forth through the long hall, busy with the daily chores that are the mainstay of a hunter-gatherer society. Penghulu Miri had fresh coffee, grown in the Highlands, brought to Harrisson and asked him to join the chiefs for breakfast. Harrisson walked down the long hall to where the chiefs were sitting about a fire pit and discussing what their policy should be toward Harrisson and the Japanese. All the men had bowls of rice next to them, and it was obvious to Tom by the way the food was only partially consumed that they had been too busy to eat. Tom sheepishly stepped close enough to the fire to be seen, then smiled and nodded to the men when they noticed his presence.

"Of all places," began Penghulu Miri, "how did you come to the Kelabit Highlands for this mission?"

"It is far from the Japanese, and it has a clearing in the forest where we could land with our equipment," Harrisson answered. "We were able to locate it through the clouds by flying to the big mountain to the north, what we call Peak 200, then turning this way and jumping when we had traveled the correct distance."

Miri's eyes widened and he stared at Tom for a moment, then translated this into Kelabit for the other men. When Miri spoke of the flight in, the men gasped, then looked back at Tom in astonishment.

"We will need some more time to talk," Miri said. Tom was led back down the hall, then brought back to the chiefs only a couple of minutes later.

"Do you understand the significance of this Peak 200 to us?" Miri asked. "Do you know what this mountain is?" Tom shook his head to say no, momentarily forgetting that for the Kelabit the gesture was not a clear answer. Somehow Miri understood.

"That mountain is called Batu Lawi," he replied. "It is actually a man and a woman, now turned to stone at the edge of the Highlands. A long time ago, Gunung Api, the fire mountain from Mulu, came here as a giant flame to burn all the Kelabit. The man and woman that are Batu Lawi gave their lives to stop Api. Now they stand over the Highlands to protect us." He paused a moment, looking into Tom's eyes with an intense stare. The other chiefs were staring as well, slowly nodding their heads back and forward. "We don't see how the evil means of the Japanese, the arrival of you and your men, and the sighting of Batu Lawi can be a coincidence."

The Kelabit chiefs, especially Miri, were generally quite logical and down-to-earth when it came to policy matters for their people, but the Japanese had been hard on all the people of Sarawak, killing many of them. Tom and the Allied commanders didn't know it, but for months the chiefs of all the lowland tribes in Sarawak had talked of how the invaders should be pushed from the shores and Rajah Brooke brought back to his throne. The problem was that no one knew how to do it. Now, as the invading army was on the brink of entering the Highlands, an outsider had been drawn to help the Kelabit people by the protector, Batu Lawi. The fact that he was a white British man, like the Rajah Brookes, and that like them he had come to the aid of the people of Borneo, could not be dismissed.

"Lawai, myself, and the other penghulus conferred over your presence all night long," Miri said to Harrisson in Malay. "We had decided to let you work from here to rid Sarawak of the Japanese before they come to the Highlands." He paused and said a few words to the other penghulus. "But the fact that you have come by the way of Batu Lawi cannot be a coincidence. We feel that you are the new rajah of Borneo, the man who will unite the island and bring peace just like rajahs of before."

Tom was overwhelmed. "You feel I should be the rajah?" he asked incredulously, stumbling over the words. He had expected to be told that the chiefs wished to avoid war and that he should leave. Instead, they wanted him to be king.

"It has already been decided," Miri replied.

Tom looked at the faces of the men around him, glanced back down the hall to his comrades, and took a deep breath. "It's very difficult to tell a man you don't want to be his elected king," he mused in English. "And I will make no effort to do so."

"I accept your allegiance with all the respect it deserves, and thank you for your loyalty," Tom said as best as he could in Malay. He knew that later he would have to answer to commanders in Darwin, Morotai, and the Philippines for this utterly unanticipated turn of events, but there was no way he would insult these men by saying anything other than "yes" to the idea of sovereignty. "We will work together to overcome a common enemy."

In just two days Harrisson had succeeded in winning the trust and the hearts of the Kelabit people, and already they were beginning to win his. Not only would it be advantageous for him to be the acting rajah, he reasoned, but the arrangement could very well prove to be beneficial for the Kelabit as well. If the Allies were going to win the war, as one had to believe, then they would someday be deciding the fate of Borneo and its people. It would be good for the Kelabit and every one of the Dayak tribes to have a military man on their side. Tom Harrisson accepted the position of rajah, and with his acceptance the chiefs went about spreading his plan across northern Borneo to all the Dayak tribes.

CHAPTER 7

March 5, 1999

THEY WANT TO BREAK THE LOADS DOWN into a more equal share of weight from bag to bag," Larry informed us. Jacob stood next to him, glancing over the piles of equipment and then back to me as Larry assured us that with a little rearranging, everything would make it to the mountain.

"I understand that the loads are pretty cumbersome," I said. "But the cameramen are worried the equipment will be damaged if it's not wrapped up in certain ways." Eddy had given me an earful about this earlier when the Kelabit had started divvying up the loads.

"It will be okay," Larry said. "They understand that you need to protect the gear, but they don't want to die trying to get it to Batu Lawi. Crossing a log bridge with these loads is going to be very dangerous."

The camera and media equipment not only took up three porters for every one who carried climbing gear, it was often more difficult to pack. I surely didn't want the job the Kelabit had accepted, and unless the film guys wanted to carry their own gear, all five hundred pounds of it, they were going to have to let the porters divide it as they wished. I acquiesced, gently reminding Larry that if any of it arrived damaged, it would be my ass, not his, so to "please be careful." He smiled to let me know he understood.

The loads were broken down and divided between the bags.

Roughly an even amount of large, bulky items, such as ropes, and small, dense items, like camera batteries and pitons, were distributed among the porters. Each North Face expedition bag came with shoulder straps for easier transport, but the Kelabit had no use for them. They had their own personalized backpacks made of rattan, dried vines, and bamboo onto which they had lashed each of the huge duffels with vine straps. The majority of the porters wore either army fatigues or Adidas-style jogging suits, although a couple were in shorts. Their feet were mostly protected with long-spiked football cleats, and at their sides hung twenty-inch parangs in hand-carved teak scabbards.

Scott, Volker, and I loaded our personal gear into our own brightly colored nylon packs, deftly stowing the Gore-Tex rain jackets where they could easily be reached. The camera guys went about filming all of the preparations, scampering around the bags and backpacks as they were hefted onto the men, while Chris stood back and took still photos of the scene. Each porter looked grossly overloaded and topheavy, the huge duffels towering above them and swelling off the rattan frames like balloons. One glance at the few wearing shorts, however, and I knew that they could handle the loads. Their legs, conditioned by a thousand generations of walking through the steep jungle with a dead boar or deer over their shoulders, had built them up like the strongest Himalayan mountaineers.

All the families of the longhouse came out and watched the loading, joking in Kelabit about the size of the packs. The Kelabit men taunted each other, each man poking at his own bulging muscles and pointing out particular traits of his load to prove it was heavier than all the others. Moments after stuffing our packs we reached for our jackets as a slight drizzle began and thunder boomed up the canyon. The Kelabit paid no attention to the change in weather, knowing already that being wet was just a part of hiking in the jungle. They strapped on the last of the duffels as the penghulu, the chief of Pa Ukat, descended from the longhouse and said a few words to Larry.

"It is tradition," Larry said to me and Volker, "that the penghulu lead us in a prayer before we leave. This is very important to us. Packs of this size in the terrain we must cross are a matter of life and death." I nodded, and the penghulu began a prayer in Kelabit. Everyone except Dave and Eddy, who continued moving about with the cameras, dipped their head. The prayer went on for a minute or so, not finishing with a general amen but a moment of silence. The ritual completed, twenty-seven men began walking toward Batu Lawi.

Only one trail leads up the canyon in the Tama Abu Mountains from Pa Ukat, and it was easy to follow. I led the way, with Volker and Scott in tow. The film guys and Chris roved about, staying behind the porters to shoot them leaving camp, then running out in front of us to get a scene of "the team" hiking through the paddies. Jacob and Larry, carrying lighter loads than the porters, stayed close to the front of the band, with us.

We walked along a trail that followed the stream up-canyon, occasionally crossing from one side to the other on bridges. The stream, perhaps ten feet below, flowed fast and deep but had few rapids. Each bridge was built of giant stems of bamboo, perhaps a foot or more thick, lashed together with rattan. The bamboo poles were smooth and wet from the rain, and with each step they bounced and shimmied from side to side. Because the bridges were rickety and generally unnerving to look at, Dave, Eddy, and Chris regularly made us stop and traverse them for filming purposes.

Occasionally the trail moved away from the stream and out into the rice paddies. Walking out front meant watching my feet and constantly glancing into the grass on either side of the trail. The paddy dikes, made of packed mud and grass, were a couple of feet wide and easy to balance on, but the thick grass along the edges is known to be a favorite haunt of cobras.

When we did look up, the view from the open canyon was tremendous. Small huts made of bamboo and hardwood planks, brown and gray with age, stood at the edge of each field. The flat terrain, either recently planted with rice or just harvested, contrasted between pale green and chocolate brown. When the sun managed to pass through a thinner bit of cloud cover, the slender rice shoots would brighten to a shade of day-glow green. They were beautiful but so brilliant that one couldn't stare at them for long without getting a slight headache.

"Larry," I called back as we walked past a small hut. "What are all these smaller houses for? I thought everyone lived in the longhouse."

"Many of these houses are just farm sheds," he said, "but some are for sleeping in when we don't want to hike all the way back to the longhouse. It's not good to walk the trails in the dark." He paused a bit and then continued, "Many of the Kelabit have tried to live in their own homes rather than the longhouse, because, well, that's what the missionaries told us that everyone from America and Europe does. It didn't work. It's very lonely out here and we have always lived communally. Also, our people are getting old. Many of the younger Kelabit are well-educated and want to use that education in the cities. This is good for them, but it means the population of the longhouses in Bario Asal is mostly elders. It's much easier for them to care for each other by living in the longhouse together."

"We have similar problems at my longhouse near Mulu," offered Jacob. "But there is something else as well. Visitors come to stay in the longhouse, and huge parties can be thrown in the main hall. Sometimes we have maybe a thousand people lined up in there, all sharing in one great meal. It's festive, and living close together makes you into one large family. But the cities are different. I have lived in Miri for four years now and I still do not know my next door neighbor's name. To me, that's sad."

The sky varied from a pale white to a dark gray, and thunder rumbled in the Tama Abu Mountains, telling us that heavy rain was only a few minutes off. More rain really wouldn't change things much, though, as we were all already soaked to the bone. I had traveled in the tropics for years and even lived right on the beach in Thailand, but had never experienced anything like the near oppressive dampness of the Kelabit Highlands. Relative humidity is a mea-

surement of water content in a given space of air. Since air is generally more dense at lower altitudes and lower temperatures, one
would think that a 90-degree day on coastal Thailand would feel
much more humid than an 80-degree day at 4,000 feet above sea
level. But it didn't seem to work that way. It wasn't warm enough
for us to sweat, but our skin and clothes were constantly damp, and
when we passed near or through the forest the air grew even more
heavy with moisture. Evapotranspiration, the process that occurs
when the trees of the rainforest have gathered so much water that
they release it through their leaves, meant that walking under a large
hardwood was somewhat like stepping into a sauna. Out in the open
the air was not white with mist, but tiny water droplets formed on
everything. Even without actual rainfall we were still dripping wet.

The North Face had given us a new product line of thin, syn-
thetic shirts and pants that were designed to dry quickly as they
didn't absorb water. We'd used them in Thailand and they worked
great, but the Kelabit Highlands were more than the most advanced
sports clothing could handle. The fabric is designed to pull moisture
away from your skin and then allow it to be evaporated from the
clothing. But it soon became clear that the process only works when
the relative humidity in the surrounding environment is less than
that of your body. Since the surface of our bodies was covered 100
percent by moisture, we could only assume that the relative humidity was also 100 percent. There was never a dry moment or a dry bit
of air to evaporate the water from our clothing. The moisture was
simply everywhere and nothing could have kept us dry.

After perhaps an hour and a half of hiking the flat ground we arrived at the base of the canyon and foot of the Tama Abu Range.
Steep canyon walls canopied in green jungle rose on all sides of the
paddies except in the direction we had come from. An ever-
thickening mist could be seen swirling in the trees above and the distant rumbles were now constant and much closer. At the edge of the
forest two water buffalo wallowed in the mud of the paddy, snorting
at us as we approached.

"This is my brother's place," Larry said as we approached a small hut. "Steve, come out and see our friends."

Steve stepped down off the hut's porch, wiping sleep from his eyes and waving as we approached. He greeted us with a warm smile, then began chatting with Larry in Kelabit. We slid off our packs to rest and wait for the porters to catch up.

"He wants to know how you found out about Batu Lawi," Larry said, obviously translating for Steve. I got up and began thinking about how to abridge the story of how we'd located the peak.

"Well, we found a picture of it in this old French atlas," I began. "But we weren't sure where . . ."

"Hey, let's do a few interviews while we wait," Eddy interjected. He had put on his raincoat and was holding the camera under it in a futile hope of holding back the mist.

"Um, okay," I said, slightly embarrassed by the interruption. "Just a moment." I briefly told Steve how we had made our way there, then excused myself and walked over to where Eddy and Dave were crouched near the edge of the paddy. "You want me or the other guys?" I asked.

"We'll start with you," Dave replied. They had me move out from under the small saplings that grew around Steve's house and sit on a log with my back to the buffalo. A microphone was wired through my shirt with a transceiver and battery pack placed in my back pocket. The porters arrived and dropped their heavy packs as we did a couple of countdown tests to get the sound right, then they started the interview.

"So, as the team leader, what are your thoughts about the climb?" Eddy began.

"I'm not really thinking about the climb, actually. We have to get there before we can climb, and from everything I've read and everything the locals are saying, the trek is what we should be focused on. Besides, the hiking is beautiful. We're walking along the edge of a hundred-million-year-old forest, past the homes of people who have lived off the forest for untold generations."

Eddy sort of rolled his eyes, as though he didn't like what he was hearing. I continued, saying a few words about what we needed to do from this point to make it to Batu Lawi before he lowered the camera.

"Okay," Eddy said. "That's enough. We'll do more later." He mumbled something to Dave about a lack of focus on climbing, but then went on filming the porters reloading and starting up the trail. We slid on our packs and followed.

Perhaps a hundred yards from Steve's house the paddies stopped and the forest began. Almost immediately we were in a different world. The constant, distant hiss of cicadas gave way to the rhythmic chirping of tree frogs, and the bright colors of flowering plants and trees all but disappeared. What little sunlight managed to get through the dense clouds over the Highlands was now blocked by the towering trees, leaving the trail dark and soggy. No one had trimmed back the undergrowth and the path was far less distinct. We were in untouched territory, and with its untempered wildness came the first moments of our constant contact with Borneo's most prevalent form of wildlife: leeches.

Leeches are carnivorous annelid worms, usually no more than an inch or two in length. They are well known as the most aggressive animals in the forest, honing in on any warm-blooded animal that passes by through special thermal receptors. Two species are common to the forests of Borneo: the tiger leech and the ground leech, both of which are ultimately harmless. They latch onto their prey as it passes and inchworm their way to a suitable spot for dining, then break the skin with three teeth and inject an anticoagulant so the blood can flow freely. As it does, the leech grows to many times its normal size, gorging itself on the warm food. Eventually it drops off, lays a few thousand eggs, and dies. Some scientists say that leeches regularly consume enough blood to overwhelm the anticoagulant, thus allowing the blood to clot within their tiny digestive tracts and bringing on the ultimate case of indigestion. Anyone bitten by a leech would probably dismiss this as a possibility after seeing how much a leech bite bleeds. The hole is too tiny to be seen, but the anticoagulant is so strong that blood pours from the wound for hours afterward.

Eddy was the first to find a leech on his leg; the rest of us began finding them almost immediately after. Having experienced these unsavory creatures before, I had told everyone to bring along Spandex shorts as underwear to deter the leeches from the most sought-after soft skin. I personally had brought along a pair of leech-proof socks, as had Jacob and Chris, which gave us a slight advantage over the others.

"I've got socks on," said Scott. "That should slow 'em up."

"No, not at all," said Jacob. "They will slither through the eye-holes in your shoes and then pass between the large fibers of the socks. Leech socks work because they are a very tight linen fabric. Rub the tobacco on your feet, or put on mosquito repellent."

We stopped to rest and to make adjustments to our packs and clothes, and to take leech precautions with various repellents. The mist had developed into full-on rain, dripping through the canopy and soaking our packs. We slid them off and put on the nylon Gore-Tex jackets, then began smearing on the tobacco. The rain immediately washed it away.

"Try the mosquito repellent," Jacob offered. "When you're wet it stays on your skin longer than tobacco." Volker had already begun rubbing it on his pants, then turned to me with an inquisitive look.

"Does DEET break down nylon?" he asked no one in particular. I wasn't sure, but I instantly remembered a trip on which a vial of mosquito repellent had broken open in my pack and soaked a tent. The tent had later torn where it got wet.

"Yeah . . ." said Chris. "These pants are tough but they're made of a really fine fabric. If we wear that stuff we might actually melt the material. It won't look good in the photos."

"I don't feel like doing this climb in my underwear," Volker said with a wry smile. There was a pause and everyone looked at me.

"Try not to get it on your pants," I said, "but I suggest using the stuff. It's that or lose a pint of blood every mile."

Trying to remove a leech with your fingers is next to impossible, as their teeth grip skin far better than your fingers can grip their slimy bodies. We were forced to dab them with pieces of cloth doused in tobacco or DEET to get them to drop off. It became important to catch them before they got under our clothing.

Volker did his best to put the leeches in perspective by getting us to worry about other nasty possibilities. "Leeches are harmless," he said. "They are even used for medicinal purposes in Western hospitals. Maybe you could get a small infection from the bite, but they really won't hurt you." He paused a bit, then went on for an hour or so about all the parasitic, viral, and bacterial exotics that call tropical Borneo home. Volker loved to see us squirm over all the health hazards in the developing world. Slowly laboring up the trail, we heard about Dengue Fever and malaria, both carried by mosquitoes and quite common, the latter of which kills over a million people a year and is pandemic in Borneo. Then he described the parasitic worms that live in the water, food, and dirt of the tropics and infect some 70 percent of the Kelabit population. A common worm, *Ascaris limbricoides*, often enters the body through contaminated food. As we tried to catch our breath on the steep incline, Volk threw out lots of technical terms about how the creature, which can grow up to two feet long, burrows through the liver and lungs, thus weakening the host's ability to breathe. Another, one of the most common parasites in the Highlands, is a pinworm called *Enterobius vermicularis*. "It descends from the lower intestine at night and lays eggs in the skin of the anus," he said with a smile, then paused and noted that a couple of us had been scratching ourselves throughout the day.

"All of this disease conversation is reminding me of another parasite I've run into in much of the Third World," I said. "It's Volkeris Germanicus, a pain in the ass rock climber and doctor who likes to get under the skin and cause irritation."

"Ya, ya. The more you scratch, the worse that one gets," he said, letting us know that we'd be subject to this psychological manipulation for the next few weeks.

The trail grew even more difficult and the rain maintained a full

downpour for much of the afternoon. We made numerous stream
crossings, passing over moss- and algae-covered logs and rocks as we
moved in and out of the rushing water. Often the rocks were big
enough that we had to move on all fours to steady ourselves, and
none of them offered any traction. It was a bad place to break a leg
or ankle, but the lack of traction made an accident quite likely, so we
moved with the utmost care. Any injury of that sort would have
spelled the end of the expedition for everyone.

"I can't imagine hiking up here with one of those loads," Volker
noted, regarding the porters as we stood in the middle of the
streambed. The video guys had gone ahead so they could film us
wading out of the water, leaving us on a small patch of gravel between the steep hill and the raging stream. Rain poured through the
canopy and our packs had gotten a fair bit heavier with the water
weight. The trekking was very rough, much more difficult than any
of us had expected, and it seemed that we were crawling over logs
and rocks on all fours most of the time. Not a single snake or mosquito had been seen during the previous hours of hiking, but the
leeches were a constant presence. Their persistence, the interminable wetness, and the darkness of the rain-soaked forest con-
tributed to a gloomy mood. No one said anything, but we all had a
hard time visualizing ourselves climbing Batu Lawi if the deluge continued.

"Did Tom Harrisson ever come through here?" Scott asked. At
that moment it was comforting to ponder the shared experience of
Harrisson, his men, and our group.

"As far as I can tell, he passed through the Tama Abu at least
once during the war," I said. "He might have used this trail. His
memoirs go into great detail on the darkness and the depressing feeling one gets while trekking in the Highlands."

We continued on through the afternoon, talking some about
Harrisson and a lot about the forest, then stopping to film every
twenty minutes or so and waiting for the porters to catch up. They
looked worked to the bone, completely exhausted with the loads,
but they maintained cheerful smiles whenever we met. Sometime

around four the trail flattened out a bit, so we stopped again to wait for them. Giant hardwoods towered above us, their crowns holding back the white and gray glow of the clouds. Smaller trees of the same species, most less than two or three inches in diameter, grew densely near the forest floor, leaving little light to nourish ground plants. The stream had broken into a number of different forks, meandering through the area and giving the ground a somewhat swampy appearance. To say this made it wetter would be an exaggeration as we were already standing in an absolute downpour. Looking up into the torrent was difficult, so we amused ourselves by counting the leeches on the trail, their brown bodies inching toward us or extended upward to reach the coveted heat source. Volker had two on his leg, Chris four on just one shoe, and I counted nine within a three-foot perimeter of my stance. It was a bad place to wait unless we all wanted to be a meal. Nevertheless, Larry took one look at the approaching porters and said, "This is where we will camp."

"Here?" Volker and I said in unison.

"Yes, it is the most level place we will be before the pass at the head of the canyon, and the last spot where we will have a decent source of drinking water," he replied.

He said a few words in Kelabit to the porters, and they immediately dropped the packs and started hacking down the smaller trees with their parangs. Despite the conditions at the site, they were serious about camping here. It was highly unlikely we would find a Holiday Inn if we kept going, so there wasn't much talk of pressing on. We too dropped our packs, grabbed the parangs we had bought in Miri, and began chopping out clearings to set up our tents.

Within an hour we had set up a small camp. The porters had actually built small shelters by using the foliage that grew around the site. Their first order of business had been to make a drying rack for wood, which they did by tying saplings horizontally across several two-foot-tall stumps. Green vines were used as cord and a small roof of bark was built above the rack to keep the rain off. Using a bit of oil from a small can, a fire was started under the bark-covered rack. More saplings were cut into short pieces and placed on the rack or stacked nearby. The hot smoke from the oil fire dried a couple of them out, then those were burned to dry a dozen or so more. Soon there was a pile of wood drying on the rack, our fuel source for that evening's cooking.

Due to the limited amount of space at the camp, we would be doubling up for the night. We went about unfolding our tents, spinning them this way and that so our heads would be uphill, and constantly looking for twigs and branches that might poke up through the floor and give the water and leeches a route into our only safe havens. The porters constructed their shelters in much the same way they had built the drying rack, then used ponchos instead of bark to cover the platforms. Their shelters were level and dry, off the ground where the leeches, centipedes, and snakes were, and had taken less time to put together than our tents.

As the last rays of daylight faded away in the already darkened forest, we prepared and ate another meal of rice and beans. The downpour continued as we ate, forcing us all under a blue tarp that Jacob had strung between some trees. The Gore-Tex jackets and pants were still working, but our feet had been soaking wet since the moment we entered the forest. We remained standing through dinner, eating by the light of headlamps and exchanging few words. The leeches had honed in on us as heat sources, forcing us to move about every few minutes. Each step was accompanied by two different sloshings, one from the mud of the forest and the other from the cold water squeezing out of our boots. After a while we realized that moving was fairly useless, as we simply stepped from one spot to another person's previous spot, thus giving a new shot to a whole different group of leeches. We ate quickly, then headed for the tents.

"I hope the leeches can't get through the mosquito netting in the tent," I said as Volker unzipped it.

"If they can, it will be a long two weeks in the jungle," he muttered.

Getting into the tent without bringing in rain or a few unwanted visitors required some diligence. After unzipping the rainproof fly and the mosquito net door, we checked each other's back to make sure nobody had inched his way up inside our coats, then removed the Gore-Tex jackets and tossed them in the tent at the end opposite the sleeping bags. We then sat in the tent with our feet out, checking our pants and removing our shoes. This inevitably meant spending a few minutes with a lighter or DEET-soaked cloth, removing the little pests. This done, we slid off our wet rain-pants and tossed them on top of the coats, then pivoted around and into the tent and zipped up the outer doors. Because of the tent's design and the amount of time we spent with the doors open, there was a fair bit of water inside the shelter, but water beat leeches by a long shot. I laid down on my elbows, setting the headlamp to the side so I could read from *World Within* as Volker thumbed through his medical field guide.

"You know," he said, "there really is no clinical reason I can find for leeches *not* to carry some disease." He tossed the book in a dry-bag and slid to the far side of the tent, then turned off his own headlamp. "Maybe you will get something that hasn't been found yet. All the really good hemorrhagic fevers come from the rainforests: Marburg, Ebola, Lassa. You'd be famous, and if I diagnosed it, so would I." He paused, then said, "Sleep well." I could hear him snicker for at least ten seconds.

I rolled away, glancing up at the mosquito netting to see a dozen or so leeches inching across the rain-fly and netting. A whole host of insects crawled in and out of the light, all of which had possibly never been charted by science. The rain pelted hard off the tent fly, so loud that the chirps of the tree frogs were all but inaudible.

My best friend was right beside me, and another twenty-five people were sleeping within a hundred feet of where I lay, but somehow I still felt lonely. The stress of keeping the porters happy, getting the film guys the footage they felt they needed, and being the liaison between everyone in such a challenging environment was proving taxing. I thought of my wife . . . what she was doing right then and how much I would have liked doing that with her, whatever it was. No doubt she was dry and had very few leeches crawling within inches of her face. Reality then bit in and I pushed those thoughts from my mind. They only whittled away at the resolve required to get to the mountain, climb to its summit, and then safely get back down.

I opened *World Within* and began reading. Volker would have been amused to read the first passage, where Harrisson talked of how, while in the Highlands, he had contracted typhus from a tick bite.

CHAPTER 8

April 1, 1945

T HE ISLAND OF TARAKAN is perhaps fifteen miles long and
several miles wide and lies off Borneo's east coast in the
Celebes Sea. For most of recorded history it has been an
unimportant mangrove swamp with a fishing village and some part-
time inhabitants. Poisonous snakes, twenty-foot-long saltwater crocodiles, and malarial mosquitoes ruled its shores, and very little about
the island invited the outside world to pay any attention to it. But
around the turn of the century a company called Royal Dutch began
probing around Borneo's east coast, and before long they hit oil on
Tarakan. Since then Tarakan, and Balikpapan to the south of it, had
been major sources of this prized commodity, and combined with
Miri in Sarawak were some of the largest oil producing areas in the
Far East. As such they figured prominently into Japanese war plans
and had been seized in the early months of 1942. Tarakan was pump-
ing out half a billion barrels of oil a year for most of the war, and for
that reason it was essential that the Allies reclaim the island. Its location, just off the coast and perhaps 180 miles due east of
Harrisson's Highlands headquarters, made it the first target for
Allied landings.

Within a few days of their arrival the team had been completely
accepted by the Kelabit leaders. Lawai had even offered Tom his
own section of the Bario longhouse, but with Miri's prodding and

some exploration of the area it had been decided that Harrisson's camp be moved to Bawang. Lying near the base of Gunung Murud and the headwaters of both the Baram and Trusan Rivers, it was the best strategic position available. Runners from either direction could signal days ahead of time if a Japanese patrol was approaching. Bario remained an outlying base, as its open plain figured very prominently in Harrisson's operation. It was remote, and since jungle covered most of the surrounding terrain, Bario was the only area where supplies could be dropped in without being lost or alerting the Japanese to the Allied presence.

Over the coming days they went about transferring the equipment to Bawang. The radio room and any equipment that might give away their location had been set up in a small farm hut near the edge of the jungle rather than in the main longhouse. A couple of men had gone off to establish another camp to the west, but Harrisson and a few others had moved into the outlying hut where the radio was kept. Edmeades had gotten along with the locals so well that he was put in charge of recruitment and began traveling through the region with a few of the Kelabit. Due to Harrisson's quick success in creating a guerrilla force, the plan to have him fall under the command of Toby Carter had been dismissed and Tom was given free reign in northeast Sarawak.

"I don't know about you gentlemen," Tom said as he awoke on his first morning in Bawang, "but I slept a lot better last night than I have in a while."

"Yes, sir," agreed Bower. "No dreams of bayonets through the chest."

"And no roosters, either," remarked Sergeant Hallam.

"We've got a storepedo drop coming this morning," Tom reminded everyone as he stepped outside onto the veranda. "No time to waste."

Early on it had been agreed by all parties that bows, arrows, and parangs were excellent weapons for hunting and up-close fighting, but a full-scale battle with a modern army, like that of the Japanese, would require modern weaponry. Almost all of the chiefs who had signed on with Harrisson knew this, and their men were eager to fight with the new weapons. Radio contact with Allied bases in Morotai and Darwin, tapped out in code, was established within days of the team's arrival, and over the coming weeks load after load of Sten machine guns and ammunition were to be dropped onto the plain at Bario, along with more Allied special forces operatives to help train and lead the guerrilla army. This morning's load would equip another hundred or so warriors, and the ammunition would be put to use in their target training.

Word that a rajah had returned with a plan to push the invaders out of Sarawak spread through the interior like wildfire. Getting recruits outside the Highlands had been easier than anyone expected for reasons that no one in Australia or England had foreseen. Many of these recruits were from different tribes, like the Iban and the Kenyah, who lived west of the Highlands and knew to fear the Kelabit. A ferocious reputation as well as the remoteness of the Kelabit Highlands had done far more to protect the Kelabit from headhunting raids by other tribes than the sentinel peaks of Batu Lawi. Many of these tribes had been at war with each other for all of fabled history, so it was with great reluctance that they made the trek to Bario and Bawang. However, trade disruptions and acts of brutality by the Japanese were so common in the lowland areas and at longhouses more easily accessed from the coast that virtually everyone in those areas longed for change. Tom spent a good bit of each day being introduced to his new recruits by Miri while his men went about training them with the Western weapons.

Bower stepped out onto the porch behind Tom and noted that far more people were camped near the longhouse than the day before.

"It looks like a couple hundred more, sir," he said.

"Yes, Sergeant," Tom said. "Although I suspect that the policies of the Japanese army can only account for part of this enthusiasm. Supposedly the Brookes had put an end to large-scale warfare and headhunting between the tribes, but it seems that refraining from these activities is not something that comes naturally to these people."

"Yes, sir," Bower agreed. "From what I've seen and heard, their songs, artwork, and even religion have always glorified warriors and battle. In all the local longhouses I've noticed wood carvings of powerful figures in attack positions, tapestries dyed in patterns that show men holding the heads of their enemies in their hands, and Edmeades saw more heads hanging from the rafters like trophies. They are born fighters and place a lot of value on how tough a man is."

"It's a bit funny how this has worked out," Tom said. "I never expected the locals to have this much will to fight, and you can be sure that the idea men at Allied Command never envisioned it this way." Hallam stepped onto the veranda with three cups of coffee. "Thank you, Sergeant," Tom said. He continued, "When you think about it, the famously bellicose spirit of these people is what kept other men from accepting this mission. Now it has become our greatest advantage."

"I would never have guessed that we'd be in this position either," Hallam agreed. "We've only been here for three weeks but already we have a standing army of hundreds, maybe thousands, of warriors. The Japs don't know it yet, but they are in a lot of trouble."

The days in Sarawak had been busy yet peaceful, although as they stood together on the veranda that morning, the stress of the coming war was beginning to gnaw at each of them. The cool mist that enveloped the Highlands every morning seemed to blanket and protect Harrisson and his men as well as the Kelabit and other tribes in training from the cruel reality of what was taking place on other parts of the island. The aircraft making equipment supply drops were put in a very dangerous position, as almost 50 percent of the Allied planes flying over Borneo had been shot down. Enemy fighters patrolled the sky throughout the day, and Allied pilots also had to deal with both the horrid weather and the distinct possibility of a catastrophic mechanical problem on such a long flight. Sadly, among these aircraft had been Commander Pockley's Liberator, the plane that brought Tom and the original SRD men to the Highlands. Apparently it had never returned to Morotai, and its fate could only be assumed. When news that the aircrew was presumed dead reached them, it upset everyone who had flown in on the Liberator, but it was especially devastating to Tom. He and Pockley had really hit it off while planning the mission. They had flown numerous reconnaissance flights in search of the future drop sight over Borneo, always with the knowledge that they might be shot down or have a mechanical failure five hundred miles behind enemy lines. The two had released the stress of these flights by throwing wild parties when they returned to Morotai, including one where they'd been put on report for sending the camp into alert by firing pistols off at 3:00 A.M. and then almost burning down the officers' mess by holding a barbecue inside the tent. On the day Harrisson jumped they had made plans to meet up after the war.

Tom found the irony of their two fates almost shocking. Here it had always been assumed that he was in the more dangerous position, parachuting into Borneo, while Pockley remained safely in command aboard his plane. Pockley's demise only reinforced just how dangerous this out-of-the-way branch of the war was, and how lucky Tom had been to make it this far. Harrisson had seen men die before and knew that losing friends was one of the greatest hardships of war. For now there was nothing he could do save vent his feelings for his lost friend, but he vowed to eventually do something that would honor their memory.

Nearly fifty more Australian soldiers had dropped into Bario since Tom's initial descent, then fanned across northern Borneo to remote outposts. They had been given command of any number of local recruits, all of whom were in training, and were working with a few standing orders. Their first priority was to gather information on the Japanese for the Allies, but to do so without being detected. Harrisson knew that as supplies of rice, poultry, salt, and other products were being used by his new army, they were no longer available to the Japanese. Eventually this would set off alarm bells to any wise Japanese commander at Labuan, Tarakan, Jesselton, or Kuching, and they would undoubtedly send out patrols to ascertain why they could no longer get these necessary supplies. If any local soldiers were seen in their newly equipped condition, complete with Sten machine guns and hand grenades, the element of surprise would be lost. Nevertheless, the Allies needed crucial information on places like the Tarakan oil fields and the only way to get it was to disperse across the region and get in close to the enemy.

Tom was worried about being discovered, but he was also pre-occupied with the mechanics of the battle itself. Drinking his coffee on the veranda, a miniature drama playing out on the railing had gotten him thinking. A troop of red ants had killed a young butterfly as it crawled from its cocoon, ready to unfurl its newly sprouted wings. The large insect was being carried off as the spoils in a harsh and constant jungle war. Tom glanced at his men, then looked at the long-house.

"Do you know what I see more than anything here?" he said, looking across the plain. Bower and Hallam shook their heads, and Tom registered the gesture without looking back. "Every morning I sit here and watch men move buffalo, women harvest pineapples and bananas, and children play with puppies while older women weave rattan baskets and their men sit about telling stories of 'the good ol' days.' " Bower and Sanderson smiled at the happy scene below them. "This just seems like the calm before the storm, and I'm re-minded of just how bad that storm will be when I hear the roar of a B-24 pass overhead. A parachute drops out of the mist, and suddenly the worst of the twentieth century arrives in Borneo. I hate to be sentimental, gentlemen, but I suspect that the aftereffects of this war, not to mention the battles themselves, will be pretty bad for the Kelabit, and I will bear a lot of the responsibility."

"I guess we'll have to deal with that as it comes," remarked Bower.

"Yes, there's not much we can do about it now," Tom agreed as he sipped the rich coffee. "But I wonder," he continued quietly, "who are the ants, and who is the butterfly?"

"Excuse me, sir?"

"Never mind. . . . Now what was it that you were mumbling about to me as we went to sleep last night, Bower."

Sergeant Bower cleared his throat. "Major, I fear that the various camps and teams are getting too spread out to communicate safely."

"Are you referring to all the English signal-code bouncing through the stratosphere that Emperor Hirohito's boys are graced with each morning?" Tom replied with a wry smile.

"Yes, sir," Bower said. "The real problem lies in masking our whereabouts. When there were just a couple of us it was obvious from context to tell who was who and where they were reporting from. But soon that's going to be impossible."

"Yes, I've been giving this problem some thought," Tom said. "Miri and I have been working on this together and I believe we have a cunning plan. As we see it, each station needs a name that identifies where they are signaling from that cannot be understood by the Japanese. For a radioman to send a signal saying, 'Long Semado reports a Japanese patrol of six men moving up the Trusan,' is to tell the Japanese that there are English-speaking people at Long Semado and thus ruin General Tojo's surprise party. The same goes for any written messages that might be taken from a captured runner."

"Yes, sir," said Bower.

"As we have all seen over the last few weeks, Borneo's jungle is the home to some of the most voracious parasites and pests the world knows, and each region generally has one unsavory nasty that truly stands out." Tom turned to face the sergeants. "For example, no one can spend a night in Bario without noting the mosquitoes, or pass through the region of the upper Limbang without being stung by a few sweat bees. Pa Main seems to be the preferred residence of the sand fly, while that little forest camp on the Trusan has more than its share of tiger leeches. No one who has traveled to these places could forget these very particular vermin, so it should be easy for us to remember each if we simply name it for its given pest."

"What about all the recon patrols that are constantly on the move?" Bower queried.

Tom glanced back at the carnage on the railing, noting that the butterfly had been divided into pieces. "Any recon group can simply be known as Ants."

"I can't wait to put this plan into place," Bower chuckled as he headed toward the radio room.

It was a good code and it added a bit of fun to each of the morning's and evening's reports. Starting that day, the few radio signals and all of the messages carried by runners ran the full gambit of Borneo's parasites, insects, and diseases as names such as Tiger Leech, Sweat Bee, or Amoebic Dysentery appeared in their daily reports. The Japanese, having spent as few nights out in the jungle as possible, never became wise to the system. Perhaps they just assumed that the Allies had started naming things in a very odd manner.

With each day they spent in the Highlands, Harrisson and his men had grown more fond of the Kelabit. They were bright, hardworking, and friendly, always supporting of the cause and pleasant while carrying out any task. Most of the men were hardy and rarely complained. In their day-to-day life one could see they valued a certain machismo. At the end of the day it was always noted who had hit the target most during Sten gun training, who could carry the heaviest load, and who could run the fastest. However, it wasn't just competition with each other that drove them to excel; even the most mundane tasks were done as best as could be expected. The Kelabit seemed to work hard simply because that was what one was supposed to do.

Tom and his men soon discovered that there were difficulties in having a Bornean rather than Allied army that would have to be overcome as quickly as possible. The SRD men had learned bits and pieces of the Kelabit language and gotten a grasp of many of the social mannerisms and taboos around the longhouse, but there were nevertheless moments of inexplicable behavior. At times, though, it was as if the Kelabit would go from asking for an order, actively seeking something to do, to outright refusing the order the moment it was made. One afternoon during a military exercise this phenomenon was explained to Tom quite clearly by Penghulu Miri.

"Tuan Major," he said in Kelabit. "We and most of the other inland people of Sarawak live in a world that is of three different levels. You and your men are paying attention to the people but not the other levels."

"I'm afraid I don't follow you, Miri," Tom replied. "Are you saying that we are not seeing what the men are actually doing?"

"No, Major," he replied. "There is much more here than just us. Every day we Kelabit, as well as the Kenyah, and even the Iban, go through our lives as we do right now; we harvest rice, hunt wild boar, and take apart and clean Sten guns. While we do that, all around us is the spirit world. This is filled with ghosts, and they are to be feared as they can be mischievous and easily angered. Above us is the world of the gods and the great warriors, and both they and the spirits do things that influence our lives. One cannot do something here without noting what the gods or the spirits have to say about it."

Tom knew that the Bornean tribes had always been animists. Their religion infused what Westerners consider as random events, such as the direction a bird flies, how the trees move in the wind, or the sound a deer makes at a certain time, with some degree of spiritual significance. Because the moods and whims of the spirits are often related through an event in the natural environment, decisions and plans are drawn up with these events in mind. What Tambon was saying was that ordering the men to "practice taking apart your guns," when a bird had given the sign that everyone should remain still, was a contradiction. These signs could prove to be a serious hindrance when it came time for actual combat. A squad of Kelabit might pull out of a battle with the Japanese because a hornbill squawked as it flew over or a barking deer was heard near the fight. Furthermore, since the spirits were believed to be more active at night, most of the tribes of Borneo rarely went outside the longhouse after dark. This would not do, and Tom asked Penghulu Miri if he could meet with the other headmen to discuss the matter.

"I believe that I, to some degree, understand your religion," he began, "and I don't want to do anything to change the beliefs of the Kelabit or any other Dayak or *Orang Ulu* people. But your men will not be able to engage the Japanese if they follow religion during battle." Penghulu Miri listened patiently as Tom explained. "The

Japanese do not hold your beliefs, so they will continue to attack no matter what signs your people see."

Penghulu Miri made sure the other Kelabit leaders understood what Tom was saying. Tom could see by the grave expressions on their faces that they understood his point, but that it was not information they wanted to hear. Nevertheless, they recognized that the new rajah was thinking of the Kelabit above all else. "I will talk to the other leaders and the men who know most about these things because I understand what you are saying," Miri replied. "I cannot say for sure, and I should not speak for the other men yet as we have not discussed it, but I think we will be able to fight anyway."

Tom knew that for better or worse, his own culture made such exceptions. Only recently, during the blizzard at the Battle of the Bulge, Gen. George Patton had called on a chaplain to write a prayer for good weather. The chaplain felt odd about writing a prayer that requested better conditions for killing people, but saw the logic in it. To defeat the Germans was a higher priority at that time, and so it was done. The prayer was written and, heard or not, the weather conditions improved. To Tom there was a certain backward logic to it. War was basically immoral, so relying on one's religious morality to influence an ultimately immoral enterprise made no sense.

This was the confrontation that Tom Harrisson had begun to fear more than any with the Japanese. He was not bothered by the fact that they would be participating in something "immoral," like war, as the indigenous people of Borneo had been fighting wars as far back as their stories extended. For Tom the real concern was that he was asking them to modify their ways to accommodate the needs of the outside world. The rajahs had never asked the people to change to fit Victorian ideals of correctness, and Tom believed in their philosophy. The people of inland Borneo, especially the Kelabit, had a unique and wonderful culture, and the thought of manipulating it to suit his or his culture's objectives weighed heavy on his heart.

From the day he'd first learned of the mission, Tom had known this moment was coming for these people. But now that he was in the Highlands and living with the Kelabit, sharing in the daily exchanges and rituals that made up their lives, it was that much harder to take. Tom tried to consider the situation rationally; either he could come in and do what he could to minimize the negative effects of a head-on encounter with the outside world, or the Japanese would eventually bring the Kelabit into the twentieth century their way. The preferred methods of the Japanese left little room for discussion, but the pain of witnessing these changes remained. When Penghulu Miri returned to tell Tom of the Kelabit decision, it was bittersweet.

"Sometimes these things are in conflict," he said in Kelabit. "And one must be put aside to accommodate the other. We won't let the signs of the forest or the spirits get in the way of fighting the Japanese." With that, the Kelabit had opened the door to the modern world a bit wider.

As the recon groups spread farther across the island, the fate of many downed Allied fliers was discovered. In an unexpectedly pleasant turn of events, thirteen Americans from various planes were found alive in the jungle and in longhouses throughout the interior. However, Tom was particularly disturbed by the story of a downed B-17 crew that had not been so lucky. Apparently, after they had bailed out of the damaged plane and climbed down from the forest canopy to the ground, the men were divided as to the best course of action. They decided to split up, with four going east and four going west. The group that went west was eventually found by the Murut, a tribe closely related to the Kelabit that lived a bit north of the Highlands. After weeks in the jungle the soldiers were malnourished and suffering from numerous tropical ailments, but the Murut nursed them back to health. However, having them live in the longhouse was very much a concern. The Japanese had sent out patrols looking for the downed plane. Eventually they came across a few of the Murut men out hunting. The men said they knew nothing of the crew, but the Japanese were suspicious and took them in for interrogation anyway. The Murut men were tortured and ultimately killed, but they never revealed that their longhouse was holding four downed American airmen. A few weeks later the men were brought to join Harrisson's team in the Highlands, owing their lives to two men who, although they had barely known them, protected them at the ultimate cost.

The other four airmen did not fare as well. They had crossed over the Crocker Range, a rugged band of mountains fifty miles north of the Highlands, and been found by hunters from a tribe known as the Tagal, a tough group that most of the Kelabit considered untrustworthy. True to this reputation, the Tagal immediately informed the Japanese that they had these Americans and that they would bring them in if they could have their heads. The Japanese agreed. The men were never seen again, though their heads were reputed to be hanging in a longhouse somewhere in northeast Borneo.

Over the following days the recon groups near the island of Tarakan provided much needed information on the size and strength of the Japanese garrison there. Information would pass through Tom at Bawang, go on to Darwin, Australia, then to Morotai where an amphibious assault force was being assembled. Bower and Tom received messages from runners and the odd radio transmission, and then relayed them to their superiors. The Kelabit and various assembling tribes were training down near the longhouse, and soon another load of supplies would be descending from the mists. It was peaceful, and gave a false sense of what the war was like.

"With each message we send out, and each return of plans from HQ, this peaceful world we're in erodes a bit more," Tom remarked to Bower. "The people of Borneo are about to confront the worst of our world, and how they fare in it is in our hands."

CHAPTER 9

March 6, 1999

W HAT'S ON YOUR HANDS" I said to Scott as he spooned out a bit of oatmeal.

"Blood. I haven't had the chance to rinse it off yet," he replied. "A leech got into my tent last night and I didn't realize it until this morning. My sleeping bag is a real mess."

It was cool, maybe in the low sixties, and the dampness of the air was chilling. A thick mist wavered through the trees, decreasing the already limited range of visibility. The rain had stopped sometime during the night, but the ground was saturated with water. A neon-green praying mantis had perched on my bowl, its big eyes menacingly staring at me as I approached. One full day in the jungle had been enough to harden me to any insect that didn't sting, and it quickly flew away with a wave of my hand. Sweat bees, which do sting and are attracted to the salt in human perspiration, had already showed up around the camp, craving the minerals that would be seething from our bodies during the hike. Birds chirped in the canopy above, and off in the distance something made a *whoop, whooooop, whoooooooooop* like a siren.

"You hear the gibbon?" asked Jacob as he slid on his thin, cotton shirt. "They look like monkeys, but they are a different kind of primate. He's letting everyone know that this is his forest. We may see him today, farther up the trail."

We ate our oatmeal, pulled down our tents, then redistributed the equipment. Everyone's packs, including our own, had gotten much heavier with the previous day's rain. The difficult hiking had worn us all out, and each load seemed that much more dense. Once we had our packs on, Larry summoned us all to the main trail.

"This will be the most difficult day of trekking," he said. "We will have another prayer, and then I suggest that you guys and I go on ahead and let the porters come along at their own pace. It will be very steep, so with these loads they will need to move slow." I nodded and he motioned to everyone to bow their heads. The prayer was again done in Kelabit, sounding much the same as the previous day's prayer, but then continued on for another minute or two. Again, the ritual ended with a raising of heads. Larry took the point position and we were off.

Larry immediately moved out ahead of us, carrying an old 12-gauge shotgun and a few shells in hopes he might see a wild boar. The porters had split up a bit of his load to help facilitate his hunting, as wild boar was a far more attractive meal than the canned beef they had eaten the night before. The trail, almost indistinct above the camp, was frequently blocked by fallen trees and branches. Larry left broken twigs as markers, some pointing us in a certain direction and others blocking us from straying off the path. The markers were all made from the same size and type of nearly leafless shrub that grew everywhere around us, and I had a hard time even locating them much less determining whether they were "blocking" or "pointing" twigs. Jacob, fortunately, always read them well.

As predicted, the trail today was much steeper, and as we pushed farther into the Tama Abu Mountains we made numerous stream crossings to get to the better sides of the canyon. Eventually we moved out of the canyon and onto the ridge that forms the skyline north of Pa Ukat. After perhaps three hours the forest made a fairly abrupt change from towering hardwoods to smaller trees covered in moss. The canopy was much thinner, and branches poked out from the trunks at all levels, not just the crowns. This was the cloud forest, known to the tribes of Borneo as *Kerangas*, or "place where rice will not grow." Because of its high elevation, mist and clouds hang among the trees most of the time, and this day was no different. It was extremely wet, and a cold wind whipped across the ridge at perhaps twenty miles per hour. We kept moving, wanting to wait politely for the porters but unable to endure the cold even with our many layers of clothing.

"There are three kinds of wind in the jungle," Jacob volunteered from behind me. "There is the cold wind, like this one," he began, and he proceeded to give a fairly detailed rationale on how the cold, while being uncomfortable, wasn't really that important if you knew that comfort and warmth would eventually prevail. "It is the other winds that we have to be wary of," he continued. "We fear the stronger wind that blows through the trees because it regularly kills people by tearing off branches." He explained how orchids, moss, lichen, and ferns will grow on any tree branch in the jungle, increasing its biomass and water weight and making it a potentially deadly overhead object. Eventually the branch becomes so heavy that the slightest push, be it from an animal or slight breeze, will knock it down, and deaths from falling trees and branches are not uncommon. No sooner did he explain all this than we heard one crack and crash into the underbrush in the distance. "But there is also another wind, the worst wind, a downdraft that comes at the head of thunderstorms," Jacob went on. "This wind hits the upper canopy of the forest as if it were a sail on a ship until large sections, all connected together by the vines and branches of the canopy, come crashing down, killing anyone underneath it. I have never seen this wind, though I have seen the forest afterward. I never want to be there when it comes."

The cloud ceiling was low and reminded me of a piece of information I'd learned about the war. Harrisson had been dropped with a number of loads of gear, all stashed in cylindrical containers called storepedoes that were designed to push their way through the canopy. One had been dropped on the ridge above Bario Asal, probably somewhere near where we walked now. Filled with weapons and ammunition, this particular storepedo had been vitally important to Harrisson and his new army's objective, so many men were sent out to search for it. The storepedo wasn't found until three years after the war ended. Passing through the dense flora, I realized how easy it would be for the forest to swallow you up. Just a few steps off the trail and you could be lost forever.

We continued on the ridge, a thin rail of green vines and small trees dropping at sixty-degree angles on either side, for another hour then began descending into a large valley. The rain was falling quite hard, forcing us to stay under our hoods and avoid looking up. At times we were forced to crawl under logs that crossed our path. The ground beneath was loose and wet and had the look and feel of expensive potting soil. Near the bottom of the ridge we entered a large boulder field and were again forced to our hands and knees as we crawled over the moss-covered sandstone blocks and cobbled creek beds. The boulders were anywhere from six inches to ten feet across and rarely stood in a fixed position. Even those weighing a ton or more might sway as we rolled over them, and the chances of breaking an ankle seemed high. Eventually we caught up with Larry, who was standing on top of a midsize boulder and somehow smoking a cigarette in the deluge.

"This trail we are on is ancient," he said. "And this is one of the markers." A man, a stick figure, had been carved into the boulder. About two feet tall and etched perhaps two inches into the hard Melingan sandstone, it must have taken years to carve. "Our ancestors put it here to mark the trail through the Tama Abu and to the lowlands beyond Batu Lawi. That was when we were headhunters and had a reason for the journey. Now, we don't call it the Happy Headhunting Ground," he said with a smile. "We call it the Fifth Division, a name for the political area like one of your counties. We are now in the upper reaches of the Limbang River and the region is under the administration of Limbang Town, not Miri."

We continued on, moving beyond the boulders and onto a flat but muddy trail. Only the night before I'd read Harrisson's account of passing through the forests of the Tama Abu: "*. . . dense jungle, endless brown fallen leaves, the awful smell of dankness, and (what*

*appeared to be on every leaf) a leech of some inches long, sitting up
and just waiting to get his bloody suckers on to you. . . ."*

The rain continued to pour down, forcing each of us into our
own tiny universe under our Gore-Tex coats. Staring forward out of
the hood, I'd watch the rain drip off the brim and down the front of
the coat. My gaze shifted from my toes to perhaps five feet in front
of me, continuously moving from side to side as I watched for
snakes. Walking the trail put me in a trance. Green leaves on the outside, brown leaves on much of the ground, then mud and an occasional root or stone. It was constantly changing, but always the same.
The weight of the pack, the cold water in my boots, even the leeches
fell out of focus, leaving just the trail for long periods of silence.

After a while we stopped, overlooking a ravine where a narrow
river raged below. It was large enough that had it been in the US, a
few dams and bridges would have spanned it and perhaps a town
would have rested on its banks. But here in Borneo, its origins and
destination hadn't even been ascertained. It was one of the many
unidentified streams from the maps, and its lack of a name, route, or
terminus reminded us of just how remote we were.

A large log, perhaps three feet in diameter and a hundred feet or
so long, lay across the twenty-five-foot-deep ravine. Covered in moss
and soaking wet, it was still the obvious way to cross the deep
stream. Larry went first, wobbling a bit at the start, then gaining his
balance and quickly moving across. It was impressive, as his plastic
football cleats provided far less traction than it appeared.

"Hey," said Eddy, "why don't you guys do this a couple of times
so we can film from both directions." Scott and I could clearly see
that it was dangerous to cross the log, but we said nothing. I caught
Jacob making a wide-eyed expression at Larry, who was standing
safely on the other side.

"It's pretty slick," Larry said. "And you wouldn't want to get
hurt . . . not here."

"They can handle it," Eddy replied, all but ignoring Larry's
words. Volker and Scott looked at me and quickly nodded sarcasti-
cally at Eddy's remark. "I'll film from that side," Eddy went on.

"Dave can stay out of the picture, then you guys can do it again with me moving out. It won't take long."

A few minutes later I was crossing the log. The stream seemed fairly far below, but the distance appeared to double when I reached the middle of the log. The weight of my pack, too, was more noticeable, and I silently thanked the Five-Ten Company for giving me a pair of boots with soles that had a special sticky rubber used on climbing shoes. Despite its size I could feel the massive tree bounce a bit with each step I took. As I moved I fixed my gaze perhaps four feet in front of my toes, stepping somewhat to the side of the apex in order to get the most traction possible. I reached the other side quickly, and was then followed by Scott, Chris, and Volker. After some discussion, Scott and I did the whole thing again with Dave filming. Volker, who had been lagging behind the rest of us for much of the day, asked politely not to have to cross again. He hadn't been talking much and I got the impression he was not feeling well.

"I would never do that with one of the packs the porters are carrying," remarked Scott. "The last thing you need on the middle of that is to be topheavy."

"The porters can handle this easily," said Jacob. "They have been walking in this forest and traversing places like this for a very long time. It's second nature to them. The question is whether the *log* can handle the weight of them and the packs."

Larry led on, with Dave and Eddy in close pursuit, hoping to get a shot of a dying wild boar.

"I can't believe they made you do that twice," Jacob said to me as soon as they were out of reach. "This is very dangerous business. That tree trunk is laying there because it is too rotten to stand. It could break, or you could slip. How would we get you out of here?" He shook his head, then smiled at Volker. "How come you're so smart, Doc?"

"I'm not," said Volker who was resting on the end of the log. "Remember those diseases I was talking about yesterday?"

"Yes," Jacob replied. My heart sank as I took a closer look at

Volker and saw that his face was unusually flushed. I sensed what was coming; Volker could make a joke in the worst of any situation.

"Well, I've got them," he said with a weak smile.

"Volk, what do you mean?" I asked, alarmed. "Give me some symptoms."

"Hey! Who's the doctor here?" he joked.

"Okay, give me a diagnosis." Scott and I exchanged concerned looks, as we knew what this could mean. At best he was just getting a virus like the flu, and at worst, malaria, Dengue Fever, encephalitis, or a disease no one had even heard of yet.

"I have a fever and chills," he said matter of factly. "At certain moments I have no balance and have to support myself on the walking stick. It could be malaria, but it doesn't feel exactly the same." Volker had contracted malaria on a previous trip to China, so he knew the symptoms better than your average small-town doctor.

"I thought all of you were on malaria medication, Doc," Jacob said.

"We are, but it could be a resistant strain," he replied.

"What about Dengue?" I asked. I had been through that bit of viral hell once before in Borneo, and if he was getting it, or malaria, we needed to be on our way out and headed for a good hospital in Singapore.

"I don't know what to tell you, but we aren't turning around on my account," he said. "Just keep going and keep me in sight."

Jacob looked at me and shook his head as I rolled my eyes. Volker glanced up and caught us in silent conversation.

"Look, let's not make a mountain out of a molehill," he continued. "It's probably nothing. I had a patient a few days ago with severe tonsillitis and the guy coughed in my face. It's about the right incubation time . . ." He paused and looked down the muddy trail. "Just keep going. I'll be fine." He stood up from the log and continued on along the trail.

No matter what Volker's illness was, our trip was in jeopardy. I had spent the previous nights next to Volk, breathing the same air, then walking through a cold rain each day. If Volker had tonsillitis, I could be next. With only four days scheduled to get up the mountain, it could be bad news for our trip. Climbing Batu Lawi would require at least two climbers, and if I were to get sick like Volker, that would leave only Scott. The mountain would be lost, and Chris, Dave, and Eddy would find themselves filming an awful lot of jungle foliage.

Taking the advice of the team doctor, we pushed on, making a few more stream crossings on fallen logs and occasionally wading through the water. The film guys and Chris had us redo a number of them, but nothing seemed as dangerous as the first crossing. As the afternoon progressed the rain stopped and eventually the sun came out. We took off the Gore-Tex and almost immediately our moods lifted. Smiles and laughs were common as the conversation grew more lively, and we seemed to walk faster, though Volker still lagged a bit.

By 3 P.M. we reached the second camp, a small hut that stood in a clearing of the forest next to a stream. Everyone was feeling upbeat. For the first time in two days we were able to look up and see patches of blue sky, and the leeches were far less common here where the grass had been trampled down. The hut, our camp for the evening, was solidly built and roughly twenty feet square, with large panels of hardwood wrapped around a post-and-beam timber frame. A tin roof capped it, and though there were no closable doors, a large fire pit inside could keep all occupants warm. Apparently it had been built eight years earlier by the men of Pa Ukat and three other Bario Asal longhouses. The wood was milled by hand and the trail had been opened up a bit more at that time so the tin for the roof could be carried in. The Malaysian government had paid for the project, hoping to increase tourism to the region. Of course, the government planners who thought this up had never walked the trail or they would have nixed the idea immediately. The six of us had found it very hard going, and we trained for this sort of thing all the time. Even the inhabitants of the region thought it was a silly idea, but no one was going to quash the project when the government was offering well-paying jobs.

The hut was not big enough to hold everyone, so we went about setting up our tents in the clearing. There was little space, so Volker and I once again shared, as did Dave and Eddy. Scott and Chris set up camp on the other side of the hut near a thin gravel beach in the streambed. I pitched the tent, sending Volker down to the stream to rest and wash up. The idea of sleeping next to someone who was quite sick seemed a bit foolish, but we had been in such close contact for the previous few days that I figured that if I were going to get sick, the process had already begun.

The stream, I presumed after studying the topographic lines on our maps, was part of the headwaters of the Limbang. Similar to the Colorado River in size, the Limbang meandered down from the Highlands for hundreds of miles, gaining strength until it flowed into Brunei Bay. Here, it was small, perhaps thirty feet across and only a few feet deep, but despite its shallowness I couldn't make out the bottom. Millions of tons of decomposing leaves had tinted it a color akin to tea, in the process creating a concoction that would kill most of the world's plants. As the biomass of the forest breaks down it gives off tannic acid, which then mixes with rainwater and eventually flows into a stream. In some cases the streams in the Highlands flow with a pH as low as 4.8. The waters are more acidic than acid rain, and most fish would have a better chance of survival in a lukewarm cup of coffee than in the headwaters of the Limbang.

Despite the harshness of the water, life abounded along its banks. From a log that stretched across the waterway, Jacob, Volker, and I could look up and down its course. Like a green tunnel tracking its way through the forest, the stream kept the trees at bay, forming an arch of foliage over the water. Hardwoods hung over the water in a cloistered vault, cresting above its middle in a twist of branches and vines and creating a dark half-pipe for the flow to pass through. Orchids, epiphytic plants that grow in the forks of trees or on large branches and never make contact with the rich soil, added pink, red, and yellow to the green tunnel. Butterflies the size of dinner plates fluttered in the branches, and the ever present chirping of frogs could be heard along the banks. Through the canopy smaller birds and insects were flying about, while above it all, set against the wisps of water vapor and a pale-blue sky, a pair of larger birds dived and circled.

Hundreds of species of birds are native to Borneo, but the most prominent is the hornbill. It is the largest bird in the Highlands, with the Rhinoceros Hornbill, so named for the upturned "horn" on its beak, having a wingspan of up to five feet. As the graceful creatures flew overhead, Jacob identified them as white crested hornbills. They are the noisiest animals in the forest, loudly squawking like a flock of geese as they fly. Revered by the indigenous people for their aggressive hunting abilities, they regularly take on deadly snakes with their long, sharp beaks. Hornbills are symbols of good luck and romance, as they bond for life and have an unusual, partner-dependent nesting system. After mating, the male seals the female into a cavity carved from a tree with mud, grass, and droppings. A small hole no bigger than her beak is left for him to feed her through. Without him she and the chicks will starve, but no sane predator would dare try to get through the hole with a mother hornbill on the other side. She does not chip her way out of the nest until the chicks are big enough to feed themselves.

Eddy and Dave came down to the stream for an interview, asking me questions about Batu Lawi and looking a bit bored when I ventured away from the climb to describe the large birds and the surrounding forest. Eddy almost looked angry that I was not concerning myself with the mountain, but with the current trek, the natural beauty of Borneo, and Volker's health along with its ramifications for the trip. We finished the interview and walked back into camp. Scott made a dinner of beans and rice, and we all went to bed early, exhausted from the previous two days of walking.

The jungle at night can be an intimidating and scary place, with its constant backdrop of noise always preventing you from relaxing completely. Most scary are the loud noises that can't be identified:

creaking sounds, or the scratching of two unknown objects together, the breaking of branches on the ground, and the occasional unidentifiable howl or scream. I had heard tales and read accounts of a mystical beast of the forest—half man, half demon—known to the indigenous tribes as Bali Saleng. Any major construction project in Borneo, whether the building of a longhouse or the raising of a hydroelectric dam, is supposed to be started with a ceremony for the spirits. Blood is the most important ingredient for a good ceremony, and though animal blood has been substituted in the years since headhunting was outlawed, it is rumored that the big companies, like the timber companies, have hired Bali Saleng to find more potent human blood. Bali Saleng is said to wander the forests looking for humans that no one will miss and then, in an eerily modern twist, sell their blood to these companies. It's easy to dismiss the story as hocus-pocus mumbo jumbo until you hear something shriek in pitch darkness thirty feet from your nylon tent. Then it's nothing less than horrifying, and if I hadn't been so exhausted, the noises and my imagination would have kept me awake all night.

If you are lucky enough to fall asleep in the forest, or at least slip into that almost-sleep state that is comfortable but not quite restful, you wake up at dawn. In the jungle there is a constant drone of animal chatter with frogs, insects, birds, gibbons, monkeys, squirrels, and even bats all wanting to be heard above the others. However, they don't all screech and hum at the same time, and there is a change of shifts when the sun comes up. That's when most of the insects go into hiding and the larger animals begin to call out. The level of noise perhaps doesn't alter, but the change in sounds is obvious and abrupt enough to wake Rip Van Winkle.

Volker awoke with a voice that had grown a bit deeper, and informed me that he had decided during the night that his fever spells were not intense enough to be malaria. What exactly he did have was still a mystery, but he appeared confident that his life wasn't in danger, so we ate a quick breakfast, tore down the camp, and began hiking within the hour. Like on most mornings a dense fog hung over the canopy, blocking out the sun and keeping the temperature cool and comfortable. We crossed the stream on a fallen log and followed the trail along another creek. I watched as the porters crossed behind us, then Volker, Scott, and I hung back to let them pass.

"These men are incredibly tough," Volker said.

"It's amazing how easily they move through the forest," agreed Scott. "You can just see they were born for it."

"Last night I was reading some of Tom Harrisson's observations on these guys," I said. "Or rather, their grandparents. He commented on how training the men as jungle soldiers was not difficult and that the art of war came naturally to them. They were born guerrilla fighters, well-aware of hit-and-run tactics long before the Allied soldiers explained it to them."

I related more of Harrisson's observations as we moved down the trail. Centuries of hunting in the jungle had honed skills in the Kelabit that no Westerner could ever hope to attain. Each man could move through the forest in complete silence, knowing intuitively where to step so he didn't slip on the mud or crack a dried branch but never needing to look at the ground. Though they tried very hard, sidestepping a thorny vine or avoiding a camouflaged nest of ground hornets while keeping focused on what lay ahead was not something that came naturally to Allied soldiers. The Kelabit never thought twice about it. Harrisson actually witnessed a man sneak up and touch a wild boar with his bare hands, and stories of men killing animals with just their parangs were common. They lived what Harrisson began to refer to as the code of jungle warfare: "Do not be smelled before you are heard; do not be heard before you are seen; and above all, do not be seen." For them, moving through the forest silently and efficiently was not even second nature, it was a part of being Kelabit.

The dense jungle, saturated with mist, was so dark in the early morning that it made the walk something not unlike scuba diving. The canopy, like the ocean surface, held the light back, and the farther one was from that surface the more branches and vines there were between the ground and the sky. Volker, Scott, and I began counting tree species, noting differences in the bark, the leaves, and the height, not to mention the ever present epiphytic plants. In a typical North American forest, 90 percent of the trees are of two or three species, but in Borneo a few acres might be home to forty different species. No one knows for sure, but it has been estimated that the Bornean forests contain nine thousand species of flowering plants, more than a thousand species of butterfly, 570 different birds, and at least two hundred different mammals. In just twenty-five acres there are more species of plant life than in all of North America. The book I had from the Malaysian University study of the Highlands admitted that due to the area's remoteness, "Little is known about the animals and plants occurring on this plateau." Only three serious, semi-thorough studies, in 1925, 1966, and 1995, had been conducted, and each yielded an unexpectedly large number of new species. As recently as April 1995 the University of Malaysia had discovered twenty-one new orchids. Volker, Scott, and I, walking the faint trail and counting the different species we saw, were made acutely aware of the jungle's variations. Memorizing what we had seen and comparing it to everything else was overwhelming and quickly reduced the counting game to a silent trek through a living museum.

After an hour or so we began moving up a hill, cresting it in another hour, and then we immediately received a strange jolt back into the modern world we'd left behind. As the wind breezed over the ridge from the northeast we could faintly hear something that sounded alien in the pristine jungle. It was hard to distinguish, chirping and humming at the same time. We stopped to listen as Larry and Jacob came up from behind, both with frowns on their faces.

"Chainsaw!" Larry said. "The rights to this area have been given to Samling, the big timber company. They tried to buy up Bario as well, but we fought them."

Jacob stared through the forest toward the sound, shaking his head. "It's a few miles away. The sound carries well because it shouldn't be here." He paused and then continued, "They only think of short-term profit. If you were to go on this little adventure in three years, you might be able to drive to the base of the mountain."

In recent years Malaysia has been cutting down the forests of Sarawak at a remarkable rate, with Samling leading much of the way. Concessions for timber harvesting are given out in crony fashion, with government ministers and friends of the prime minister getting first dibs. Sadly, Sarawak has been subjected to modern colonialism, this time under the rule of the Malaysians rather than the British. As a Malaysian territory, Sarawak is the Malaysian government's to do with as it pleases, but international pressure to slow down the logging has gotten quite intense. Bowing to this, the government requested the International Tropical Timber Organization to review its logging practices and help defend the policies. They found that in 1991, Sarawak had exported 19.6 million cubic yards of timber, an exorbitant number given the fact that Brazil, the second-place country, only exported 1.3 million cubic yards. The ITTO is no friend of the forest, but it still felt that Sarawak was being depleted of its largest natural resource at eight to ten times a sustainable rate. Nevertheless, no changes were made. One of the concession holders, a government minister, was told that the cutting of the forests was changing the environment and decreasing rainfall in the region. He responded quickly, saying that such results were an added bonus as the rain had delayed far too many of his golf games.

"Talking bad about the logging is dangerous in Malaysia," cautioned Jacob. "People have gone to jail for protesting the logging practices. We don't really have any say about what will happen to the land."

We trekked on, the trail angling more to the west and away from the sound. The noise soon faded away into the green undergrowth, but in the back of our minds we knew it would soon reach the uncharted places we were headed to. The jungle, despite its remoteness, was one big endangered species.

The trail soon led us up on a ridge that fell off steeply on either side, giving us the occasional long view through the upper levels of the forest. Slowly, we arced around to the north, and though it was much easier walking, Volker began to fall behind. Dave and Eddy ran on ahead to get footage of us proceeding down the trail, and Chris occasionally took advantage of the brighter sunlight on the ridge and snapped a few photos. Scott and I walked a bit more slowly than normal so Volker could have someone to talk to. His face was ashen, and the constant joking and prodding by the other members of the team had all but stopped. The temperature was great for hiking, but he complained first that it was too hot, then too cold, throughout the morning.

After a few more hours we came over a treeless rise in the ridge to see the film guys stopped and waiting for us. We approached them, trying to continue with our normal conversation even though the cameras were pointed at us, and for the first time in two and a half days we got a clear view across the vast and verdant forest. A large valley covered in green foliage and surrounded by steep hills spread to the cloud-scattered horizon. And there, forming the farthest wall of the valley, perhaps five miles away, a bright white spire stood towering a thousand feet above the sea of green. Dark-gray clouds loomed behind it, and an occasional wisp of white could be seen spinning about its summit.

I was elated. To everyone but Volker and me this mountain had been nothing more than a myth based on an unreliable image in a dusty atlas. They had joined on the trip because I had said it existed and convinced them that it could be climbed. We had all seen the old black-and-white pictures, but somehow Batu Lawi had remained a ghost. Now Scott stood staring at the spire and nodding, and Volker patted me on the back in acknowledgment of our success. Inside, I felt a touch of relief that there really was a face to go with the name.

We stood gazing out across the jungle as if from the prow of a boat and talked a bit about our possible route up the peak. The left side of the east face was the obvious standout. It looked long and vertical, rising perhaps one thousand feet from the jungle canopy. Corner systems, where there would be cracks and other weaknesses that might allow us to climb, could be seen running its full distance. Occasionally there was a bush or even a small tree jutting from the ivory-white wall, indicating ledges to belay from and perhaps even sleep on. We pointed out the various features to each other with so much excitement that none of us ever got to finish his description. It didn't matter, though, as we were talking the happy gibberish that all climbers do when they find a mountain that is truly inspirational. It looked perfect for climbing, and if the weather continued as it was then we would probably be successful. We talked a bit about our game plan on camera and gave the film guys an interview, then continued on down the trail with the anticipation of actually climbing the mountain quickening our pace.

The trail descended the ridge, crossed another stream, then started back up on the lower slope of Batu Lawi. Along the path we saw deer and boar tracks, which helped lift the spirits of Larry and the exhausted porters. In 1986, somewhere near the base of Batu Lawi, the fabled Sumatra rhinoceros had been seen. This rhino is so rare that many biologists consider it to be extinct. We didn't see any sign of it, but the porters weren't interested in rare rhinos anyway. They wanted boar, the preferred dinner of the jungle's human inhabitants.

Before we started up the last incline I stopped to check in with Volker.

"How are you doing?" I asked. The answer was obvious from his washed-out expression, but I didn't know how else to start the conversation.

"I'm pretty sure I have strep throat and tonsillitis," he replied, dropping his pack. "Do you have your headlamp?"

I retrieved the light as Volker pulled a small, stainless steel mirror from the top of his pack. He shone the light in his mouth and looked in the mirror, then let out a big sigh. "Take a look," he said. I leaned over and held the light near his mouth.

"That's disgusting," I said. "Your tonsils look like two golf balls wrapped in prime rib."

"Ya, it's a lot of pus," he said as he started into his medical kit. "Streptococci for sure, same as I diagnosed that guy with the other day." Volker took out a vial of antibiotics and popped several down, then slung his pack over his shoulder. "Let's get going. I need to sleep."

Three full days of walking in the chilly rain with wet feet and a cold, damp head had transformed what might have been a mild cold into something far worse for Volker. He had deteriorated all day from a lively, gregarious, and sturdy athlete to a slow-moving shell of a person, alternating between sweats and chills every few minutes and maintaining a distant and glassy stare. It had already become clear that barring some remarkable recovery, Volker would not be climbing for a few days. Perhaps, given incubation time, neither would we.

Late in the afternoon Larry led us into camp, a pair of clearings along two streams, one with a small wooden hut. The porters built their usual jungle shelters, cleaned out the hut, and gathered firewood, while Volker, Scott, the media guys, and I went about setting up the tents and arranging the supplies. Once the tents were up, Volker collapsed inside his, only occasionally waking up to go to the bathroom.

It rained again that day, as it does every day at Batu Lawi. Just after dark we had a dinner of spaghetti, then the media guys and Scott slipped away to their tents for a much needed night's sleep. Jacob and I filled a few water bottles in the nearby stream and looked in on Volker. When I unzipped the fly I discovered that he hadn't even had the strength to zip the inner screen, leaving an easy route in for all the nasties of the jungle floor. Volker was lying in his bag, his coat on and a hat pulled down over his ears. His eyes were shut and he was shaking like a leaf. His water bottle was laying on a pile of wet clothes, unopened and completely full.

"Volk, wake up. You need to drink some water," I said.

"No, I'm not thirsty," he replied. Somehow his tone sounded like that of a small child.

"Doctors!" said Jacob. "They always make the worst patients." It was a cliché, but coming from a Berewan tribesman standing in the middle of Borneo with a two-foot parang at his side, it seemed very much like a genuine observation.

"It's part of our education," muttered Volker. "We are taught to resist nursing at all times." He sat up and stuck a thermometer in his mouth, trembling a bit.

"Doc, there are a few things you should know," said Jacob. "If you have to piss, don't do it near your tent. Fire ants are attracted to the uric acid and we don't want them here. Also, keep your tent zipped up, and if you feel something move underneath it, don't touch it. Just let it slide by."

"Ya, I know," he said, pulling the thermometer from his mouth. "Look, 39.5 degrees. That's like 103 degrees Fahrenheit for you barbarians who can't use metric." Still shaking, he took a sip of water and slid back into his bag.

"We're less than a couple meters away, so just yell if you need something," I said. He mumbled a bit, then rolled over as we zipped up his tent.

"Sleep well, Jacob," I said. He walked toward the opening into the hut, smiled, and nodded as if to say, "You, too." I unzipped my tent and went about taking off my boots. As I did, two of the porters stepped silently past, one carrying a shotgun. "Wild boar," he said, holding the gun up and grinning. I smiled back, then slipped off my socks. My boots stank horribly, like old garbage. Sufficiently callused from years of hiking in dry mountain regions, my feet were now wrinkled and white, and large flaps of skin slid away with the socks. I zipped up the tent and dumped everything out of one of my stuff sacks, then poured a bunch of Tinactin foot powder in the bag, slid my feet in, and shook them about. Hopefully, this thin layer of dust would dry my feet and give them a short reprieve from moisture and bacteria.

Sliding into my sleeping bag, I noticed that despite my efforts to keep the tent closed, it had become something of an exotic zoo. A small spider, black with a neon-green thorax, was on my dry pair of pants. Two ants, black and over an inch long, were crawling across the ceiling, as was an orange-and-black-striped tiger leech. I gently moved them all outside, making sure that no one was hurt. The leeches hadn't been bad to me thus far, and I didn't want to upset my karma by killing this one. Checking my body over for other un-invited guests, I found a tick crawling up my leg. Ticks spread typhus and no telling what other nasty diseases so, karma be damned, he was killed and put outside. I made a few notes in my journal, then lay down and began reading *World Within*. Only a few pages into it I began to slip away, my head on a pile of fleece clothing, my mind in the Kelabit Highlands in 1945. A gunshot rang out in the distance and the porters in the hut responded with a symphonic "oooooh." Perhaps we'd be eating wild boar tomorrow. Or perhaps the Japanese were learning the folly of invading Borneo.

CHAPTER 10

May 3, 1945

ON MAY 1, 1945, THIRTEEN THOUSAND men from the Australian Twenty-sixth Brigade stormed the shores of Tarakan. The night before, the small island had been pulverized by Allied bombers and navy guns, but the two thousand Japanese who held it were deeply entrenched. The battle for Tarakan began on a typically hot Bornean day. The Allied plan was to establish a forward position that could hold troops, equipment, and an airbase, all to help support landings on the main island of Borneo. The Japanese fought hard, but shortages of supplies and a sense that they were cut off from their imperial homeland weighed against them. By the end of the day the Australians had managed to take a beach and a heavily cratered airfield. It was the start of liberating the island, but the fighting would continue on Tarakan for several months, killing or injuring almost nine hundred Allied soldiers and no telling how many Japanese in the process.

The information Harrisson's recon groups had gathered proved to be valuable to the Allies, but the Bornean tribes' role in the war was about to change. As the Australian soldiers stormed ashore, it quickly became apparent to at least one Japanese commander that Tarakan would soon be in Allied hands. He led his men, perhaps as many as three or four hundred, across the estuary and mangroves that separated Tarakan from Borneo and up one of the nearby rivers.

Their immediate need was food, which they quickly gathered by raiding longhouses along the river. The Allied commanders knew that a large contingent of Japanese soldiers had escaped into the forests of the mainland, but they could not be pursued as the primary objective was to gather and hold the small island. Someone else would have to deal with the rogue force.

Up in the Highlands, Harrisson's men were just completing an airstrip that would allow planes to come in and supply his forces as well as lift out the downed American pilots who had been rescued from the jungle. Nearly fifty more SRD men had dropped into the Highlands and fanned out across Sarawak to train and work with the new recruits. Tom was now in charge of a force that filled Sarawak's interior and—when including all the supporting families and networks of suppliers—was estimated to be nearly one hundred thousand people. They were all angry at the Japanese and eager to fight. To properly supply this new army the airstrip had to be built. But as Tom stepped onto the freshly surfaced runway, he let out a heavy sigh.

"I'm sorry, sir," a young American pilot said, noting Tom's expression. Harrisson wore an American olive drab T-shirt, an olive drab cap, a naturally died sarong around his waist, and no shoes. His appearance had become less that of a British SAS major and more the epitome of a guerrilla leader, but the nonregulation dress code was the only side of Harrisson that was relaxed, and the rescued airmen he met always showed their respect. "The soil here just isn't solid enough to support a transport plane or heavy bomber during landing," the airman continued. "Any one of our planes would rip it up on the first landing and then never get out." The young lieutenant stood somewhat at attention as he spoke to Tom. After months in the jungle the pilot's uniform was rotting and torn, but he did his best to be respectful to the leader of the resistance.

"Yes, yes, Lieutenant," Tom replied. "I believe you have managed to force me and the Kelabit into a first here." The strip had been all but completed weeks before, but the rescued American fliers had complained that it was inadequate and insisted that he put a better surface down. "Putting down the hard surface you wanted cost the Kelabit one longhouse. It also used up a lot of training hours as the Kelabit sat around conceiving of this prehistoric version of pavement." To get a better surface Tom had been forced to radio Allied Command for better building materials. In an effort to aid the construction, an American B-17 had accidentally bombed a long-house with a load of spades, picks, and shovels, all of which seemed useless to the Kelabit, who preferred to work with their own tools. In the end, Kelabit ingenuity and culture overpowered all ideas the Allies might have come up with. They had laid out the strip in un-used rice paddies and filled the surrounding paddies with water. In a very short time the paddy dikes could be broken and the runway flooded, quickly hiding it from a Japanese patrol. A solid surface was laid, the fliers were happy, and planes were able to come in as regu-larly as the weather permitted. "This is," Tom continued, "as far as I can tell, and as far as Allied Command knows, the only bamboo-surfaced airstrip in the world. You and your men should be proud of the fact that you convinced me to get Penghulu Miri's men to . . ." he paused, searching for the correct term, "to weave it."

Tom's exasperation with the American flier partially stemmed from their need for a solid-surface runway, a bit from the complain-ing the Americans had been doing for weeks about virtually every-thing, but mostly frustration came from the ramifications of the runway. The pilots had probably been right about the need to cover it, although in Borneo, a land with virtually no paved roads, the only option had been incredibly time-consuming. The pilots' complaints were also understandable, as they had been forced to live off the jun-gle for months and their bodies were seething with parasitic infec-tions. But the runway itself was what caused most of Tom's anxiety, as it would be a clear sign to any enemy plane flying over that the Allies were in the Highlands. No sane Japanese pilot would want to fly over the Highlands as the storms there could rip the wings off a small plane like an A6M2 Zero, but the rate at which the Japanese pilots were hurling themselves at American ships reminded the Allies that they were willing to do anything to win the war, sane or not. If one did fly over the Highlands, the runway would stick out like a rhinoceros on a thimble. The Japanese could show up any day, in force, and Tom wasn't sure his new recruits could handle them yet.

He hadn't really admitted it to himself, but Tom's vexation also grew from the fact that with the new runway just about anyone could come to Bario. Visitors no longer had to make the five-week trek through the inhospitable jungle or the dangerous parachute drop in order to see the Kelabit. The runway would be there indefinitely, serving as an inroad for missionaries, traveling salesmen, tax collectors, lawyers, and someday maybe even tourists, none of which were needed by the inland peoples of Borneo.

It was this deeper concern that wore a hole in his stomach, but it wasn't the one that kept him up at night. That position was reserved for the approaching enemy. The Japanese force from Tarakan had become the top priority as soon as they had left the little island and headed for the shores of eastern Borneo. Tom excused himself, then walked from the runway to the radio room to get news of their whereabouts from the radio operators.

"Good morning, Sergeant Long, Corporal Illerich," Tom said as he stepped inside the radio hut. Sergeant Bower had moved to a radio in the field and his position as head cipher had been taken over by Sgt. Bob Long. The radio and cipher work had become so constant that they were also being assisted by Cpl. Daniel Illerich, a downed American flyer who had volunteered to help despite being in very poor health. Corporal Illerich was listening intently to a transmission so he merely gave a relaxed salute to say "good morning" to Harrisson. "Any word on our unwelcome visitors today?" Tom asked.

"Yes sir, plenty," Long replied. "The new HQ on Tarakan reports that the Japanese force crossed over sometime late last night."

"Any idea if they went up the Sesayap?" Tom asked, furrowing his brow. "If they went up that river, we're in no small amount of trouble."

"No, sir," Long responded. "HQ intelligence didn't track them, but suspects they are trying to get to other Jap garrisons in Labuan,

Jesselton, or Miri. HQ also wants you to know that the moving force presents a possible logistical problem for the invasion plan as they could find our exact location and then notify the other garrisons of our existence and strength."

"It's always good to have a superior out there keeping us up on the obvious, eh, Sergeant?" Tom quipped as he poured a bit of coffee into a steel mug.

"Yes, sir," Long said with a chuckle. "Nothing slips by HQ intelligence, sir."

"I don't suppose they mentioned the fact that as the Japanese go thundering about the forest they will be bayoneting the local men, taking liberties with the women, and doing serious damage to the crops and food supplies," Tom went on.

"No, sir. It must have slipped their minds," Long replied.

"Yes, yes, it always does. They can clearly track and analyze the invasion, but can't be bothered to worry about who it is that's going to do the fighting for them," Tom said with a sigh.

A couple of special forces men along with Penan, Murut, and Kelabit recruits had gone down the Sembakong River to monitor the movement of the Japanese on Tarakan. They had kept a close watch on the imperial soldiers and Tom suspected they were now tracking the rogue force. "Any word from our men in the area yet?" Sergeant Long looked to Illerich, who had just put down his headphones.

"No, sir," Illerich replied. "Would you like me to contact them?"

"No. They will call us when they have something useful," Tom said. "Until then, we play the waiting game."

Tom knew that the Japanese were well disciplined, and though they were not comfortable moving through the jungle they could travel very far into the interior in little time. Although he knew they had to be stopped, he also knew that he could not let the new recruits engage them in battle without giving away his position. If any Japanese survived the attack and made it to any one of their coastal bases, the element of surprise would be lost for the Allied landings. So instead of forcing an outright battle, he planned to use the Kelabit, Murut, and Penan in the capacity they were very much prepared for. Over the previous two months Tom had seen that these men were born hunters and could move through the forest with more stealth than a cobra. They would serve as his forward observers, radioing back the exact locations of the Japanese through map coordinates and visual references. This would allow the Allies to formulate a safer invasion plan by avoiding and attacking Japanese forces at their choosing. Tom also planned to use the local warriors in a capacity that they seemed born for; ambushing enemy patrols.

In the days that followed, time in the Highlands seemed to speed up. The war had arrived and the invasion of the main island, now planned for June 10, was barely a month away. The anxiety of sending the locals into battle was a heavy burden for Tom, and he kept Penghulu Miri nearby as much as possible to discuss how they would react to this or that, and to bounce around strategy ideas to see how well they would be understood. He didn't want to get anyone killed in a war they had never asked for, and he knew that if the men could be trained properly he could limit the casualties. From everything he could gather from Miri, the Kelabit, Iban, Kenyah, Murut, and Penan men were ready and able to beat the Japanese, but Tom knew how tough the Japanese soldiers would be and he didn't want to rush a conflict that could potentially last for years.

Then late one afternoon Sergeant Long got the anticipated radio call.

"Major!" he called, stepping out onto the porch. Tom was down near the longhouse talking to Miri but still within shouting distance. "I just got a message from our Ants," he yelled. Tom turned and ran toward the radio room.

"What did they say?" he asked as he came up the steps.

"They were able to stay very close to the Japanese after they came ashore without being noticed," Long said. "They notified HQ that the force was big, perhaps four hundred strong, well armed, and in good shape, and that they were moving along the Sembakong River."

"That's a much larger number of men than I was anticipating." Harrisson frowned. "We have no hope of taking a group that large in a direct fight, and they could be out of the Sembakong and into the Highlands in just a couple days. This little piece of paradise may very soon become a war zone reminiscent of Guadalcanal."

"Yes, sir," Long said.

It was clear that something had to be done to slow the progress of the Japanese, but neither Tom nor the Allied commanders wanted to commit the new recruits to a large-scale battle just yet. They were trained, and no one was more eager to fight than the Kelabit, but a well-armed and well-trained Japanese force would be more than his guerrilla soldiers could handle. They would have to come up with a way to slow the force without actually engaging them.

In early morning light two days later, as soon as the Japanese had begun crossing the Sembakong and moving toward the Highlands, Tom put the new recruits to work. As the Japanese crossed the river they emerged from the dark, wet forest and its protective canopy to find themselves beneath the pale-blue sky. But within minutes of this exposure, American planes roared in overhead with a clear view of the Japanese force. Bombs rained down on the troops, killing many soldiers and disrupting the movement of the entire unit. Chaos and terror erupted and for a minute or two the Japanese could not figure out where to run. The heat from the explosions was tremendous and an unpleasant surprise to the Kelabit recruits hidden in the forest just downstream from the crossing. This kind of war was beyond their imagination, and they watched as the bodies of Japanese soldiers were blown into bits or vaporized by the explosions. After each bomb fell the recruits could hear the Japanese screaming, and they cringed as they watched the enemy soldiers fall to the ground in agony. Within minutes the Japanese were completely disorganized and terrified, and as the planes flew off the survivors became caught up in caring for their injured and dying comrades. In war, an injured enemy soldier is often worth two dead ones, as the injured can't be left behind, but often can't keep up the regular pace and thus slow down the entire unit.

Amid the cries of their enemy, the Kelabit recruits pulled back and began heading for the Highlands. They and their SRD leader had made the attack possible by signaling perfect coordinates to the Bawang headquarters. That information had then been relayed to the pilots and bombardiers in the air. The new recruits had used a radio and a map, something none of them had even conceived of two months earlier, to win their first confrontation with the Japanese. This one bombing attack had cost the Japanese dearly, and the Kelabit could already see that the enemy would spend the days ahead just trying to survive, and that their even reaching the Highlands much less attacking was very improbable.

It wasn't long before another group of Kelabit and Iban, who were watching the Japanese garrisons near Brunei Bay, alerted Tom to another roving band of enemy soldiers. Over the past months the various tribes had made sure that rice, buffalo, and vegetables had all but stopped flowing from the interior to the Japanese contingents stationed near the coast. The Japanese commander at Brunei Bay, a man experienced in dealing with local discontent in occupied countries, had become suspicious of the sudden scarcity in local supplies. He queried one of his conscripted aides, a Dayak named Bigar, as to why the well of provisions had dried up. Bigar naturally knew of the new rajah and had been passing information, from one longhouse to another, on to the Highlands for weeks. To conceal Harrisson and the newly formed Bornean army, he told the Japanese commander stories about plagues of locusts, horrible storms, and various hand-of-God events that could slow up deliveries from the interior. These explanations had sufficed for a while, but as supplies dwindled further the commander grew impatient and sent an armed contingent up the Limbang River to investigate.

Bigar immediately notified Tom of this through the longhouses, and Harrisson in turn sent word out to his superiors at Allied Command. Everyone agreed that if the Japanese were sending out troops to ascertain why locally grown food was no longer available, they would eventually find his army. The men at the new HQ on Tarakan, giving little thought to the horrific effects an angry band of Japanese soldiers would have on the local population, were adamant that Tom's men not give away their position by engaging the enemy before the larger Allied invasion took place. But Tom argued other-wise. If his Bornean force could completely wipe out this band of Japanese, there would be no one to inform their commanders. The Japanese would simply disappear into the forest just as so many out-siders before them.

"This is a risky idea, Major," Sanderson remarked gravely as they pored over river drainage maps of the area. "Just one straggler could ruin the entire invasion, and it will be the first time the Kelabit and Murut go up against the Japanese."

"I know," Tom conceded, glancing back and forth from an aerial photo to a map. "And many of the Japanese soldiers on Borneo have seen heavy fighting in China, the Philippines, and Malaysia, so they know how to react in battle. How our boys will fare in a real fight is none too certain, but it doesn't seem like we have any other choice. HQ doesn't want to admit it, but if we don't do something, those soldiers will walk back to Brunei Bay knowing everything, and shoot every local between here and there. You're just going to have to make sure you get every last one of them."

"You're right," Sanderson acknowledged. "So what will our plan be?"

"We're going to reorganize the squads so we can send in our best-trained men," Harrisson answered. "We will form a special unit of the Kelabit and Murut soldiers who have been training with us the longest. They'll go into this drainage here," he continued, pointing at a stream that flowed into the lower Limbang. "The Japanese will ob-viously come up here, through this low-angle canyon, as no one would want to climb over this ridge." Sanderson nodded. "Our men will need to be led by Allied personnel, and I'd like you to take the job, Sanderson. I think Driver* Henry should go with you as well, as he has taken to life in the jungle, and the Iban seem to really respect him. I suggest we get started first thing tomorrow."

They went out and gathered the men, then put those that they felt were best prepared in one group of roughly a hundred. The men

---

*Driver is a rank in the Australian Army roughly equivalent to private.

were informed of the mission, with Miri translating from Malay. The Kelabit, Murut, and Iban held Harrisson in such high regard that they didn't question how the group was formed, and though everyone wanted to go on this attack it was understood that some had to stay behind. The soldiers who had been chosen to go went about gathering the gear that would be needed for a few weeks in the jungle. Everyone slept a bit uneasily that night, and then left early the next morning.

It took only a few days for Sergeant Sanderson and the recruits to locate the enemy. Japanese tactics, not to mention their policy toward the locals, left telltale signs of their movement. The Japanese were loud, sloshing through streams, allowing items to clank about on their packs, and breaking branches as they thrashed through the forest. Tom had a standing order that his men, like the Kelabit, go bootless. This was hard on the Australian SRD men, but it proved effective as it left the Japanese as the only people on the island wearing boots. Their soles left an unmistakable print in Borneo's black mud, and the recruits were able to easily identify them. The Japanese were tracked to Long Semado, a longhouse perhaps seven days upstream from Brunei Bay and less than thirty miles from Bawang.

"The trail they left behind shows they have little respect for the lives of the local people," Sanderson reported back to Tom from his forward position. "Longhouses have been raided, people have fled to the woods, and those that were found were often mistreated or killed."

"It's shockingly suicidal behavior," Tom commented darkly. "If they have mistreated the locals, they have alienated their guides, the only people who might possibly help them." Tom and his SRD men had recognized early on that befriending the locals was key to survival in Borneo's jungle. To an outsider the forest was a sea of green with less than fifty feet of visibility. Jungle trails were only barely discernible and so difficult to find that a well-trained soldier might pass right over one without noticing it. If a man found one and then stepped off it just five feet, he might never find it again. The thick forest canopy made it impossible to navigate by using distant objects like mountains or even the sun as reference points. And of course there were no real maps. The power of man to wage war paled in comparison to nature's fortitude.

"Yes, sir," agreed Sanderson. "The Japs' approach to this war seems to be that the only way to win is through domination, rather than cooperation or pacification. It's a bad policy. By the way, some of the scouts have reported that this group is not entirely Japanese."

"That may very well be true," Harrisson replied. He knew that as the Japanese had stormed across East Asia, men from Java, Sumatra, and Indochina had been conscripted into the Imperial Army as slaves. They were often forced to walk in front of Japanese soldiers as human shields that would take the first hits in battle. "We must do whatever we can to avoid killing the men who are not Japanese. Those people are just as innocent as anyone in this mess."

"Understood," Sanderson radioed back.

The following morning the heavily armed Kelabit, Iban, and Murut men moved in close enough to listen to the Japanese soldiers talk, though they had no idea what was being said. The Kelabit could tell that the Japanese were scared and very much out of their element. With soggy, wet feet, rotting clothing, and no true destination in mind, the forest was becoming an overwhelming force in itself, rattling their nerves in the way that miles of glittering snow in the arctic will push a lost explorer to the edge of madness. A paranoia about their alien environment had set in. Shadows had begun to move when there was no wind, and the sudden silences that broke up the roar of insects sounded unnatural. The Japanese were lost in a sea of green, and they were losing touch with reality. But they would have been far more nervous if they'd known that a hundred Murut and Kelabit were silently moving in all around them.

As the Japanese made their way up the canyon they passed bushes, logs, and boulders that hid Kelabit and Murut warriors. Completely oblivious to the coming ambush, the Japanese soldiers had inadvertently put themselves in a surrounded position on low ground, the worst of all possible scenarios.

Without a sound the Kelabit warriors stood up and opened the battle from behind with a horrid barrage of machine gun fire. The Japanese, having put their Javanese conscripts in the front, were totally exposed to the short-range attack. Not only was the ambush completely unexpected, but no one would have thought the attackers could be so close. Kelabit and Murut soldiers fired at point-blank range, cutting down scores of Japanese soldiers before any of them realized what was happening. The soldiers cried out in terror and a few tried to run for the cover of the forest, only to find parang-wielding Kelabit hidden among the elephant-ear palms and rotting logs. The groans of the wounded echoed through the forest, and the Kelabit and Murut quickly followed them to their sources. No mercy was shown. The Sten guns were fired until there were no more bullets, and anyone still standing was finished in the traditional way, with parangs. It was over in less than a minute, and entirely one-sided.

Sanderson had a big grin on his face and was wanting to congratulate his men, but he soon realized that for them the battle was not over. He watched as one of the recruits nearest him walked up to a Japanese soldier he had just dispatched and lifted the man off the ground by his hair. With one slice of the parang across the back of the dead soldier's neck he freed his prize. Blood spouted from the man's severed neck as his headless body dropped back to the jungle floor, and Sanderson took in a deep breath to hold back the nausea. Glancing across the battlefield, he saw that all the men were following suit. Headhunting had begun again.

Sanderson immediately radioed Tom at Bawang to inform him of the outcome.

"The fight is complete. None of the enemy escaped, and no Ants were wounded or killed," he tapped over the radio. "But there is something else." He paused a moment to think of a way to convey what had happened after the battle, then thought better of it. If HQ was listening there could be trouble. "You'll just have to see for yourself, Major," he concluded.

"I can only guess what he is referring to," Tom said to Long and Illerich back in the radio room.

"The heads, sir?" Illerich queried.

"Yes, Corporal, the heads," Tom said with an almost imperceptible smile. "The Japanese should have never ventured here. But the important thing is that we won with no losses." He paused a moment, then continued, "Tell Sanderson to send Driver Henry and as many recruits as can be spared on down the Limbang to watch for other patrols. Sandy can bring the conscripts back here."

The message was tapped in by Long as Harrisson stepped out of the hut to find Miri. Tom was ecstatic with the results. No one would have predicted such a landslide in the first engagement between crack Japanese troops and a band of Bornean guerrilla fighters who just a few months before had never seen a gun. Miri too was pleased with the news, although he seemed to have expected it. To the Kelabit it was never a matter of whether or not they could beat the Japanese, only of whether or not they wanted to.

A few days later Sanderson and a dozen or so Kelabit and Murut warriors marched into camp with twenty Javanese prisoners. Hanging at the guerrillas' sides and from their packs, woven into vines and rattan taken from the jungle, were their trophies; the heads of Japanese soldiers. Tom had been steeling himself for this sight, and somewhat to his surprise he found that the knowledge that it was coming had already numbed him. Tom understood that headhunting had been enormously important to the Kelabit for many years, and despite its illegality by the Brooke governments they had continued to do it from time to time. All the tribes involved in the fighting considered it an important part of warfare, not to mention their religion. However, if Allied Command ever found out about it there could be trouble. As far as he could remember there was nothing in the Geneva Convention about taking heads off corpses, but there damn well would be if it became common practice, and Harrisson didn't want to be in charge of an army that set a precedent in what troops *shouldn't* do in war.

Nevertheless, he also knew that the rape and murder of Rajah Brooke's administration by the Japanese, not to mention the mistreatment of Allied prisoners of war, were policies these heads might have smiled on these past four years. When it came right down to it, the treatment of them, especially considering they were dead, was hardly something he could allow himself to worry about, and he wasn't about to order his newfound army not to wage war on their terms when it was their turf.

"That's a grisly sight," Illerich muttered as he stepped up behind Tom. "But I suppose the important question here is, what are we going to do with those conscripts?"

Tom took in a deep breath. "We shall figure out something," he replied. "In the meantime let's go down and congratulate our men. They've done a great job."

Still, Tom couldn't help but feel that the victory was bittersweet. The old rajahs had gotten the people of the interior to accept a reluctant peace, putting an end to the large-scale warfare and headhunting that had dominated Borneo for so long. Now another outsider had come along and restarted it.

That night he, Illerich, Sanderson, and Long were invited to a giant party where the guests of honor had been brought in without their bodies. The heads were dried over the fires as everyone gorged themselves on wild boar, fern shoots, and various fruits. Borak was poured in copious amounts and the warriors danced about the fire pits mimicking the taking of heads. The good old days were back, and the longhouse reveled in its victory. Later, in a borak stupor, Tom and his men wandered back to the radio hut to roll out their mats and get some sleep. The party continued on through much of the night, and Tom was lulled to sleep by the soothing hymns of glory in battle.

CHAPTER 11

March 7–10, 1999

I AWOKE TO A CHORUS OF CHANTING. It was early Sunday morning and the porters, devout Christians, were praying. The air was damp and chilly and the inner walls of the tent were wet, but there was no time to lay around and think about the uncomfortable surroundings. I unzipped the tent screen to see a heavy mist hanging in the giant trees, then slid on my wet shoes and rotting socks and looked in on Volker. He was sleeping and breathing hard, his water bottle still mostly full.

Chris was up and rummaging through the food bags, complaining to himself aloud that they hadn't been properly organized. He found some muesli, dehydrated milk, and dried fruit, then put them back when he realized that, although it was 6 A.M., the porters had already boiled us rice. I helped myself to a bowl and added some dried pineapple, then went about eating and preparing the climbing equipment. Soon Scott was also up and eating as he organized the ropes. The film guys spun around the camp, getting different angles on us doing various chores, then poked inside Volker's tent and woke him to see how he felt about not being able to climb that day.

"It's Sunday," Larry informed us as he appeared in our clearing. He had been to the stream and returned holding two large buckets full of water. The veins in his forearms bulged beneath the skin so much that it looked like his muscles had been wrapped in cargo nets.

"And normally on Sunday we do not work. But the porters feel that your climb is very important and that for this occasion they can help. They will carry your extra gear to the base of the mountain."

"Great," I thanked him. "We'll need the help."

"Oh, and you will be eating wild boar for dinner tonight." He smiled, then turned and headed toward his shelter on the other side of the stream.

"Can we get going?" Eddy prodded. "We have a video to make." Each day he seemed to get more exasperated with the little inconveniences of the jungle, and his tone that morning was the worst yet.

I checked on Volker one last time, then rallied everyone together and led the way through the dense forest. When we started we couldn't see the spire at all, not even a glimpse through the fog, but knew from our view across the valley that it towered above the streams where we'd camped. The hiking was very steep and the game trail we followed was all but imperceptible. Generation after generation of leaves had fallen and no one, save a few wild boar and a deer or two, had walked it in months, if not years. As we gained altitude the branches of the canopy grew lower and thinner, until after about forty minutes we found ourselves back in the Kerangas, or cloud forest. Twiggy plants and trees stunted in growth by the continuous cloud cover survived as best they could in the harsh surroundings and held the black soil to the hillside. Vines and creepers still grew from bush to bush, but the mammoth, buttressed trees had vanished, although their smaller cousins still grew twenty to thirty feet above us. Occasionally through the thinning forest we would catch a glimpse of an ivory wall, but never gained enough of a view to truly look over the spire.

Eventually we clambered over a large boulder, then another, then up a gully that ran between rocks at a forty-five-degree angle. Suddenly we arrived on the saddle, the ridge that ran between the spire and the smaller peak that formed Batu Lawi. The mist was lifting quickly, exposing an incredible view. To the south a ridge of moss-covered boulders and small cliff faces ran a few hundred feet up, fusing together in a smaller knob of stone that was the south, and lower, summit of Batu Lawi. Opposing it to the north, like a sword pointing into the air, stood the main peak. A steep face of light-gray stone and verdant moss, perhaps sixty degrees in angle, rose from the saddle to this main spire. Small shrubs no more than five feet tall and with only a few leaves grew from cracks in the rock. Pitcher plants, carnivorous plants that survive in weak soil by consuming insects, grew around the shrubs, their orange and red openings adding bright swatches of color to the otherwise green and gray face.

Perhaps a few hundred feet up, this low-angle slab of rock and moss abruptly became a steeper, dark-gray wall. This was the beginning of the true spire, an imposing tower that seemed to defy gravity. It loomed out over us like the Empire State Building, its summit obscured by the swirling mist. We stood there a moment, taking in the view, each of us quietly looking for weaknesses in the rock that might allow an ascent. There were thin crack lines, perhaps a finger's width or smaller, and large chimneys, cracks that were big enough to wedge a whole body into. Smooth gray faces separated the crack lines, and shelves of vegetation showed that ledges existed every forty or fifty feet. Whether or not the rock was strong enough to climb would be a mystery until one of us actually grabbed ahold of it.

"It's amazing," said Scott.

"It's damn big," Dave affirmed.

"We don't have that much time," I reminded them. Standing that close to our mountain, after the countless hours spent passing over history books and travelogues searching for the exact peak and its location, I was filled with awe. But I was already worried about our limited schedule. Despite the imposing nature of this side of the mountain, it was obvious from our view the day before that the east face just beyond our view would be even more difficult. "Maybe we should think about plunging for the summit right now on this south ridge and give the more difficult east face a go after we have summited," I suggested. "We only have a few days and all of us have been exposed to whatever Volker has. Hell, I slept in the same tent with him for two nights. We could all end up sick and unable to climb before we know it."

"I agree," said Scott. "It seems like there are a number of possible lines we could take on this side, and a bird in the hand is worth two . . . uh, on the east face." He grinned at the wordplay, then looked back up the wall.

The media guys, all steadily filming and clicking away, put down their cameras. Dave and Eddy looked at each other and nodded as if to say, "We knew it." Chris lowered his camera, then tilted his head a bit and crossed his arms.

"I don't think AAP is paying for you guys to do some sort of 5.8 jungle climb," Dave said, referring to the easy degree of difficulty that he presumed the south ridge would have.

"And I know The North Face doesn't want that," added Chris. "Anyone looking at this mountain is going to see that the east face is the best objective."

There was a bit of silence. Larry looked at me and raised his eyebrows, then stepped away. Scott looked my way, while Chris, Dave, and Eddy all stared, waiting for my response.

"It seems to me that neither sponsor is paying for us to *not* climb the mountain," I said. "The number one goal is to get up the thing, isn't it? What kind of story are you going to have if we fail altogether?" I paused a moment to see what their response would be, but I didn't get one, at least not verbally. "We only have four or five days to pull this thing off."

"It's not just a matter of getting up it, it's how you do it," said Eddy. "It has to look good on film or it's not worth filming."

"Failing is not an option, and you shouldn't even be talking about it on the first day," said Dave pedantically. He and Eddy stared at me and Scott, as though trying to be intimidating. Chris shook his head and smirked, then stepped away.

"I didn't think you guys would be such quitters so fast," Eddy said with a wry smile. I pretended not to hear him. There was no sense in taking a vote as the lines were drawn, three to two. It would have been nice to have the good doctor with us right now, his logical Phi Beta Kappa–German mind always able to argue a point.

"Actually, failing is an option," I said, sliding on my pack. "It always is, and I would expect climbers of your caliber to know it. But, I'll tell you what. We will go up this slope and then try to traverse out onto the east face. If it looks do-able, we'll move out there, even though it will be a much longer and more difficult climb. If we get sick and don't make it, so be it. You guys can explain to your bosses why there was no 'summit shot' for your home viewers. I'm sure they'll understand the need for the east face over the south ridge." My facetious tone was probably a bit much, but at this point I didn't care. They had been giving us orders and speaking in a somewhat condescending tone for days, and now they'd begun to be outright insulting.

With the porters in tow, we began our ascent of the low-angle face that led to the main spire, pulling on shrubs and vines and occasionally jamming our feet into cracks. The leaves of the plants were quite sharp and easily cut the raw, wet skin of our hands. It was too steep to casually hike up, but not enough of an angle to necessitate getting out the ropes and equipment, as a fall would only be a few feet and onto some sort of bush. Ropes would never even have the chance to catch us, and their use would eat up a lot of time. When we reached the base of the spire we went east on a ledge that ran where the two slopes converged, traversing below the big, gray south ridge. The media guys didn't speak much, occasionally mumbling this or that about the gear. Scott and I continually discussed climbing options as we moved along the wall. Eventually we reached a flat clearing at the base of the south face. A steep chimney rising at perhaps seventy-five degrees and filled with small trees and bushes ran up the face above us. To the east, the mountain dropped off towards base camp like the side of a skyscraper.

I looked out over the valley from the edge. A blanket of leaves and vines lay across the ridges, clouds and fog rising up between them. The canopy grew steeper and steeper as it drew closer to the mountain, eventually becoming vertical directly below me. Looking straight down, I realized that I was standing on a heap of moss and plant life that hung out over the face, and not a rocky ledge. I stepped back, feeling the whole thing shake under my feet as I moved.

After some discussion we decided to make a foray up a gully that ran upward and to the east to see if the face could be accessed that way. Pulling on vines as much as rock, we worked our way up the cleft but had to retreat when we hit a wall as sheer and blank as the side of a building. The debate over which route to take bubbled up again, but before it could escalate into a full-on fight I rappelled off the moss heap and traversed further east onto another mossy ledge. From there a large vertical inward corner could be seen starting below us and running partway up the face. A crack in the back of the corner was a weakness in the mountain and could be climbed, though what was above it was still a mystery as the face angled off just beyond my sight. I climbed back up to the main ledge to find everyone eating energy bars in silence. Scott was sitting a few feet from the other guys.

"There is the beginning of a line out there, but I don't know how far it will get us," I said. "Still, it looks pretty cool and is worth giving a go. Getting there, however, is going to be a bit weird. We're going to have to rappel back down and traverse out to it."

"Why not start chopping a trail directly from the camp to the base of the face?" Chris suggested.

"We won't be able to tell when we are under it because the jungle will block our view," I said. "Also, that would take at least a day, which we can't spare. This gets us there in an hour or two. We will fix a rope in place and if we decide that this is the best possible route to the summit, we'll ask the porters to start making a new trail. Why waste time, not to mention kill a few plants, if we aren't even sure that face can be climbed for more than a pitch* or two?"

I looked at Scott, who was staring at Chris. "This is way contrived," Scott said forcefully. "We ought to be climbing right up here, right now." He pointed up the chimney.

---

*A pitch is defined as a length of climbing as determined by the lead climber. He may only go 35 feet or so between two ledges, or he may go the full 165 feet that is considered a standard "full" pitch, as defined by the maximum length of a rope. Most climbers try to make their pitches long as it means less changing time between leaders.

"There are climbs all over the world that start this way," Chris responded. "You descend to the absolute base, then you climb up."

"This *way*? You mean *this plan*? *This* isn't about mountain climbing," Scott said. "*This* is about getting the right pictures and film. If it were about climbing the mountain we would take this route here," he said, pointing back up the chimney. "*This* is about you, Chris, and selling a few photos and a video." The film guys had the cameras running. I realized, right then, looking at their expressions as they taped the argument, that the tension made for good footage. They were getting what they wanted.

"Scott," I said, pulling him aside. "Listen, we'll start this way and put in a couple days of trying to do this face. If we get sick, so be it. We fail. You're right, but the camera guys are here so let's give it a go." He stared at me for a moment, then dumped out his pack on the mossy ground and started organizing the gear for the rappels.

Scott put on a bandolier (a set of slings that distributes weight over your shoulders) and began clipping our protection gear onto it. Since I had gone down to check the area out, it was assumed that I would be going first, and Scott knew the order I liked the gear hung in. He placed the smallest Friends, camming devices that can be wedged into the cracks in the rock, on one side of the bandolier and hung Wall-nuts, aluminum wedges that can be snagged inside even smaller cracks, on the other side. Pitons, the steel pegs that can be hammered into thin cracks, were placed behind the Wall-nuts according to their sizes and shapes. Dozens of carabiners, the snap links of aluminum that serve as a medium between the protection gear and the rope, were clipped on behind the pitons, and larger Friends were placed on the opposite side in case we came across a wide crack. All together, the "rack," as we call it, of gear, weighed about twenty pounds. To add to that gear, I hung numerous devices from my own harness, including the hammer for the pitons, the friction-creating devices used in rappelling, and the ascenders, small rope cams that allow a climber to ascend back up the line.

I uncoiled the rope and began placing an anchor as Eddy leaned in with the camera to get a good shot of what I was doing. I tested the anchor, which consisted of a few pieces of protection gear that the rope could be tied to, and clipped the rope onto it. I did not have complete faith that the rock was solid enough to handle my weight, so I asked Chris to wedge himself in the moss and tie into the rope as a backup. That done, I grabbed the rack of equipment and a couple of ropes and took a last swallow of water. I now had all the necessary equipment for the descent. I clipped my rappel device, an aluminum tube that creates friction on the rope and thus controls a climber's rate of descent, and put my helmet on. I leaned back and within a few seconds had slid down to a second, lower ledge. After traversing right a bit, I placed a piton and Friend. This would be our anchor for the descent and, perhaps, the climb back out. I tied the rope into both, equalizing the tension with a sewn loop of webbing, then clipped my rappel device into the line and leaned back so my weight pulled against the rope. My harness came tight and I stepped back a few feet to the edge of the cliff.

Every rappel is different, and though it is a safe form of descent if done correctly, it never feels "old hat." The peculiarities of this one were that it started off a large ledge of moss, shrubs, and soil all held together and in place by the plants' roots. On bigger, snow-covered mountains such as one would find in the Himalayas or Alaska, the snow consolidates on ledges into large blocks known as seracs. Scott and I had already dubbed these "moss seracs," which was apt and fitting but unsettling nevertheless. Seracs eventually break free of the mountain, tumbling down the face and taking everyone on it with them. A disconcerting thought, but an ugly reality of mountain climbing. None of us liked the idea of facing a moss-serac avalanche.

When rappelling, the rope and gravity pull the climber in a straight line between the anchor and the earth's core. If the rappel is less than vertical, your legs hold you out from the wall and you walk down backwards. If you're a Marine you make big jumps backward, but this is not advisable because each swing out equals one swing back in and heightens the possibility of getting hurt. On this particular rappel I would be forced to walk backward over the ledge, which protruded from the wall like the eave of a roof, then jump off and swing in under the moss serac. The whole thing might come off when I hit its weak underside. Worse, it looked like the perfect place for a snake to live. With the doctor comatose at the base of the mountain, I wouldn't be receiving any antivenin for a bite. Still, it had to be done. There was no other way, given the time frame, to reach the face.

I leaned out over the void, looking straight down a hundred and sixty feet to several boulders that pointed at me like daggers. The slope, choked with vines and small shrubs, fell away from the spiked rocks for another few hundred feet at roughly seventy-five degrees. Trying to push the ugly possibilities from my mind, I jumped off the ledge and let out a bunch of rope, the idea being that if I descended fast enough I might miss the roots on the swing in. Unfortunately I wasn't quick enough and found myself racing back toward the face before I could gain control. The release of rope actually added to my momentum and I swung in hard under the serac, my helmet streak-ing across its dirty ceiling and my right side slamming against the wall. Something flashed past my left arm and into my face, and I felt a scratching across my forehead. I clung to the rope with my right hand but let go with the left to deflect whatever was hitting me. If it was a snake I would already be too late. I swung back out and it shot past me again, this time squawking as it went into the air. A bird, or two as it turned out, had been living under the moss serac, and I had literally dropped in on them unannounced.

I waited a moment to regain my senses as I swung back and forth over the jungle, then slid down the rope, still breathing hard. Near the end of the cord I reached the exposed blocks, freshly fallen and without the usual covering of moss. Still clipped into the rope, I gen-tly moved over them, traversing along the east face until I reached the corner. I called out for Scott to come down the rope, warning him of the birds.

Within an hour he was with me at the base of the cliff and we began our ascent of the corner. Scott led first while I belayed him. Belaying is the act of using the same friction devices used in rap-

pelling to safely control the leading climber. In this case the combination of pitons, Friends, and Wall-nuts, with the rope clipped
through them and my belaying, would arrest a fall if Scott were to
suddenly lose control.

Scott worked his way up the corner but immediately found the
crack to be quite difficult. He first tried free climbing, that is, using
his hands and feet alone on the rock to achieve upward movement.
Free climbing requires a lot of strength and agility and is done by using the protection gear as merely a backup to catch the climber in
the event of a fall. But any pulling on the Friends, Wall-nuts, pitons,
or rope turns free climbing into aid climbing. Aid climbing, commonly used when ascending big walls, refers to using any type of protection gear to gain ascent. With free climbing you use the edges,
cracks, and pockets in the wall to place your fingers and toes and
move up; in aid climbing you place the protection gear in those
"holds" and pull yourself up on the gear. Aid climbing is much slower
and generally what a free climber will resort to only when the holds
become too small for him to grasp.

The crack proved to be too small to get his fingers into and the
wall was mostly bereft of edges and pockets to hold onto. Eventually
Scott had to nail pitons into the thin seam that ran up the corner and
then hang from them, pulling himself from one placement to the
next to ascend the wall. By 3:30 we were only halfway up the corner, but thunderstorms had begun to envelop the mountain. Looking
up, we could see the white face above us being rapidly obscured by
an almost black cloud. The wind was gusting across the jungle
canopy below and I occasionally felt the splash of raindrops. To top
it all off there was a constant rumble coming from the clouds, and it
seemed like any moment lightning could strike and cook us off the
mountain side.

"I think we better go down," I called out to the camera guys, still
clustered on the moss ledge. "The skies are about to open up and this
mountain is the best lightning rod I've ever seen."

"It's not even dark yet," Eddy yelled, then he said something under his breath so it couldn't be heard and let out a laugh. Scott looked down at me from his hanging position and shrugged his shoulders.

"We don't really know the return trail," I yelled. "And we're about to be hit by a big tropical thunderstorm." Eddy mumbled something to Chris and they both snickered. Scott and I began organizing the equipment, which we planned to leave on the mountain, so it would be somewhat protected through the night. Some equipment, like harnesses, collect salt when the climbers sweat, and the salt can attract small mammals, like rats, who will chew the gear up to get at the precious mineral. Other equipment, like ropes, are stronger when dry, so we placed them inside dry-bags for the night.

We used ascenders, devices that will slide one way on a rope but not the other, to climb back up the rappel line. Pulling yourself up a rope that is hanging a hundred feet out in space is hard work, like doing fifty chin-ups, but it was the only way back from the corner and the east face unless we wanted to start chopping our way down through the jungle. We made our way back onto the first ledge, located the trail, rejoined the camera guys, and were back in camp by 5 P.M., all in a raging downpour.

Camp, however, had changed during the day. Our large blue tarps had been strung up around the shack to form a large tent, and a picnic table made from sheets of tree bark and held together with vines sat underneath. A rail for our feet had been built under the table so we wouldn't have to worry about ground leeches while we ate, and the kitchen supplies had been organized and put up on stilts. An afternoon of creative work had transformed the camp from a rough bivouac in the woods into a relatively comfortable campsite.

"This is incredible," I said as the porters gathered around. Jacob looked proud, and he should have, as he'd designed and organized the whole thing. "This will really make our stay here more comfortable," I said. "Thank you." They wanted to know how the day had gone, wondering if we'd already been able to climb the mountain. I explained the whole endeavor, giving explicit climbing details to Volker, who had managed to crawl out of his tent to greet us.

"Currently," I said, "we are lower than where we began." Volker, understanding the concept of rappels to the start, knew what I meant, but the porters seemed a bit lost.

Jacob was already cooking in the wok. It was still raining, but we stayed dry as the blue tarps held the cold rain at bay. The wild boar, cooked in oil with garlic and pepper, was gamey but delicious.

"Did Harrisson eat this sort of food when he was here?" Dave asked. I was a bit taken aback by his sudden interest in the history, but it occurred to me that while Dave was generally a quiet guy, there were clearly other facets to his life besides climbing.

"Actually, he did," I answered. "The food everyone was to eat was listed as one of a bunch of rules Harrisson kept concerning the way the men could behave; they had to learn the Kelabit ways in the jungle, there was to be no fraternizing with local women, no wearing Allied army boots. . . ."

"Why couldn't they wear boots?" Scott queried.

"Harrisson's thinking was that anything alien in Borneo would be noticed by the Japanese," I explained as I took a sip of water. "The Kelabit didn't wear shoes back then, so any bootprints in the mud would have stood out." Scott nodded in appreciation as Eddy got up and walked from the table, presumably to relieve himself.

"As far as food went, it was one of the things that the Allied men really disagreed with Harrisson on." Dave nodded as I spoke. "They wanted the normal rations, I guess those canned C rations that you always see in movies. But Harrisson didn't let them have that food, or at least not much of it."

"Why is that?" Volker asked.

"He thought the Kelabit, Iban, and other tribes would also want it, and there was no way to supply everyone with that many meals," I said. "But the other reason was that it forced his men to live closer to the locals and thus become more accepted." Dave nodded in appreciation as Eddy returned.

"And no ladies?" Volk asked.

"No. He didn't want any jealous rivalries to come up that might divide everyone," I replied.

Throughout the dinner we thanked Jacob for cooking. After a few minutes of conversation on Bornean history, Eddy grew bored and began talking to Dave about a climb in Black Canyon of the Gunnison in Colorado. From then on the conversation was mostly confined to the two groups. Volker, Scott, and I talked about the forest and what Volker had seen the porters do that day, while Chris, Eddy and Dave all talked about big expeditions to cold Himalayan peaks. Eventually they wandered off to the clearing where their tents were set up. Scott, exhausted from the climbing, went to bed and Volker and I crept inside the hut to see what the porters were up to.

"We will be having services soon, but come in. We want to hear about your lives," one man said, putting down a recent copy of *Time* magazine. "Do you think Monica Lewinsky has ever heard of the Kelabit?" he asked.

"I don't know," I said. "She seems like a pretty smart girl, but I don't know if she would have studied Sarawak much. Maybe so."

"Doc," said Jacob, "did you vote for Kohl or Schroeder in the election?"

"Uh, Schroeder," he replied, taken aback, then looking at me in amazement. "But I usually vote for one of the smaller parties."

"The Greens?" someone asked from the dark.

"No," Volker replied. "The Liberals."

"The Greens seem to have their heart in the right place, but they don't think about much other than the environment," Jacob added. Volker just nodded.

"You guys sure know more about our world than we know about yours," I said.

One of the men, who I couldn't make out as he was lying back in a shadowy corner away from the fire, responded quickly. "Sam, you keep talking about Tom Harrisson. Did you know he built our first schools? We had schools in Bario long before any of the other interior villages. The Kelabit owe that man a lot, including our ability to read *Time* and *Newsweek*."

We talked for a while about American politics, possible war in

Yugoslavia, and the economic crunch that was hurting much of Malaysia but having almost no effect on the Kelabit. "We grow our own food and don't really need much more," one of the men explained. After a while Volker and I slipped out of the hut and into the damp night. A slight drizzle fell as we entered our tents. Ten minutes later I was falling asleep to a hymn that echoed through the trees, mingling with the other forest sounds. It was sung in Kelabit but had the same soothing notes that I'd heard in Sunday school as a child.

Early the next morning I was awakened by a clamoring of bowls as Jacob went about preparing the morning's rice. I'd been asleep for six and a half hours but was still exhausted. It took a major effort just to raise my head, and my face felt flushed. Both of my hands were red and sore, the branches and leaves on the climb having made numerous small cuts that were now growing septic. It had been seven days since my last malaria tablet so I took another one, slid on my wet shoes and socks, and stepped out of the tent. Filling my water bottle, I noticed that the boar's entrails had been thrown in the creek above where we had been getting water. Hopefully the filters we used to siphon water from the stream were working well.

Volker, who had a raging fever and tonsils the size and color of golf balls, again remained in camp. The hike up to the spire took me over an hour and I stumbled much of the way. My throat burned, I was dizzy, and when Scott asked me a question I couldn't concentrate well enough to answer. During the rappel down to the base of the corner I almost fainted with exhaustion. It was not a pretty picture and didn't bode well for our chances of getting up the mountain. When Scott arrived at the base shortly thereafter, I asked him if he could lead on. I just didn't think I had the strength.

Scott moved up the wall at a snail's pace, the aid climbing eating up lots of time. Placing a piece of protection like a piton in the incipient crack, then hanging off it to place another took up way more time than quickly climbing ten or fifteen feet with just his hands and feet. A climber has to move fast in free climbing, as the more time is spent on the wall, the more strength is sapped from the muscles. But with aid climbing he had no choice but to move slowly. Each placement of gear had to be done exactly right, and there were a lot of them. Scott eventually got to a wider part of the crack and was able to free climb, making it onto a large ledge perhaps a hundred feet up. As usual the clouds were already building into cumulonimbus giants that would chase anyone with half a brain off a wall, but we had to push on. I followed Scott up to the ledge, figuring out a way to free climb the pitch and removing his gear as I went. While doing this I could hear Chris, Eddy, and Dave thrashing about on the moss serac we had descended from. Eventually Chris and Eddy managed to maneuver themselves into positions so they could film us, and Dave came down to my belay position to get a few close-ups.

From our new high point we had a clear view up at least another rope length of wall and a 180-degree panoramic view of the Kelabit Highlands. We were perhaps fifteen hundred feet above the creek drainage where the base camp was, but the forest completely obscured our tents. Across the valley and over a ridge stood Gunung Murud, and we could make out a thunderstorm in the valley where we had camped the second night.

Looking up, we could see three possible routes over the next section of rock. Two possibilities, both rising from the left side of the ledge, were very thin cracks that would require the use of the thinnest pitons. On the far right was a wider crack, easily capable of accepting our bigger pieces of protection and probably free climbable, but it ended in a thin crack through a roof, a section of rock that projected horizontally away from the main wall. All three lines looked to be difficult and would require a lot of upper body strength as they loomed out beyond vertical.

"It looks to me as if we ought to go for the right crack," I said, leaning back and out from the wall to look up. Just lifting my head was a strain for me, and when I leaned back and out from the wall the whole world seemed to spin out of control. I definitely had fever.

"Yeah," agreed Scott. "These cracks are pretty thin. Still, these on the left stay in line better with the last pitch."

"Hey!" Eddy yelled to get our attention. He and Chris were

filming and taking pictures from atop the mossy ledge of the access rappel, perhaps a hundred feet to our left. "If you guys go up that wider crack we're gonna lose our filming position. We can't see you over there."

"Yeah, but it looks like the most probable line," I said. My head was pounding and just yelling the words took considerable effort.

"Well, this thing is being funded by a film company, and we won't have any decent film if you go that way." He made another remark to Chris and giggled a bit.

"Are they filming a documentary or a movie?" Scott mumbled to me.

I felt like crap and just didn't have the energy to fight. "Let's just go their way," I said to Scott. "It's like six or a half dozen either way." He nodded in agreement, but we both knew that the decision had been made without the higher level of thought it deserved. Making a mistake in choosing the climbing route could cost us days, and thus cost us the ascent. It happens that quickly. Just a single moment of feeling bad and not wanting to think things through is what separates us from good and bad decisions. As it turned out, I had just made a bad one—that being to act on advice other than my intuitive knowledge of how the mountain would play out—and we would suffer the consequences.

I organized some of the equipment, then lay down on the ledge to rest while I belayed Scott. The jungle spread out below us in a smooth flow of greens, rising over ridges and dipping into river systems as far as the eye could see. Birds, insects, and various primates could be heard calling to each other in the canopy, and wisps of white water vapor slithered from the trees like ghosts. It was a beautiful sight, but I wasn't able to completely enjoy it. Whatever was dragging me down was getting worse, and I had laid down on the stone ledge because I simply didn't have the strength to stand.

Scott assembled the gear he felt he needed, then started up the hairline crack on the left. Initially he tried a free climbing move, pulling on the edge of the crack and smearing his right foot on a vertical bit of the coarse sandstone. Before his second foot could be lifted from the ledge he was stymied by the power required in the move, and soon resorted to the time-consuming aid climbing. He hung from a Friend, then reached higher in the crack and placed a midsized piton. This done, he tested the gear by yanking down hard on it, then pulled himself higher and clipped his harness to the thin piece of metal. Again he reached high up the crack, this time placing a Wall-nut, and again moving himself up to hang from it. In this manner he was able to gain altitude on the wall. All the pieces were solid enough to hold his weight, but they might not hold a fall. His body weight was roughly 165 pounds, but if he fell onto the piece he could generate as much as 3000 pounds as his body accelerated with gravity's pull. If one piece were to pull out under the added force, the additional force on the next one would pull it out, starting a chain reaction that would quickly have Scott bouncing onto the ledge. Again, everything had to be done exactly right. He placed another Wall-nut, then looked at me and raised his eyebrows as if to ask for some advice.

"I hate to say it, but maybe you should place a bolt," I said, glancing farther up the wall. "This is not the place to experience severe deceleration trauma." He smiled and nodded, then glanced across the wall. Bolts, the same anchors used in heavy construction, are very small and the safest form of climber protection gear. They almost always safely stop a fall but can take a very long time to place. We had brought a drill to place expansion bolts, but had planned on using it only as a last resort.

Scott looked up, then back down at me, then up again. "We aren't going to be able to place bolts the whole way up this thing," he said.

"Go for it, Scott," Eddy shouted from the rappel line. "You're almost there. I think you guys are no more than a pitch or two from the top."

Scott and I both looked at them, the bolt issue falling to the backs of our minds. "Are they serious?" he asked, shaking his head in disbelief.

"I don't know. They have a lot of experience, but I don't see how they could actually think we are near the top," I said to Scott. I then turned to Eddy and yelled, "We aren't even as high as we were when we started. This ledge is below you guys." They looked at each other and made a joke. "Scott, do you want the drill?" I asked. "It's a rather long walk out of here, and a broken leg isn't going to make it any easier."

"Yeah, I guess," he acquiesced. We both felt reluctant to place the bolt as it was planned as the last resort, and this was just the second day on the wall. Also, placing that form of semipermanent protection on a climb that, at least in the backs of our minds, didn't seem like it would pan out, seemed a bit of a travesty for the mountain. Nevertheless, I sent up the drill and Scott placed the bolt, securing himself for at least a few more meters of upwards travel.

We spent the rest of the morning and much of the afternoon repeating this process. Scott would work this or that piece of gear into the crack, continually trying new ways of stacking them together or equalizing the weight between two particularly weak pieces. Chris and Eddy would yell out words of encouragement, none of which seemed to make any sense, and I would lay there and occasionally offer advice. By the time the storms began to settle in, Scott had moved perhaps eighty feet up the wall and had placed four bolts. It had been slow going, and demoralizing. Eighty feet was next to nothing, maybe 10 percent of what we should have done in a day. Still, it was late and there was no way to retrieve the lost time. We descended the corner, traversed across, then ascended up the tied-off ropes as before.

Dave, Eddy, and Chris had all already left, knowing that the rain was coming and that they could avoid a dousing by getting down sooner. Scott and I hiked down the muddy trail by ourselves in the rain, entering the silent camp just before dark. Volker was sitting at the table, waiting for us to return.

"How did it go?" he asked.

"It's hard. Very thin cracks and thin aid," I said, dropping my pack in the mud next to my tent. "And, to top it off, I feel pretty bad. Slight fever."

"Yes, I've already received a report on what a wimp you are and that you are trying to get out of climbing the mountain." He laughed as he said it, but then realized that I wouldn't be able to dismiss the insults so easily.

"Which one said that?" I asked, forcing a smile.

"The asshole!" he said, grinning at his joke.

"That's a pretty vague answer," I replied, "but I can narrow it down to any one of three people." I paused. "You know, we are just even with the rappel point, and *they* think we are a pitch or two from the top."

"I know," he said, grabbing a bag of peanuts from one of the storage sacks. "They told me you were close, but it seemed a bit unreasonable, so I went to the far edge of the clearing to see how much of the wall was visible. I can see the top two hundred or so meters of wall, but I can't see any of your gear or ropes. That's a lot more than a pitch!"

"I guess it's a bit late for this," I said with a weak smile, "but I'm beginning to rethink the idea of bringing people we don't know on our expeditions."

"I haven't said anything because I didn't want to start any bad feelings," Volker continued in a low voice. "But I've felt like Eddy has had a beef with us from the beginning. It's more than the lack of pleasantries . . . he has lacked civility. In an environment like this, on a timetable, and in potentially deadly situations, it's really important that we each do those extra little things, like say 'please' and 'thank you,' so we can get along and work as a team. With his experience you would think he'd know that, but he doesn't act that way at all."

I nodded in affirmation. "It seems as though he really doesn't like me, and I'm not exactly sure why."

"We just have to forget about what he says and play our own game," Volker advised, making his way toward his tent. "I overheard him questioning our skills as climbers, which is absurd. I mean, between the three of us we have fifty years of experience climbing on virtually every kind of rock on the planet. If anyone can climb this thing we can, and we don't need to be told how." He took a big breath, then collapsed on his back and slid back into his bag. Checking my ankle for leeches in the cold rain, I really felt for him. The jungle is a horrible place to be sick.

I walked down to the stream to rinse off. The rain had increased the runoff and left the creek a dirty brown. Using my food bowl, I poured water on my legs, arms, and face, rinsing away the caked mud that had accumulated there throughout the day. Carefully spilling water over my shoulders and down my back, I began to feel a slight pricking on my hands and neck. I glanced down to see a large leech biting the back of my hand and another in the bowl I'd been using to pour the water. The scratching on my neck was one as well, all obviously coming from the stream. The heavy runoff had carried them out of the soil, causing the creek to literally flow with leeches. That pretty much put an end to cleaning up.

Dinner was chilly. The rain had stopped, the air temperature was fairly pleasant, and the barking deer the porters had shot that afternoon was delicious, but the conversation was stone cold. The media guys talked to each other while Volker, Scott, and I talked with Jacob, but not much was said between the groups. Until dessert.

A chocolate bar was passed around and each of us helped ourselves to a chunk. Eddy, generally the most confrontational, cleared his throat and looked straight across the table at me. "So, I think you're talking your way off the mountain," he said, giving me a hard look. "You complained yesterday that we might get sick, then whined for both days about thunderstorms. You didn't lead any of the climbing today, and I didn't hear one word of encouragement for Scott." He raised his eyebrows for emphasis and held the stare.

"Was I upbeat yesterday?" I replied. I was taken back by his aggressive tone and it took me a moment to come up with a response.

"Yeah, I suppose."

"So I'm not allowed to feel sick?" I asked. "I don't need this, Eddy. It's not good for the expedition, and it certainly isn't good for me. Just keep it to yourself."

"Well, I don't like the way you're doing things," he replied, "and we are supposed to be making a documentary about this climb."

I was about to say, "Fine, then start documenting and stop directing," but Volker nudged me in the ribs as if to say "Shut up" before I spat it out. Instead, I let it slide. What good was fighting with him over his opinion of me anyway?

Eddy and Dave looked at each other and took deep breaths. "Should we get out the *culture* cam tonight?" Eddy asked, with an obvious disdain for the word culture.

"I'm feeling a little tired," Dave replied. "Let's do it tomorrow or the next day."

"What's the culture cam?" Scott asked quietly as they stood up from the table. Volker and I sat without saying a word.

"The producer wants cultural footage, so at some point we have to film these guys doing their thing," Dave said in reference to the porters. "Good night." They walked off toward the stream.

Volker, Scott, Chris, and I sat up a bit longer, knowing that nothing was resolved and that the tension would still be there in the morning.

"I'm glad you guys are here," I said. "It's really stressful to have all of this crap thrown onto my shoulders. This is not how I planned for this expedition to go."

"Sure it is," Chris said with a laugh. "You're the expedition leader. You get to take all our crap. It's a rotten job because you're caught in the middle of two opposing points of view—yours and ours." He chuckled a bit as he dropped a tea bag in a hot cup of water, then said good night and wandered to his tent.

"Yeah, I suppose, but it wasn't this way when we were in Laos or the Philippines," I said to Volker in reference to two previous trips we had made with several climbers we hadn't known well. I took a swig from my water bottle and looked down to the creek where Dave and Eddy had gone. I could see their headlamps flashing across the boulders in the stream. "Just because I don't say 'Yeah, dude, way to go, you're the best' all the time doesn't mean I'm not supportive of my team."

"I hate to say this," said Volker slowly, "because I know I come off as some sort of European snob, but Eddy seems to want a very

American way of communicating from you. He wants you to high-five, to yell a lot, and to cheer. As long as I've known you, that has not been a part of your character. It's very American to have cheerleaders, and I don't mean that as an insult, it's just a fact. It's part of the American culture. It's why European tennis players get flustered at the U.S. Open. We just don't do that, and for whatever reason you never have either. Maybe it's from hanging out with me, or being married to a Swede, or just being a bit shy. But that's not you, and you shouldn't feel bad about it."

"I don't do it either," offered Scott. "Never have. Never really cheered at Junior Nationals for Biathlon, and didn't care if anyone cheered for me."

"And why is it okay for you to be sick, but if I'm sick I'm trying to get out of the climb?" I asked Volker irritably. "And why would I fake it? Do they really think I worked to climb this mountain for eight years, only to decide not to climb it when I finally got the chance?"

"You're missing the key points," Volker replied. "And there are only two. One is that Eddy just doesn't like you. You have been in different cliques in the US climbing scene for years and have known of each other's accomplishments, but never hung around together. That is probably because of the second thing, which is that Eddy is not a big thinker. You walk through the jungle talking about plant adaptations, he talks about a climb he did in Colorado." He paused and stared at me for a moment. "You shouldn't worry about what he thinks, you really shouldn't."

Scott nodded as he stood up, then patted me on the shoulder and strolled off to his tent.

"Come on," Volker continued. "Let's go see the porters."

We stayed in the hut for an hour or two, learning about the crop rotations the Kelabit have always used to maintain healthy rice, and telling them about the climb and where we had climbed before. As we explained things they listened intently, then asked questions that brought together numerous points. They really paid attention and never seemed to get caught up in the "thrill-seeking" aspect of the sport, recognizing that free climbing for us was like a chess game. Each climb was a physical equation, and we only reached the top when we had solved it.

The next morning I awoke feeling considerably better. Perhaps I had just been reacting to the malaria medication, or had a passing illness, but I felt much stronger. Before leaving the tent I could hear the loud *whooop, whooooop, whooooooop* of a Bornean gibbon. It continued through breakfast, and we later found him swinging through the trees about halfway up the trail. Volker was feeling well enough to come along as well, figuring he wouldn't lead any climbing but could help manage the equipment and support the effort. Perhaps because of the awkward conversations the night before, the film guys left camp after us and we walked up to the base of the climb as separate groups. As we neared the saddle I almost stepped on a thin, brown snake. I couldn't identify it, though the head was a triangular shape like most pit vipers. None of us had drank coffee that morning and we were all very tired, but the close encounter with the serpent inspired an adrenaline rush that was more than enough to wake us up.

Scott had problems finishing the pitch, not knowing how to continue on when the crack split apart. I took over the lead about halfway through the day, adding a number of the thinnest pitons available to the rack of equipment before making my way up the line. I ascended to Scott's high point, then began traversing left by placing small steel hooks on the tiny edges of sandstone. About eight feet from my last piece of protection I placed a thin piton into a vertical running crack. A sharp offset edge of the crack threatened to cut the rope, but it was the only way up and would simply have to be dealt with.

Suddenly a rope sliced through the air behind me and to my left. Eddy and Chris, unhappy with the slow progress and the same camera angle, had gone up the gully a bit and then dropped a rope off as close to the face as possible. They then rappelled down it and hung just behind and above me, taking pictures. For the rest of the day I had Eddy in my face telling me how he would do this or that, and snorting when I did something in a different manner.

The climbing went very slowly. From below, the crack could be seen as a black line snaking its way up the white wall, through a few bulges, and over a roof. In various places ferns grew in it, giving us the impression that it might be wide enough to get larger and stronger pieces of protection in and maybe even offer holds big enough to free climb. However, when I reached this section of the crack I found the opposite to be true. What had appeared to be a wider crack was actually a razor-thin seam with black moss growing on either side. For at least twenty feet the only protection I was able to get into it were the appropriately named knife-blade pitons. Less than a millimeter wide, these thin slivers of steel could be banged into the crack, but often not the whole way in and therefore were not up to their full strength. If the one I hung on failed, the one below it would pull out as well, and the acceleration would create a domino effect until the rope stopped me on one of Scott's bolts, forty or fifty feet below.

I stayed focused on the placement of the equipment, losing track of long periods of time, then pausing to relax and take in where I was. A few thousand feet below, the green valley rolled into the Tama Abu. The walls of the spire ran for hundreds of feet to my right and left, and looking up beyond the rock that lay ahead of us, I could see wisps of vapor twisting in the breeze around Batu Lawi's summit. It was a beautiful place, but like so many other remote destinations it held plenty of unseen dangers. Letting my guard down while climbing could be very costly.

Halfway through the afternoon a thundershower came in, but we pressed on. It was a risk, but at the height we had reached the wall was overhanging and each of us felt safer there than we would have on an exposed ridge. I was so focused on the climbing that I hadn't even noticed the rain. Glancing up at Eddy, I saw he'd quit filming and was now focused on an area just behind me. I turned to see a silver sheet of water perhaps ten feet back falling from an unknown overhang and pounding onto the outer lip of the ledge a hundred feet below. Volker and Scott, who were standing on that ledge, had moved in close to the wall to avoid the spray. Looking back up, I saw Eddy ascending his rope to get off the mountain. I hung there a moment, forgetting my precarious position and just watching the storm throw its erosion forces at Batu Lawi. Dense clouds less than a hundred feet thick swept in between Scott, Volker, and I, momentarily leaving me alone on the mountain with my rope trailing off into a turbulent sea of ivory.

The cloud bank, smooth and level like a soft blanket spread over a bed, then slid below Volker and Scott, exposing their ledge and completely obscuring the jungle below. Like the sound of a distant yet we could hear the rain falling beneath it, dousing the hillside forest. We could hear it, smell it, and see its source, but we were not in the deluge. I was reminded of all the times I'd looked out the window of a plane and thought how inviting the tops of the clouds appeared, wanting to get closer to them and perhaps even walk on their surface. Now I was hanging there, watching and listening to them, as close as one could be to the storm and not be a part of it. Occasionally the wind whipped the rain about and a heavy spray blew up from the mist. Then thunder cracked through the white fog and everything lit up in a bright white flash, bringing me back to reality.

I looked ahead up the wall, seeing very little that showed any sort of change in the razor-thin seam. If the crack widened then the climbing would become easier, perhaps even allowing us to free climb instead of using aid. If the crack stayed thin we would continue with the dangerous aid, something we did not specialize in, and our limited amount of time would become an even more prized commodity.

It was getting late so I placed an anchor to hold the rope for the night. I yelled to Scott to begin lowering me, and an hour later we were back at the packs and preparing for the walk down.

"I thought of a good name for this documentary, whenever it comes out," said Eddy, who was already there and filling his pack when we arrived.

"What's that?" asked Scott.

"How about 'Change the Channel,' " he replied. I glanced up to see him looking at me. Volker was looking at me as well, shaking his head as if to say "just ignore it." I couldn't.

"Eddy," I said in as calm a tone as I could muster, "I think you're missing the point. It doesn't matter whether this is a 5.8 or a 5.18.* You guys don't even realize it, but we are a part of something altogether new here. Few people have ever seen this mountain. Hell, the most recent scientific study of the region referred to it as a limestone peak, and we now know it's sandstone. There is a lot of discovery going on here, but all you can think about is how hard the climbing is. The real story isn't how hard it is, it's *where* it is."

He put on his pack and pursed his lips, staring out towards the obscured south summit. "That's not how the video business works," he said, then headed down the trail.

"My gut feeling," Volker said, "is that you're not going to name your firstborn after Eddy, and it's not just because he has a stupid name." Scott let out a loud laugh and we headed down the trail.

"I wouldn't be surprised if they tried to write me out of this thing," I said. "They really don't like what I have to say."

"Who cares!" Volker said emphatically. "We're here doing something totally unique. Let them play their games."

"Besides," said Scott. "Just what *can* they do?"

"Nothing, really," I replied. "But I wouldn't be surprised if they started telling you to do stuff behind my back."

After we descended below the saddle and the trail required less concentration, the conversation about sponsors, media, and all its effects on climbing resumed.

"It amazes me that we, the three of us and the other guys, see this thing from such different perspectives," I said. "After meeting the producer, I really got the impression that these guys would be making a Borneo video as much as a climbing video."

---

*A rating of difficulty; 5.8 would be an easier to intermediate grade, and 5.18 more difficult than has yet been climbed.

"I bet it turns out that way, but it's obvious that Eddy and Dave were hired for their climbing abilities as much as their filming," Volker remarked.

"Those guys do have big reputations in the aid-climbing scene," Scott added.

"And they are probably fine videographers as well," Volker continued, "but they are climbers first, or at least Eddy is, so he sees the flight in, the porters, the trail, the jungle, everything, as just something between us and the east face."

"The thing I don't like about having them on the trip is that I feel like I'm an actor or something," Scott said. "Just placed in front of the camera to fill a role."

"You are," replied Volker. "You're a product, and it only makes sense that they will try to shape you in their image. The worst result of this is the lack of spontaneity between us." He continued glancing back to make sure I was listening. "On most of our trips we spend a lot of time joking around. I only realized it today, when I saw how we behaved while climbing in front of the camera, but the usual joking around isn't there. It's as if we are being what we think we are supposed to be, not what we actually are."

"Well, considering how he wants high fives and stuff, my guess is Eddy wouldn't go for your cynical sense of humor," Scott commented.

"Probably not," I said. "But Volker is right, and I hadn't realized it until he said it. With the cameras and microphones on, without even thinking about it, we are giving up control of ourselves. It only makes sense that we would become more reserved."

"Ya," Volker agreed. "And that takes away from the fun you and I usually have on these trips."

We gradually descended into the cloud bank that we had watched from above an hour earlier. The jackets did their job of keeping the cold rain from our bodies, but our legs and feet were soaked and made squishing noises as we walked. The rain was still falling hard, washing out the trail and saturating all the equipment. When we arrived at camp we were pleased to discover that the porters had cooked up more rice for us and Jacob had prepared more of the barking deer. They all wanted to hear how things were going and invited Volker and me into the hut to explain it after dinner. I talked with them for a while, avoiding discussion of the drama between team members, and Volk went to bed as his fever had jumped back up after all the hard work in the cold rain.

The rain pounded our tents throughout the night but we awoke to a clear day. Volker's fever had returned with a vengeance, and the film guys were in no hurry to watch us spend an hour getting in position to climb, but Scott and I set out as soon as we'd finished breakfast. I left the camp a couple of minutes ahead of Scott, but as expected he quickly caught up.

"Well, you called it," he said, shaking his head with a grin.

"What do you mean?" I asked.

"The second you left camp those guys laid into you, calling you weak and scared, and telling me to quit going along with any of your decisions," he said. "Basically they said you and I should stop working together and that I should do whatever they say."

"That's good to know," I laughed. "Patton won World War Two because he had such a predictable enemy."

"Scott," I said, catching myself on my hands as my feet slid down the mud-slick trail. "Are you ready to call it quits on this face and move to the more obvious line, or do you want to keep going? Don't try to guess what I think just because I'm older than you. You're an experienced climber, too, so what do you think?"

"Those guys keep saying we're close, which makes it confusing," he replied. "But I think we're wasting time."

"Fine," I said. "Then let's quit worrying about the cameras. We've already done that too much, so let's go up and move the gear to an easier line. We don't even have to explain ourselves, we'll just do it in front of the cameras and if they don't like it, they can cry in their pillows tonight."

An hour and a half later I was at my high point. I rearranged the anchors, then had Scott lower me down. The day before I'd commented on how weak the wet sandstone seemed around the pitons, and I got a good feel for just how weak it really was while descending. All but one of my pitons came out easily, two of them pulling out with nothing more than a tug of my fingers. A small fall would have unzipped much of the protection on the pitch, increasing the length of the drop to at least 50 feet.

We filled the haul bags, large packs specifically designed for the equipment, and I lowered them down to the start of the corner. Scott then had the unenviable job of hauling them back up to the original moss ledge. Dave and Eddy arrived in time to film the retreat and said very little about it. Chris said a few words in support of our move, perhaps recognizing the difficulty of the attempted route and having gotten the necessary photos for The North Face. As the clouds gathered overhead for the afternoon deluge, we returned to the moss ledge where the argument over which way to climb had originated. We now had less than two days left to get up, and safely back down, the mountain.

CHAPTER 12

June 9–August 15, 1945

I SHOULD TELL YOU, SERGEANT, this is really beginning to concern me," Tom said as he looked out across the field in front of the Bawang longhouse. Some Murut men were there with one of the SRD soldiers, cleaning a Sten gun after an hour or so of target practice. The sun was out and it was quite pleasant, but Tom was not enjoying the morning.

"If you don't mind me saying so, Major, I think you're worrying about it too much," Sergeant Long ventured. "If these people are anything, they are flexible. I don't believe there is anything they can't handle, and that includes the Japanese tomorrow and the new world that will follow this war."

"I can't deny that, but these damn generals. . . ." Tom continued as he glanced over a map of Brunei Bay. "They concern themselves so much with winning the war that they aren't preparing for its end. These people are being forced into changes they never could have anticipated, and if we don't help them through it, no one will."

"Between Lawai, Miri, and the other penghulus, I think we are getting a good understanding of how these people are adapting," Long said as he adjusted some wires inside the radio. The damp air of the Highlands was corroding the electrical equipment faster than it could be replaced, so over the past few weeks Long had become a self-taught electrical engineer. "Besides," he went on, "you're ignoring the local legends. . . ."

"What legends?" Tom queried.

"Peak 200, or Batu Lawi, led us here," Long reminded him. "It watches over them, and I don't think we'd be here if the mountain hadn't wanted it this way." He smiled to let Tom know he didn't really believe in the legend. "Just think about how miserable their lives would be if the Japs took over the place."

"Maybe," Tom replied solemnly. "But consider how well we're adapting to the twentieth century." He pointed to one of the invasion plan maps. Long glanced up at it and nodded sympathetically. "This is the second 'war to-end-all wars,' and we haven't even made it halfway through the century yet." He paused for a moment, looking at the map. "Still, you're probably right," Tom continued, then added, "I suppose we'll know more after tomorrow."

The coming fight with experienced Japanese troops had everyone on edge, but Tom was equally concerned with what was happening when bullets weren't being fired. The economy of the interior had altered, adjusting to the trading of goods in wartime, when many of the working men were not able to be in the fields and larger amounts of commodities were being consumed. For the first time a full-time army had been created from the hunter/gatherer societies of central Borneo, and a wartime economy of sorts had sprung up, with the people producing less than they needed. It was a short-term change that meant the usual storing of food was not going to happen this season. The rice paddies that should have been planted were left empty as the farmers were off fighting the war. Perhaps more sinister, the old men around the longhouses had begun to reminisce about the old raiding days of tribal war and headhunting, and children began to "play war" in the fields. In one case a Kelabit boy who very much wanted to fight but was too young got a hold of a .303 rifle cartridge. He then went about drilling a hole into a post, pushed the cartridge into it, and waited for a buffalo to pass by directly in line with the "gun." With one whack of a rock, he had almost lost his hand and one of the tribe's buffalo.

The Kelabit and most of the other tribes in the interior had lived under the Brookes in much the same way they had for centuries. The only rule forced upon them was to stop the senseless headhunting raids that were a constant threat for each tribe. Now a Westerner whom they respected and held in high regard had asked them to reignite the flames of war and start the killings again.

While the social changes impacting the tribes of the interior were considerable, they were not nearly as critical as the changes that the Japanese troops at Labuan, Miri, and Kuching were facing. Driver Phil Henry's force of Iban and Kelabit recruits had ambushed a number of Japanese patrols, and word of their attacks spread through the people of the interior faster than the men could actually move. Drums were beat in an age-old code that told of a rebellion, and Japanese sent to gather supplies from the local people had suffered for giving out harsh treatment in the past. On a number of occasions Driver Henry's recruits came upon a longhouse expecting to set up an ambush, only to find that the people there had already done away with the visiting Japanese. Virtually every patrol coming out of Brunei Bay had been wiped out, and headless Japanese corpses were filling the jungle along the Limbang and Trusan Rivers with a horrid smell.

By June the Japanese garrisons in Miri and around Brunei Bay had been on high alert for over a month, as much of the Dutch Indies, the Philippines, and Tarakan had fallen to the Allies. Between the missing patrols and the Allied movement across the region, their morale was low. The alert helped to keep them ready, but it is hard to truly prepare for the horrors of an attack until it actually strikes. A few Japanese soldiers, sensing the inevitable, had deserted into the jungle, but many more would have done the same had they known how devastating their final hour would actually be.

On the morning of June 10, 1945, Tom Harrisson stood by the radio listening to the incoming reports. That morning, over thirty-one thousand American, British, and Australian troops had come ashore at Labuan, and his Bornean army had been sent into battle. Their assignments were prearranged and everyone in the Allied

Forces was waiting to see how they would do. Harrisson was more tense than any of his men had ever seen him.

"Sir, I've got something for you," Long called to Tom, who had stepped onto the veranda for a bit of fresh air. Having anticipated the attack all night, he'd been next to the radio and didn't get a wink of sleep. "HQ says we quickly overran the Japanese garrison on Labuan and have moved on to the mainland in Brunei Bay."

"Still no word from any of our boys?" Tom inquired.

"No, sir."

Tom's new army, which numbered a couple of thousand armed and ready warriors, had been divided up into small squads, each led by a member of Australia's SRD. Their orders were simple, but very important for the success of the Allied landings. They had left the Highlands headquarters a week or so prior to the invasion and waited in the jungle around the Japanese positions. Each squad had been assigned a certain area along the coast in order to locate any Japanese patrols, radio stations, and telephone and telegraph lines. The Iban, Murut, Kayan, and Kelabit men were to dismantle all the communication lines that tied the Japanese forces together. When the invasions began, the squads were to make sure that no groups of Japanese moved to support their brothers in arms at the invasion points in Labuan and Brunei Bay. Any Japanese patrols were to be eliminated, and cutting communications between the defending forces was paramount. If this could be done just as the invasion began, Japanese units would immediately be cut off, isolated, unable to warn each other, and much easier to handle. If this were not done they might all rally around one location and hold back the invasion.

Around midday the Highlands headquarters began receiving news from their forces. One by one the squads called in, all sharing similar stories. With their communication lines severed, men at small Japanese outposts and guard stations remained oblivious to the drama unfolding in Brunei Bay and Labuan. Soldiers went about their daily chores just as they had the day, the month, and the year before, unaware that Tom's army lay waiting in the nearby bushes. Their encounters were all uncomplicated, but chilling. In one instance a Japanese soldier walked outside to fetch water and was shot as he bent down near the stream. In another a soldier went into an outhouse to relieve himself, only to be relieved of his head when he stepped out of the building. One man simply stood up in his hut and received two or three blowgun darts into his back through an open window while another, monitoring a radio, watched a spear plunge through the bamboo walls of his hut and into his chest. Tom received reports like these all morning. Almost all of the Japanese manning the smaller posts were dead by noon, and those that weren't had escaped into the jungle.

"Sergeant Long," Tom instructed. "Notify each squad that they should only pursue the Japanese if they are in small groups, perhaps less than five men. I don't want our boys trying to take on platoons of battle hardened and desperate soldiers without a plan and a numerical advantage. We're a guerrilla force, not Patton's Third Army."

Tom continued to listen as positive reports from the new recruits rolled in throughout the day and into the next. The forces on Labuan and in Brunei Bay were also winning. They had taken a lot of casualties, but the ferocity of the Allied invasion, not to mention the bombardment and shelling just before it, had been completely demoralizing for the Japanese. For months they had endured the stress of knowing that an invasion was coming while being all but cut off from the main bulk of their army as it fought to hold the Philippines and Okinawa. Now, overwhelmed by the numbers of Allied soldiers, three of the Japanese commanders had chosen to change their tactics in an effort to save their forces. Instead of behaving as the occupiers of a foreign land, they would work as guerrillas.

"Sir, I'm getting something from HQ again," Corporal Illerich yelled. Tom had been going over maps outside, but stepped into the radio room to get the news.

"They say that three large forces from Miri and Brunei Bay have fled to the interior."

"Just as the Tarakan group did, eh?"

"Yes, sir," Illerich confirmed. "Their exact whereabouts are, of course, unknown."

"Sergeant Long, any further word from Buffalo Leech and Red Centipede on the other missing Jap squads?" Two groups of recruits were pursuing small bands of Japanese who had escaped from listening posts into the jungle.

"Just what I said earlier," Long replied. "They are being tracked and moving farther inland."

"One of you gentlemen please get me Allied Command on Labuan," Harrisson said. "We need as much information as we can gather about those forces." Long radioed the forward command near the front and Tom spoke with them for quite a while, getting a feel for Japanese troop concentrations and discussing the possible movement of Allied troops towards the interior.

"We're in it now, gentlemen," Tom said as he handed Long the radio headset. "The war has become a real fight, and real fights never go as one expects. A lot more Japanese have fled into the jungle than we had anticipated."

"Do they have any idea how many?" Long asked.

"Nothing is clear," Tom answered. "As our forces stormed the island there were reports of Japanese groups fleeing into the jungle in droves. However, they left their usual marks before leaving. A number of oil wells around Miri were ignited and one of the groups, which Army intelligence says is led by a Captain Kamimura, killed all the occupants of a POW camp before fleeing. They either attempted to hide the bodies by burning them or simply killed the poor souls by lighting them afire." Tom's voice held a note of disgust as he went on, "Some of the dozen or more groups are platoon size, probably less than thirty men, but others appear to be at least a few hundred."

"Did they agree with your suggestion of how to deal with them?" Long asked.

"Yes, they did," Tom said as he leaned close to the aerial map. "Rather than send the regular Allied army into the jungle after the Japanese, it will be up to us to take care of them. I hope we are ready."

Tom recognized that the separation of Japanese forces who had left Miri, Labuan, and Tarakan was a gift that would last only a short time. Groups of no more than a dozen or so were perfectly suited for his recruits to take on, but if they were given the chance to come together with the larger forces it would make fighting them that much more difficult. For the most part his men were guerrillas, with the Iban, whose culture glorified warriors who attack straight on, being the one exception to the rule. The Kenyah, Murut, Penan, and Kelabit were all stealthy jungle hunters who had a natural affinity for ambushes. A straight-on battle would not suit them, as it required completely different tactics. Tom decided to send his men against each of the smallest groups first, the logic being that they could more easily take on smaller groups and get some valuable training for the coming fight with the larger groups. This would have to be done quickly because if all the Japanese managed to gather into one force, they would be creating a whole new front in Borneo.

Working with the maps, radios, and the intuitive knowledge his men had of their forest, Tom and his men were able to move the new recruits all over northern Borneo to set up ambushes. In the weeks that followed, the ambush tactics were employed with perfection. Numerous small firefights took place, all in guerrilla style and all resulting in lopsided victories for the Kelabit, Murut, Iban, Tabun, and Kenyah. Japanese units, unable to communicate with one another, for the most part never expected the jungle to suddenly come alive with Sten gun–toting tribesmen. In one instance two Iban men accidentally blew themselves up while mishandling a grenade, but otherwise there were no recruit casualties.

The engagements were becoming so one-sided that Harrisson found himself having to deal with the repercussions of being too victorious. His new recruits vaguely understood that orders were coming from Head Quarters at Labuan, and frequently asked Tom and his SRD men if they needed to hand the heads of the Japanese over to the men at HQ as proof of their victory. Tom continued to hold the position that under no circumstances should Allied Command know anything of what was happening to the Japanese post mortem, so all queries in this direction were politely turned down. However, a couple of Iban were so close to Labuan after one engagement that they simply took the heads in without asking. It was quite a shock for General Wooten, the commander of all Allied forces on Borneo, to have a couple of tribesmen in traditional dress walk into his command center with strings of bloody Japanese heads at their sides. The general wanted to turn a blind eye, but Harrisson was told that this tribal custom would not be accepted by Allied forces in the future.

The Iban, one of the larger tribes in Sarawak and probably the most feared people on the island, were reluctant to accept this new kind of warfare. The Iban lived in two main groups: those on the coast, and those who resided in the interior. For much of recorded history the Iban have been known to the larger world as the seafaring headhunters and pirates that discouraged many a European ship captain from entering the waters around Borneo. Their society has almost no class structure and places emphasis on individual achievement. They have great respect for the way a battle is fought and regard the guerrilla hide-and-seek approach used by the Kelabit as cowardly and less manly than their straightforward, screaming, attacks. The Iban believe that a good warrior charges into battle, running straight for his enemy with reckless abandon. As machine guns, flamethrowers, and minefields were unheard of in their world, this seemingly reckless approach was generally effective. When the battle was over the defeated people were expected to serve some purpose to the Iban or their lives were not spared. The taking of the defeated warriors' heads was never questioned; for the Iban, it was simply a part of warfare.

In recent months Driver Phil Henry had proved to be perhaps the best SRD commander on the island. He was at home in the jungle, wearing no more than a pair of shorts, bandoliers of bullets, and the beads his Iban recruits had given him after each successful engagement. The Iban men held him in the highest regard, as his approach of leading by example and not by order was in line with the way the Iban had always lived. Driver Henry was able to get more out of them than most commanders could with any force.

In early July, Driver Henry's Iban force ambushed a fairly strong group of Japanese soldiers. Though the Japanese carried automatic weapons, the crazed tactics of the Iban proved quite effective in the firefight. The Japanese retreated into a position from which they could clearly see far enough to lay down defensive fire. Suddenly the Iban, dressed in leopard skins and brightly colored feathers and adorned with wildly shaped tattoos, stormed through a clearing towards the Japanese, waving their parangs over their heads and screaming in a terrifying high pitch. It was a horrifying sight and literally shocked the Japanese into submission. The Iban ran over the soldiers, slicing men open with the parangs and firing short bursts at close range with the Sten guns. The Japanese soldiers were overwhelmed by the ferocity of the attack and within seconds all were dead.

A platoon of Australian regular forces had been situated near the fight and went toward the scene as it came to a close, picking up one conscripted Malay who was doing his best to get away from both sides. However, the Australians then happened upon an activity their basic training had not prepared them for, as the Iban went about the chores that follow a good battle. Heads were being removed from the dead, and a conversation with the nearby longhouse led to allegations that the Malay conscript was actually a collaborator. The Iban saw no reason for him to be let off any easier than the Japanese soldiers, but Driver Henry convinced his men to let the Malay go with the regulars as a prisoner of war.

In the process of explaining the situation the Iban noticed that the Australians were having a lot of fun at Driver Henry's expense. The shabby dress, lack of boots, the beads, and general non-Western military look of this man, who was supposed to be a respected member of the Australian Army, brought out a fair number of insults, and the Iban would have none of it. Their leader was a man of integrity, and these strangers wearing strange clothes, who had seen no part of the previous battle, had no right to insult him. A fight was only narrowly averted, with Phil Henry literally standing between the two forces. Eventually the Iban calmed down, but while the Australians weren't looking the Iban lopped off the Malay prisoner of war's head.

Driver Henry was upset that this had happened before he even got a chance to interrogate the Malay, but that was how things went with the Iban. Assuming control of the situation, he told the Iban that they could keep the head. The Australian soldiers, however, were not pleased with the way things had progressed, feeling that they had lost face in front of a bunch of "backwards tribesmen." They immediately reported the incident to HQ, and Driver Henry was soon placed under arrest at the new Ninth Division Head-quarters for the murder of a British subject. Technically the Iban had indeed killed a British citizen as the Malay was from a British colony. Henry, being the soldier in charge, was held responsible. When the news of Henry's arrest reached him, Tom Harrisson did not respond well.

"I cannot believe they have placed him under arrest," Tom said to Long, Illerich, and Penghulu Miri when he heard the news. "It only illustrates more clearly just how little understanding the army has of these people."

"Perhaps we should hand over the POW as is," Miri suggested. "Maybe that will help." Penghulu Miri understood Kelabit ways, but he had a long way to go before he fully understood what a POW was.

"No, Penghulu Miri, that won't work," replied Long as he adjusted the receiver dial on the radio. "Even a general would recognize that the man looks a bit odd, not having a head and all."

"It's bloody army politics," Tom went on, "always trying to find a scapegoat. It's utterly senseless that with all this killing going on they could actually think of accusing one of their own men of murder." He paused for a moment, thinking hard. "Get me HQ, now. I want to talk to General Wooten." Long had already begun ringing Labuan.

The airstrip, with its bamboo surface, had already been put to good use by some smaller and lighter planes in the air corps. At one point a plane had landed hard and augured into the mud, but amazingly the Kelabit had repaired the broken parts with bamboo and dried vines, and it had been able to fly back to Labuan. Flights could be made almost daily, and since Tom's phone call regarding Driver Henry proved successful, he was forced to fly down to Labuan. A hearing was convened, with Tom testifying on Henry's behalf. He told of the Kelabit and Iban belief in spirits, how the original SRD men had only been accepted because of a legend about Batu Lawi, and that the headhunting was as much a part of warfare to the local tribes as the taking of POWs was to the Australians. It was simply how things were done, and to hold anyone responsible for this culture's beliefs, and to hold them responsible for the actions of the men they had only recently met and asked to fight for them, was unfair and unjust. The hearing had been shaping up as a modern-day witch-hunt, but Harrisson's explanations of how the war was actually being waged in the interior of the island swayed opinions. At its end, Field Marshal Blamey on Morotai personally exonerated Driver Henry of the charges and he was returned to active duty.

But as Tom prepared to fly back up to the Highlands, General Wooten asked him into his office for a quick word on how things were going. Harrisson was led into the prefabricated building and then shown a seat in the general's office. The general finished a phone call and then turned to Tom.

"I'll come straight to the point, Major," the general said, leaning over his desk. "Your man was let off by someone above me, and I don't much care for the way you're running your sector of Borneo. Your Semut Campaign was supposed to be in support of our landings, but you seem to feel we should be in support of you."

"Yes, sir," Tom replied. "I understand your point, sir, but I am only trying to do what's best for the men involved."

"Just remember, Major," the general said coldly, "I want things done by the book. I don't want anything else occurring like what happened with Driver Henry."

"Yes, sir," Tom replied. The general dismissed him and he was ushered out by the general's aide and on a plane back to the Highlands that afternoon.

The moment Harrisson arrived in the Highlands, he called in as many runners as possible and sent them with a message for each of his squad leaders. His SRD men were told to avoid any contact, if at all possible, with the Australian regulars, and to do their best to run things by the book. Headhunting and the practice of not taking POWs were to cease immediately, although he knew it would be far easier to simply keep those actions from the men in charge than to change the culture of his army. He was also concerned by how close the two groups had come to a fight when the Australian regulars had confronted Driver Henry. Tom knew that if a fight between any squad of his army and any squad of Australian soldiers were to break out, the Australian men would suffer in the short term, but the indigenous tribes would never be given a fair shake by the Allied commanders down the road.

In the days that followed, skirmishes between the smaller Japanese groups and Tom's men continued, all conducted as ambushes, with every one of them ending in complete victory for the new troops. The Japanese were being beaten on all fronts while the only new casualties reported within Harrisson's army were a couple of Murut on the Lower Trusan.

Through interrogations at various longhouses, the Japanese learned of the guerrilla attacks and were left wondering what was worse: Allied bombardment or Rajah Harrisson's tribal warriors. When moving through the jungle they had to be suspicious of every rock, tree, or bush, as any one could be a guerrilla hiding place. As the ambushes continued, one group began to stand out as the most feared of all the Bornean tribes: the Penan.

The Penan were a relatively small tribe in Borneo, numbering less than five thousand, who lived in nomadic groups of twenty-five to forty. They spent all of their lives on the move in the forest, eating what they hunted, a few vegetables that grew wild, and sago bread made from the heart of the sago palm. The Penan looked upon the forest as their domain and were quite protective of it. Anyone who disturbed the hunting or was viewed as a possible threat was warned off with signs, usually in the form of broken branches or twigs left in their trail just before they arrived. The Penan were rarely seen, never heard, and hunted almost exclusively with the blowgun, a silent but lethal weapon.

When Tom had first begun outfitting the recruits the Penan had not received guns. While most of the recruits craved the new weapons, the Penan didn't want them. Since guns were in short supply but high demand, Tom didn't question it, and he didn't question the use of their blowgun instead. A Penan can hit a coin with a blowgun dart from a hundred feet away. The darts, made of bamboo and balsa, are not very big, but each is tipped with a poison that either attacks the nervous system or shocks the heart into stopping. No one alive can say which poison is worse, but those that have seen them work have a healthy respect for the blowgun warriors. The most common poison works like strychnine, exciting the nervous system until convulsions and muscle spasms begin to contort the body and even break bones. On one occasion one of Harrisson's officers accidentally scratched the tip of his finger with an old dart. He was quickly unable to speak and within hours completely immobilized. They transported him to Labuan, and he was then sent to Australia. Eventually he recovered but not until long after the war ended.

One cool morning, as a rogue Japanese contingent moved across a stream near the Sembakong River, the Penan silently moved in. An all but imperceptible, high-pitched *floop* was heard twice, then several more times before any of the Japanese realized what was happening. It was the sound of air passing through tubes, and seconds later a rain of small blades of bamboo pierced their legs, backs, arms, and faces. Within minutes the entire squad was screaming, gasping for air, and then convulsing and writhing over rocks in the streambed. None survived, nor did they ever see who their killers were.

This attack took place just a few days after the Iban headhunting incident, and the Highland camp was consumed in the flow of war, charting the Japanese movement on maps and moving supplies

and soldiers around to meet the enemy. The Penan, who had duti-
fully been fighting without an SRD commander, let it be known that
they had pulled off the ambush. But upon hearing how it had transpired, Tom got a bit nervous. The descriptions he'd heard of the
darts and the way in which they killed a human being didn't sound
like something the world beyond Borneo would accept. If HQ on
Labuan found out about it, there could be more trouble for his men.

Tom convened a meeting the following morning in the Bawang
longhouse with penghulus Miri and Lawai and a few of the other
Kelabit leaders. "I feel slightly awkward bringing this up," Tom began in Kelabit, "but we may have a problem with some of the troops
and I need your advice." The Kelabit men nodded. Harrisson asked
for their advice regularly and they were honored by the gesture. "As
I have explained to you in the past, we have rules within which we
are forced to fight. If we break these rules, the other side breaks the
rules and it is bad for everyone."

"These are the same rules that say we shouldn't take the heads
of the Japanese?" Miri asked.

"Yes," said Tom. "The rules also say something about torture and
the use of poisonous chemicals to kill a man." The Kelabit men all
looked at one another with puzzled expressions.

"Why is it okay to use the Sten guns or drop the bombs but not
use poison?" Lawai asked.

"Well, it does seem rather silly," Tom admitted. "But that's what
the rules say and I don't think we will be able to change them this
afternoon. I bring this to your attention because the Penan have just
killed a squad of Japanese on the Sembakong. A fair number of your
men have been using the blowguns, and I really hadn't given it much
thought, but events concerning Driver Henry make it so I must ad-
dress this. What I need to know is, when using the blowguns, will
the darts do the business or must they use the poison?"

"It is the poison," said Lawai.

"The poison is horrible," said Penghulu Badak. "You should not
even touch the plants it comes from."

"It turns your teeth black if you shoot the darts," Penghulu Malong chimed in.

"If your rules say that poison is illegal, then the blowguns are definitely illegal," said Miri. "Perhaps the Penan need to be told they must come here to get Sten guns?"

"Yes," said Tom nodding his head. "That is what we must do."

Runners were sent out that evening to track and find the Penan, no small task as the tribesmen had quickly moved up the Sembakong away from the attack. Eventually the runners located the men and passed on the message that they were to stop using blowguns on the enemy as it was too brutal a means of killing. They were offered guns, which a few took, but they were rarely heard from again. The Penan simply didn't feel a need to fight according to anyone else's rules.

Over the next few weeks the few remaining smaller groups of Japanese, who numbered less than a dozen or so troops each, were picked off using guerrilla ambush tactics. By mid-July they were of little or no concern. The larger groups were being tracked and occasionally harassed with random shots or the occasional taking of anyone who wandered away from the main group. It wore them down but did not wipe the forces out. Everyone knew that any group of considerable size would eventually have to be dealt with in a manner other than guerrilla warfare. The Tarakan and Brunei Bay bands of Japanese totaled in the hundreds, and the Miri group had been reported to be as big as fifteen hundred, all well-armed. Although no one knew for sure, it was suspected that the groups may have previously agreed to meet at an unknown location if an invasion ever did take place. If so, they would be a very formidable force when united, not capable of knocking the Allies off the island but certainly able to wreak havoc on the tribes of the interior.

Tom recalled many of his forces in order to discuss the next phase of the plan. In the days that followed, many of the Bornean troops made their way back to the Highlands where they were greeted as war heroes. The SRD men had grown accustomed to life in the jungle, and though their clothes were rotting and most had lost a lot of weight, they were now very much at home in the forest, having accepted the perpetual rain, leeches, and insects that were a part of everyday life. One morning after most of the men had returned, a meeting was convened in the long room of the main longhouse at Bawang.

"It seems that Allied Command has decided that the Japanese in the interior are of no concern," Tom began as he faced the group, "and that they would disappear if left alone. They are now looking at our operation as a mopping up of what has already been done." He paused, looking intently at his men. "We all know that this is silly—fifteen hundred trained and equipped Japanese soldiers don't just disappear. They won't disappear. They will fight us until their end. However, the official Allied position also means we get to decide for ourselves how to deal with the remaining forces and won't have to worry too much about HQ asking us to employ tactics that make no sense in the given environment. Sergeant Edmeades, what do you know of the Miri contingent?"

"Our scouts tell us that it's large, Major, very large," Edmeades said. "Some of the Kelabit boys think it's over a thousand men, not including conscripts. We've been safely using hit-and-run tactics against them for the last few weeks, so I think they know we can take them in the forest." He paused, then added, "They are going to be looking for a clearing to fight from, and if they get to it, we'll be in trouble."

"There are only a few places that fit that description," Tom said, "and we're sitting in the biggest one."

"Outside of the Highlands," Sergeant Mills began, "there is a spot in the Crocker Range, and Lawai told me that there are a number of large, grassy clearings south of here in the Dutch territory. But the Japs would have to come through the Highlands to get to any of those places."

"There is something else to keep in mind," Edmeades continued. "The scouts got the impression that the Japs were running out of salt." With that, the whole group erupted in a low murmur, acknowledging the horror of such a situation. Travel in the jungle is hard work, and the humid heat of the region drains fluids from a man by the buckets. Salt, which allows the body to absorb water, is lost in the process of sweating. Without replacing that salt you can drink all the water in the world but will eventually die a miserable death from dehydration. "It appears that they don't know how to get salt from the jungle, but if they have heard of the salt deposits here in the Highlands, they will soon be coming for them."

All of Harrisson's men had been taught how to extract salt from the forest by the Kelabit. The main source of the life-giving nutrient is other animals, and if you know how to hunt you will have your necessary salt. But the Kelabit generally didn't have to worry about getting the mineral from animals as there were a number of springs in the Highlands that poured forth salty water. Deposits of salt around the springs could then be packed and carried from there on any mission. It was just one more advantage that made the Kelabit homeland a peculiar sort of paradise: everything they needed was readily available in abundance.

"Rather than wait for them to come to us," Tom decided, "let's keep on with what has worked and go forward with more attacks. Again, we'll go after the two smaller groups from Tarakan and Brunei Bay first."

The next morning the squads of Bornean recruits were reorganized into a few larger units with their SRD leaders, then started down the Trusan and into the Limbang river drainages to track the Japanese movement and harass them from behind. They left Bawang in a cool and somber drizzle. Tom watched as they marched across the paddies and then disappeared into the dark forest. It had gone better than expected so far, with only a couple of casualties, but everything pointed toward an impending showdown with the Japanese. It was hard for Tom to believe that their good fortune could last.

Knowing that the Miri contingent of Japanese was the largest and therefore most formidable, the SRD men and Bornean recruits went about tracking the two smaller forces first. Within a few days they had caught the Japanese in the river basins north of the Highlands and established a radio link back to the Highlands. The forward observers, sometimes blending into the foliage less than ten feet from the imperial soldiers, kept a constant watch and were able to observe that Japanese morale was very low.

"Some of the men are starving and all appear to be in dire need of salt," Sanderson radioed to Harrisson.

"If they had kept up a better relationship with the locals," Tom remarked to Long and Illerich, "both problems might have been solved."

"We've been living pretty well out here," Sanderson continued. "There's plenty of wild game in the jungle, but the Japanese are so noisy and inexperienced in the forest that they even have a difficult time hunting."

"If you journey to Antarctica, you'd better know how to live in the cold," Harrisson said. "The jungle is every bit as extreme. They are good soldiers, but they are poorly prepared for this sort of fighting." From their very first encounters it had been readily apparent that everything about the jungle was a mystery to the Japanese. For them, wandering through the forest was like being lost at sea.

The Kelabit, Murut, and Iban warriors spent the next few weeks taunting the soldiers throughout the night and picking off the occasional straggler. This fed the soldiers' constant fear of ambush and compounded the stress of trying to live in the inhospitable environment. Still, the Japanese never made an attempt to surrender. Instead, they forged ahead, their growing desperation becoming their greatest liability. One group raided a longhouse and, half mad from starvation, ate raw, unhusked rice. The result was a slow and painful death as the rice swelled in their stomachs and burst their internal organs. Their existence had become an interminable nightmare as they roamed through the forest with little food or water and slept on the ground at night, often waking with leeches in their eyes and hundreds of malaria-carrying mosquito bites. Beriberi, dengue fever, and dysentery added to their misery and lowered their numbers day by day. After a few weeks the Bornean recruits began to find Japanese hung by their belts from tree branches, as suicide was far more acceptable than surrender and anything was better than continuing in the dismal jungle.

Eventually, Harrisson ordered his men and the recruits to launch an outright attack on the Tarakan and Brunei Bay groups. The latter of the two made their way to a small clearing, thinking it would give them an unobstructed view of the enemy and thus a reprieve from constant guerrilla aggression. They were quickly surrounded, then harassed by the Kelabit throughout the night before being fiercely attacked straight on by the Iban during the day. In just one day fifty-five Japanese were killed without a single loss of life by the Bornean side. Eventually hundreds of Japanese died, but only a few Iban and Murut men were killed in battle. A number of imperial soldiers managed to escape over the Crocker Range and into British North Borneo, only to be bombed by Allied planes and then greeted in the forest by the fierce Tagal tribe. The group from Tarakan that had moved up the Sembakong had also suffered from constant air attack as well as the guns and parangs of the Tagals. By the end of July, Harrisson's tribal warriors had killed at least seven hundred Japanese soldiers. Those remaining had been starved, dehydrated, and antagonized to the point of exhaustion and were now isolated in small clusters and surrounded in various valleys and canyons in northern Borneo.

Except for one group, that is. The Miri contingent, still considered to be the largest with as many as fifteen hundred troops, had moved progressively further into the interior. They had traveled east, up the Tutoh River and through the Mulu Region. The Karst Mountains of Mulu, which lie directly between the Highlands and Miri, are surrounded by lowland jungle and deep gorges and make up the most desperate terrain in all of Borneo. The group had been forced to move south by the rough territory, then back east around the mountains. This put them on the banks of the Limbang, a river that flowed right past Batu Lawi as it left the Highlands. If they went any higher, Harrisson's HQ and all of the Bario longhouses would be threatened.

With the other groups weakened, surrounded, and contained, the Miri contingent became the principal focus of Rajah Harrisson's Bornean forces. Many of the Kelabit and Murut recruits, having seen what the Japanese had done to other longhouses, pulled away from the weakened forces and regrouped at Bawang to protect their homeland. Tom, Edmeades, and the other SRD men knew this was not the best way to take on the Japanese as the location favored the enemy's strengths, but they had little choice. For the majority of men from the Highlands, the thought that this ruthless army could be doing to their homes, wives, and children what had been done elsewhere in Borneo meant they had to return to protect the Highlands—and no foreign leader, no matter how much they respected him, could convince them otherwise.

Tom and his men began putting together a plan to meet the Miri contingent in what would probably be the final battle on Borneo. They recognized that although it would be difficult with such a large force, ambush tactics might still be employed once the Japanese reached the Highlands. Then, in mid-August, while the Japanese were still lingering on the Limbang, Tom received an urgent message from the HQ at Labuan. Dumbstruck by the news, he walked out onto the veranda where the ranking members of the SRD were enjoying lunch on a rare sunny afternoon.

"That's an odd look you're sporting, Major," Sergeant Long said as Tom stepped onto the open porch.

"We are to stand down, gentlemen," he said, staring out over the paddies. "The Americans have just dropped atomic bombs on two Japanese cities. Both were completely destroyed, and Hirohito has surrendered."

All was quiet for a moment as the men sat together, stunned that this colossal war could be ended with something as simple as a radio call. They had devoted their adult lives to preparing for and fighting a war, and now that war was over. Everyone silently wondered what would come next, but Corporal Illerich, having become very good friends with a number of the Kelabit men, asked perhaps the most crucial question.

"Perhaps this is a foolish question," he ventured, "but has anyone informed the Miri contingent of Japanese?" Harrisson looked across the paddies to the Tama Abu Mountains, then looked back and shook his head.

CHAPTER 13

March 11–12, 1999

A S A THUNDERSTORM hammered the north slopes of the Tama Abu, we made our way along the south ridge of the spire in search of a weakness that would easily give us some altitude. Volker had made his way up to the mountain, ignoring his slight fever in hopes that his contribution would get us to the summit. Our first attempt to ascend the center of the south ridge failed miserably. I led sixty or seventy feet up a nice hand crack, quickly free climbing through a series of roofs, but then reached a dead end when the cracks clogged with overhanging moss seracs. I spent an hour or so trying to climb over the moss heaps, blindly reaching out and over the serac, then sinking my fingers into the wet carpet of tiny plants. I'd begin pulling over, then the moss would tear free and I'd drop into space and onto protection placed in the crack. I'd hang there a few minutes—seventy feet above the ridge and several thousand over the valley—then claw my way back up and try the process again. After a few tries Scott gave it a go, then Volker, all with the same result.

Dave, expecting us to get high on the ridge that day, had decided to carry a camera across the saddle to the south summit where he would have a clear view of the entire spire, while Eddy, who was filming us as we tried to climb the hand crack, had been more or less quiet for the morning. His usual insults and rude remarks about our climbing abilities, how poorly the video was turning out, and his overall negative attitude about the trip had all but ceased. He had rolled his eyes a few times at our retreat from the east face, but now appeared to accept the fact that there simply hadn't been time to aid climb its razor-thin cracks. Also, the realization that their filming effort would not be well received by the producer if we didn't reach the summit had finally sunk in and he in turn became more supportive of our plan.

Volker and I decided the seracs at the top of the hand crack would not allow us through, so we set an anchor and retrieved the equipment from that line. Meanwhile, Eddy, Scott, and Chris took a rope up the gully Scott and I had originally wanted to climb near the far right side of the ridge. Eddy and Chris had already been up this gully while getting in position to film us on the east face, so they were familiar with the terrain. They knew it would get us above these lower moss seracs and with a bit of luck onto easier ground. By the time Volker and I had removed the other equipment they already had ascended a hundred or so feet up to a spot where the gully closed up and forced a traverse out onto the ridge.

Volker and I followed them to this point, then as the sun rose higher I took the next lead, working my way past a series of heavily vegetated ledges. The climbing was vertical and the vegetation as dense as I'd ever seen. Nevertheless, I had to move through it fast on account of our rapidly approaching deadline and was left with little time to keep an eye out for vipers. For years Volker and his brother had joked that I was a snake freak because I had made a point of studying wildlife—reptilian or otherwise—on each of our trips to Asia and Africa. I was well aware that a number of known, deadly species were living at this altitude in Borneo, and though none were as quick to kill as the lowland cobras, we needed to be mindful of them. Some, like the Popes viper, the Wragglers viper, or the Bamboo viper, live much of their lives in a single bush or tree. As ambush hunters they are well-camouflaged and small enough to be easily overlooked. Despite their small size, each snake has very long fangs and a poison that can kill a man in a matter of hours, if not less.

I had purchased antivenin in Bangkok for Volker to administer, but the complex proteins of the antivenin were created from horse serum and could easily cause a deadly allergic reaction in a human. Also, the antivenin was specific to only a few species, and on the remote slopes of Batu Lawi there were likely to be numerous species that hadn't even been discovered yet. It was clearly better to avoid getting bit, so after a few minutes of thrashing my way up the vertical jungle I moved out onto a blank face and free climbed on the small edges and knobs that protruded from the stone.

About eighty feet up I came to a large chimney. Pressing one foot on the left wall and another on the right, I was able to take the weight off my hands and stay fairly stable on the damp rock. The rope trailed off below me, descending through space without coming into contact with the mountain until it slithered over a bush perhaps thirty feet below. It then disappeared into the vertical jungle, eventually meeting with Volker and his belay equipment roughly eighty feet below that. The wall fell away beneath me in a blur of gray rock, moss seracs, and brightly colored plants. Even further down I could see a couple piles of our equipment, damp with the morning mist and standing out in neon colors against the natural hues of Batu Lawi. From this height the ridge began to look thinner, and the multiple-thousand-foot drops into the valley were much more pronounced.

I smeared my feet a bit harder against the rough but wet walls and worked my hands up an inner edge of the chimney. There was little in the way of protection to save me if I fell, but somehow, knowing that my fate rested in the power of my own hands was more comforting than having to avoid the possible deadly snakebite. About 350 feet up I found a large, mossy ledge that looked perfect for me to set up a belay for the others. A giant flake of sandstone perhaps thirty feet tall and fifteen wide leaned against the wall, forming a tunnel that could shield us from an afternoon downpour. I fixed the rope in place, called down to Scott to let him know the line was ready for ascending, then walked through the tunnel to look for a possible climbing route on its far side.

I stepped out of the far end of the sandstone cave to an incredible view. The jungle, undulating with the eroded topography of highland Borneo, stretched as far as I could see. It was early afternoon and the sun was out, so what was left of the morning rain was quickly evaporating into a mist and rising from the canopy like smoke billowing from a dark-green fire. As I stood, observing, I could see the rainforest working to create its own climate. Storms were forming as millions of gallons of rainwater were pulled skyward, forming nimbus clouds towering twenty or thirty thousand feet. As they cooled, the water would condense, recycling last night's rain and rehydrating the forest. It had gone on like that every day for millions of years and, barring human intervention, would go on for millions more.

I was happy to see us progressing up the mountain so quickly, and to be honest I felt a bit vindicated as well. Scott and I had pushed for the team to climb this line five days before and had suffered a litany of insults for bringing it up. Now this route was appearing to be our saving grace, and though it lacked the blankness of the east face that Dave and Eddy wanted to catch on film, it was enjoyable climbing. The rock was solid and well textured, we could get in good protection gear, and we could climb it fast. On top of that we were being given a gift of a day with perfect weather, and Volker had been able to come up and take part in the climb. Whether we made it to the summit or not, this had already turned out to be the best day of climbing so far.

Eddy suddenly emerged on the moss ledge, complaining that he wasn't getting the proper video footage. Apparently, now that we were on free climbing terrain we were moving too fast, and he had elected to ascend ahead of Scott in hopes of securing some better shots as the rest of the team made their way up behind him. Scott quickly followed, as did Chris and Volker. Dave, now at the lower summit perhaps a thousand feet south of us, had a clear view of our progress. Using a couple of walkie-talkies we had brought for just this type of situation, he radioed in that we were now nearly halfway up the mountain.

Scott grabbed the gear and passed through the tunnel of rock formed by the flake. The flake rested on the corner of the ridge so that from one side of the tunnel you looked out on the south ridge, but on the other side you were above the now familiar east face. The face, now well above our previous day's high point, ran out and away from the belay in a maze of corners and roofs of white rock. Scott chose to climb the next pitch on that east side, moving over a series of large holds and somewhat loose rock. Any one of the stones if pulled on incorrectly could come off and crush us at the belay, but Scott had a lot of experience with this type of stone as it was much like our old stomping grounds in the Tetons of northwest Wyoming. He gently moved up perhaps sixty feet, then around a corner and onto an all but blank stretch of wall. The climbing was a bit tougher there, and moving around the corner had created a lot of friction on the rope. Known as rope drag, this friction can all but stop a climber's progress, so he placed a few pieces of gear in the middle of the face and set a belay with no ledge to stand on. He hung from the equipment and belayed me up. I removed the gear along the line Scott had ascended so I could use it on the next pitch of climbing.

"Nice lead," I said, making reference to the fact that Scott had just been the first to climb that section.

"Like the Tetons, huh?" he replied. "I just couldn't go on with that rope drag." I nodded in appreciation, then climbed over him and moved on another forty or so feet to a corner system. I pulled up over one very dense moss serac, complete with shrubs and other bushes, then onto a bit more rock and up to a slightly larger ledge. I anchored myself to the wall using a couple of Friends and a Wall-nut, then tied a second rope to the anchor so the other guys could ascend.

By this time it was the middle of the afternoon, and daylight was already fading as the usual thunderstorms gathered off to the east. We couldn't afford to waste any time. Everyone had been concentrating on coiling ropes, organizing gear, and doing the little things required to move safely and efficiently, but we had only a couple hours of light left and the summit was still above. Eddy again came first up the pitch Scott and I had just done, ascending the static rope as it hung in space just to the right of my climbing route.

"I need to get some footage of you guys from above," he said, looking over the anchor to make sure I had set it up to his liking.

"Eddy, we pretty much lost that option a few days ago when we didn't immediately start climbing this line," I replied.

"Well, the video is gonna suck if I keep getting shots of you from below."

I just shrugged. It wasn't worth the breath of an argument.

He and Scott continued onward with Scott leading as I began trying to flip the cord more into my climbing line. A slight breeze had pushed the rope to the right of our line and I could not see what rock formations were there. If there was loose rock or a sharp blade of sandstone, it could cut the line or crush the person coming up. I flipped it back to where it had been and yelled for Volker to ascend it. I then went about adjusting the anchor so the smallest amount of gear could be safely used, thus freeing more equipment for use on the upper face. We weren't sure exactly how much more rock climbing there was, or how difficult it would be, so every Friend, Wall-nut, or piton might be needed.

"Sam, I need your help," I heard from below. It was Volker, speaking quietly but deliberately in an odd monotone. I could hear the concern in his voice and leaned out on the anchor to see where he was. The wall fell away for perhaps five hundred feet below the ledge, broken by moss seracs and vertical crack lines and blurred by wisps of mist. Roughly twenty-five feet down Volker hung motionless, his hands fixed on his rope ascenders and his face staring straight in front of him. His body was halfway over a serac and bent out at the waist as if trying to avoid any contact with it.

Roughly six feet tall, Volker is regularly ranked as one of the twenty-five best climbers in Germany, and was in the Hochzug, an elite special forces group of fifteen men that fights only in the mountains and could be compared in stature to our navy SEALs. As one would expect, he carries his head high, but when I looked down off the ledge I did not see the fearless individual I had traveled with for so many years. I saw someone who appeared to have shrunk in size, as if he'd just learned how insignificant he was in Borneo's great forest.

"What is it?" I called out. I was startled by his tone, hearing that rare but unmistakable bit of fear in it, and was already guessing with a sinking feeling what the problem was. But how? How could there be anything there when I had just climbed over that serac myself?

"There is a bamboo viper right here," he said with the unmistakable calm that flows from genuine terror. "She is pulled back in a striking manner, and no more than twenty centimeters from my right hand and thirty from my face. I don't think I should move and I probably should not speak."

He didn't look up as he spoke, and although I couldn't see the snake I could ascertain that the shrubs were less than two feet from his hands and face. He was no doubt right about the snake's anger. She was used to living alone but had just seen me crawling through her living room and was now face to face with another stranger. Any motion might set her off. I pulled my pack off my back and hung it on the climbing anchor. Normally I don't climb with a pack, but the weather and varied types of climbing terrain on Batu Lawi had me carrying many different pieces of equipment and odd climbing tools. Among them was a parang. I clipped my rappel device into the rope, grabbed the knife, then started down the line.

"I'll be there in a second," I called down in my most reassuring voice.

Sliding just a few feet down the rope I could see Volker's face, ashen with fear. He hadn't moved since calling to me and no doubt his arms were getting tired. His ascending line ran fairly close to my rappel line, and with gravity pulling me straight down I was forced to hold myself off to the side with my feet. I quickly realized that this was not going to work if I had to do battle with the snake, as the animal would be below me and therefore get the first shot, at my ankles.

"Volker, I'm going to lower the parang to you," I said. "I know you can't grab it right now, but if we wait long enough the snake will pull back. You can then grab the knife and use it if you have to." I clipped the parang into the rope with a spare carabiner, then lowered it through the remaining ten feet of space that separated us. The wall was steep enough that I had to swing the big knife from side to side to get it within Volker's reach.

"She's moving," Volker said tersely. "She sees it and is moving to defend herself. No, she's pulling back. Okay, okay, she's gone into the crack. Keep swinging it."

He slid his right hand and ascender far up the rope, then yanked hard and was over the serac. Within seconds the adrenaline of the moment had him level with me, and a minute later we were both at the anchor. Volker was breathing hard, as much from fear as from the quick ascension up the rope. We leaned out on the anchor a bit, resting our arms and letting the stress and excitement dissipate.

"They have bad eyes," I said, patting him on the back. "The snake probably thought that thing flapping out away from the cliff was a hornbill or some other genuinely threatening creature."

"Ya," he said, reorganizing some of his equipment. "Maybe so. That is as close to dying as I want to get today."

"If you want to lead a pitch of this climb, you better get up there. We may not be that far from the summit," I said. Volker quickly took advantage of the snake-inspired adrenaline rush and moved up the rope. I adjusted the lower line so that it lay a few feet to the right of the snake's serac, then called out for Chris to come on up. He reached the anchor, then moved past me on a line that Volker had trailed behind as he climbed. I unclipped from the anchor and slowly followed him up.

I reached the next ledge, another hundred feet up the wall, to find that no one was leading us further up the spire. Chris and Eddy were hanging on their lines, taking photos of this and that, while Scott sagged against a pile of the smaller day-packs. Volker was sitting on the ledge looking at me.

"I couldn't go on," he explained. "I had a bamboo viper inches from my face a few minutes ago. I just don't have the mental energy now to push myself up the next bit of rock and vertical jungle."

I looked at each of the other guys. Scott leaned against the wall, looking exhausted, while Chris just continued to click photos as if that were his only reason for being there. It appeared that no one wanted the lead, which left me to do it.

"You're the big jungle guy here," Eddy said with a smirk. "Let's see it."

He pulled the video camera between his face and mine, and Volker just stared at me with a faint smile. I glanced up the wall and saw perhaps twenty feet of clean rock split by a thin crack, then a long stretch of overhanging moss followed by vertical jungle. This possibly led to the summit, but the amount of foliage between us and the highest point visible meant that running into another snake was more likely here than anywhere else we'd been so far.

"I can understand your fear, Volk," I said. It now seemed to me that no one wanted the pitch because of Volker's run-in with the snake. That made sense. We're all human, and a strong dose of fear is a healthy thing when dealing with deadly wildlife. But it irked me to see that despite the abuse I had taken during the previous days, I was expected to take the lead on what was obviously the most dangerous bit of climbing. However, Eddy's rude remarks aside, I knew that this was what the sport often called for, and what Batu Lawi required right then.

"Give me the gear," I said, staring up the wall. Minutes later I was above the rock face and pulling into the vertical jungle. Glancing down, the ridge from which Batu Lawi rose now appeared to be far away and the same color and texture as the jungle in the valley below. The difference in height was all but imperceptible, and the airy spot just before the jungle overhang seemed to be a couple thousand feet above the ground. I glanced down at the rest of the crew, all standing on what was a relatively large and safe platform. Jungle and moss poked out above me as a serac and appeared to offer very little in the way of protection. It was an airy, scary place, but we were so close to the summit that there was no thought of not doing the pitch. I stepped out of the crack and then worked my bare hands up in fistfuls of shrubs, smearing my feet on the dirty wall just under the vegetation. The shrubs and moss bulged out almost two feet, so eventually I could no longer keep contact with the slippery rock. I worked my hands up a bit higher, then kicked my feet into the underside of the moss. I could feel it giving way and allowing me only a second or two of support, so I threw both hands higher to the next clump of shrubs. It was all perfect snake terrain, but I didn't have time to look around. If one was there, I was going to get bit.

Equally nerve-racking was the lack of climbing protection. The last piece of gear I'd placed was a Friend fifteen feet down in the crack. If I failed to grab ahold of the bushes, if my footing gave way, or if a snake was spotted, I would drop out of the vegetation and tumble at least thirty feet. If that one piece of equipment failed, the force of the fall would come squarely onto the anchor. One hundred and fifty pounds, thirty-two feet per second squared, thirty feet. That would be over three thousand pounds on the anchor, which might pull it from the wall and take everyone with it. If a moss serac didn't stop us, Dave would get a great shot of the whole team tumbling down the six-hundred-foot face.

I focused, then grabbed in front of me, sticking solidly to the bushes. I took a deep breath, then brought my feet up and kicked them a bit higher in the moss. It was a bit more solid, so I reached farther. Forcing the vipers from my mind, I struggled through the vertical jungle. After another twenty feet the angle eased off and I found myself on another ledge. The bushes grew larger and less dense and a carpeting of moss covered everything. It was Kerangas forest again, the same vegetation that existed on the slabs below the spire. Up here it was just a bit more stunted in its growth because of the altitude. I worked my way across it, dragging the rope through fifty feet of moss and branches until I reached the back of the ledge. Above me was a forty-foot-high knob of rock, then nothing but pale-blue sky.

The weight of the rope dragging through the moss forced me to stop at the wall and think through the situation. It was 5:50 P.M., and though thunderstorms had passed around the peak all afternoon, we had lucked out and stayed dry for the first time since arriving on Borneo. However, the sun would be down in another thirty minutes. If we climbed on, the others would have to come up and belay from the big ledge, eating up valuable time and putting us on the summit at dusk. We would then have to rappel down the wall, cleaning all the ropes and equipment, with only our headlamps to light the way. We had come so far, and it was a tough call, so I radioed the rest of the team for opinions.

"How far is it to the top from where you are standing?" Volker asked.

"I can't be sure, but it looks like twenty meters or so," I replied.

"I think that's about right," Dave offered from the south ridge.

"It looks like twenty meters, Volk," I went on, "but it might require a couple of belays as the obvious route winds back and forth through jungle. If we make it, the film guys are going to have some fairly dark shots of us on the summit." I paused a moment, then added, "One option would be to sleep down behind that flake a few pitches below and get a really early start." Sleeping out in the open, exposed to the weather, the insects, and the snakes, was not what I wanted to do, but it would almost assure us of a successful climb in the morning. If we descended tonight and didn't get up right away tomorrow, the weather could move in before we reached the summit and keep us off it all day. And tomorrow was the last day before we had to start the trek back to Bario.

"Okay," he replied. "Give us a minute."

I began working on a secure anchor that we could all rappel from. Just as I got it set Volker called back.

"Come down," he said. "We think we should take our chances and come back first thing tomorrow."

We descended, leaving all the ropes in place so we could reach this high point before the storms came in the next afternoon. If we ended up sick or held down by bad weather, then those were the breaks. Success is never a certainty in climbing, and we all knew it.

The rappels went well. By backtracking over the way we'd come up and avoiding that obviously dangerous spot where Volker had met the bamboo viper, we were able to make our way down with some sense of security that there were no snakes in our path. Granted, they could have easily moved in after we climbed by, but the knowledge that they hadn't been there before was a strong reassurance.

We made our way back down the muddy trail and into camp, where Jacob had already begun preparing us a dinner of beans and rice. Everyone was so exhausted that the only dinner conversations were discussions about the objectives and time frame for the morning's climb. We had a bit of chocolate for dessert, then everyone except Volker and me crept back to their tents. We stepped into the hut to talk to the porters just before going to bed.

"We want to come up tomorrow," one fellow said to me across the fire pit. "You will need help carrying the equipment down because it will all be wet, and we want to see you on the summit." We thanked them, then filled our water bottles and went to bed. It was one of my last nights at Batu Lawi and I wanted to sit up with the porters, but I just didn't have the strength. As it was I would only get five hours of sleep before waking and, for the last time, marching back up the mountain.

The next morning we ate and were up the fixed ropes and on the high ledge by 10:30. I took the final lead up the block, weaving back and forth around detached bits of rock, then over another moss serac. From below I could see that this last pitch would be more of the vertical jungle thrashing I'd pushed through the day before. I moved up on rock, then grabbed handfuls of moss on a bulging serac, working my feet up the wall and reaching higher for the shrubs. This time, however, I had no branches to grab, just a verdant headwall of moss. With no other options available, I sank my fingers into the weave of moss and began clawing my way up the green wall. Just as my feet reached the overhang of the serac, I was able to grab the stems of shrubs. I pulled my feet up as high as possible, grabbed the next bits of vegetation, and stood up to reach to the next bush.

There was none. Standing, I could now see that what looked to be an overhanging wall of vegetation was actually a mushroom of moss and small shrubs. I was all but standing on top of it, on top of Batu Lawi.

The summit was perhaps 150 feet long and 100 feet wide, with low bushes and one small tree near its center. As I walked away from the mushroom edge I could feel the summit cap of moss shaking under my feet. Like a giant sponge covering the summit, the moss grew in thick heaps around the widely spaced bushes. Small pitcher plants with crimson rims hung from the taller shrubs, and a mass of purple orchids grew in the stubby tree. Butterflies flitted about, and the whole summit buzzed with the sounds of sweat bees and wasps. The heat from the direct sun was cooking the moisture from the moss. It was so intense that I could feel a difference in the humidity between my face and the back of my neck when I looked down at the wobbly ground.

The view from the summit was of a dark ocean, rolling up and down in green waves as far as the eye could see. To the east was Gunung Murud, to the west Batu Iran, and way off in the north, only faintly visible in the pale haze, was Gunung Mulu. Sadly, I could see a thin line stretched between Mulu and Murud. It was the first logging road, and reminded me of Jacob's prediction that in three years we would be able to drive to Batu Lawi.

The Limbang River, the river that had led the Japanese deep enough into Borneo to become a threat to Bario Asal, snaked through the forest far below. Just beyond the far ridge ran the Trusan, the river that Jacob's longhouse lay on and the stream that had guided the Miri contingent of Japanese towards Harrisson and his men. Gunung Murud, the headstone to the final battle, stood in such a dark and violent thunderstorm that it was hard to discern where the clouds ended and the shadowy mountain forests began. The jungle around Batu Lawi looked so wild that it was hard to believe how much human history had taken place beneath it.

I sat on a large clump of moss for a few minutes, watching the clouds rise out of the canopy a thousand feet below and listening to the buzzing of the insects. Someone called to me over the radio, asking what I was doing, so I turned it off. They could wait. I had fought hard for this summit and wanted a few minutes of peace before the cameras arrived. My only regret was that Volker and Scott couldn't come up together and leave the media behind, but I'd lost that choice months before when the film company had first been contacted. Our meeting on the summit would be the perfect ending for the video, so we had no choice but to share it with the cameras.

I had to admit it; the old sages had been right. Bringing in the camera crew had allowed us to easily afford the trip to Batu Lawi, but it tainted the experience of the climb. Volker and I had wanted to scale this peak for years, always assuming that no matter what sort of baggage was brought along, our trip and our objectives would remain pure simply through our love of travel, exploring, and climbing. We had gullibly believed that the cameramen would come and film us doing what we normally would as if they were not there, like some sort of enlightened observer, and this had been a silly mistake. The reality of how the film would be produced lay with Dave and Eddy, who saw Batu Lawi only in terms of photo angles, powerful or weak footage, and whether or not they would be hired again by the producer. They were doing what they had been sent to do, what we had invited them to do, and we had been naive for not seeing that it would dramatically alter our adventure. I was elated to be on the summit, but I had to admit that it would have been nicer had I come to this realization a few months before.

I spent another few minutes taking in the mountain and reflecting on the events of the past week, then began looking for an anchor that I could tie the rope to. I saw no exposed rock, and the tree was too far away from the edge, so I decided to tie off one of the heaps of moss and then clip myself to the rope as a backup. This form of protection, known as a bollard, is common on snowy mountains where packed snow is utilized as the anchor. I reasoned that the moss was snuggly knitted together like a wig that covered the entire summit. If the rope cut through the moss, as it sometimes did through the snow, I would then become the anchor by snagging myself in the vegetation.

The bollard worked well and everyone except Eddy, who had traded places for the day with Dave and was near the south peak getting a long-range shot of us, was on the summit within fifteen minutes. We shook hands, I did an interview with Dave, and Chris snapped a few photos. Volker thanked me for putting together the trip, and Scott passed out the traditional summit-treat candy bars he'd been carrying for days. As we ate the candy bars there was a lot of joking around. Volker was the happiest, having thought for days that there was no way he would make it to the summit of the mountain. Scott and Chris were also pretty excited, and Dave had a fairly big grin on his face, knowing his mission for the producers was now accomplished. All in all it was a fairly low-key summit celebration, as those that are really important to any climber usually are. The fact is, if the mountain is worth the ascent and if you get a lot out of the climb, you are just too exhausted at the end to let out a lot of emotion. The happiness is there, but it's on the inside.

We spent almost an hour on top of Batu Lawi. We were each in our own world, thinking of our success and taking in the views, and as a result we didn't notice the mammoth clouds growing around the spire. A rumble in the distance woke us from our daydreams, reminding us of just how vulnerable we were in our position of triumph. All experienced climbers know that reaching the summit is not the goal; reaching the ground safely after climbing the mountain is.

A giant cumulonimbus had formed to the west and was moving toward Batu Lawi. With little discussion, Volker, Scott, Chris, and Dave descended the line. I untied it from the bollard, then tied it to my harness and began down-climbing. I would have preferred to rappel off the summit as well, but the lack of trustworthy anchor nearby meant that someone had to down-climb.

Walking to the edge of the moss, I glanced over the summit and again across the surrounding jungle. Although I'd only been there for an hour, and it was only one small piece of the vast Earth, I felt that the years I had spent thinking about the summit of Batu Lawi had created a bond between me and the mountain. Knowing that it was the last time I would see it, and that the logging roads on the horizon meant that I might be the last person to ever have that unspoiled view, made the moment bittersweet. "I'm glad I got to see it," I said out loud to no one, then started down the rock cap of the mountain.

I managed to climb down the face relatively quickly, reaching the big ledge as the clouds closed in just above the summit. Looking up at the approaching storm was downright scary. The bottom of the cloud was less than two hundred feet above us, and its dark-gray underside seemed to be boiling as bulges quickly formed and disappeared. Thunder rumbled deep inside it like the growl of a hungry tiger.

"I don't think we are going to be able to pull this rope," I said to Dave as I surveyed the vegetation that the second rappel cord ran through. Scott and Volker had already gone down to the next anchor to hasten our retreat.

"It's not very likely," he agreed. Thankfully the camera had been put away, as getting the proper shot was no longer the priority. We needed to get down as soon as possible. To descend efficiently over a lot of vertical ground, each rappel needs to be as long as possible. To do this you tie two ropes together, run them through the anchor, and descend by letting both lines slide evenly through your belay/rappel device. When you reach the next anchor you then unclip and pull one side of the rope until the other has passed through the anchor. The catch is the knot. Knots in ropes tend to get caught on things, and both Dave and I agreed that pulling a knot through the dense foliage would be nearly impossible.

"If the knot gets stuck. . . ." I began as a clap of thunder echoed through the cloud. Dave and I both ducked instinctively, then I continued, "We're going to be forced to come back up here to get it down. If this storm begins to let go with all its fury, we're going to be completely exposed on that ledge." Dave nodded as I talked. "I think we have to leave a rope behind. It's ugly, and I hate fixed ropes on mountains, but we very well might die if we don't." The wind was beginning to blow in gusts and a few droplets of rain were hitting my face. Dave glanced back through the vegetation toward the edge of the cliff, then nodded in agreement. He clipped into the line and began backing down.

Another clap of thunder sounded off and some mist swirled about Dave as he descended over the ledge. Once he unclipped from the rope, I exchanged the thicker rope he'd gone down on for a thinner cord so that the thinnest possible line was in place. Whether we were in danger from the electrical storm or not, I felt bad about leaving a rope behind; however, the knowledge that the thinner cord would disintegrate much faster in the equatorial UVs and incessant rain of Batu Lawi was some consolation. I tied it around a mossy boulder, then clipped my rappel device into the line and walked back off the ledge. The rain was beginning to come down in big drops and the rumble from the cloud was constant. With my last view back toward the top I could see that the summit was already engulfed by clouds. The storm was barely a hundred feet above me.

When I reached the next ledge the rappel was already set for me—Dave, Volker, and Scott having already gone down. I clipped into it and continued the descent. Friction built up on the rope as my device slid over it, adding to all the friction that had built up as the others had gone down. A bright flash and crack rolled across the quickly descending sky, and I couldn't help but think of what would happen if lightning struck the anchor above me. If the blast didn't kill me right away, it would instantly melt the rope and I would soon be tumbling down the face. Still, all mountaineering rules had to be applied, so I took the time to glance back up to make sure the rope wasn't running over any sharp edges. I slid down as the constant rumbling grew even louder and flashes of light streaked across the sky.

I reached the next anchor to find Dave patiently waiting as Volker descended on the rope. The wind was gusting around us, adding to the sense of cold foreboding that radiated from the dark clouds. Below us lay the stretch of rock where Volker had run into the viper, so more care was needed in the descent. While we waited for Volk to make his way down, the wind picked up and the ceiling of clouds descended below us, wrapping the mountain in a white-and-gray blanket. With a loud roar of thunder the rain began to fall hard, sometimes blowing sideways in the wind. I could almost taste the static electricity built up in the surrounding mist. Volker was moving as fast as he could, I knew that, but it still seemed like an eternity. I felt as though we were sitting ducks waiting for that instantaneous jolt of lightning.

As Volker descended, Dave adjusted the anchor, trying to conserve as many pieces of gear as possible. As always, protection equipment would be left behind to facilitate the retreat, but there was no need to leave more than was necessary. If nothing else, adjusting the anchor gave Dave something to focus on as the storm raged around us. Volker yelled up that he was "off rappel," meaning that it was safe for one of us to descend. Dave was still messing with the anchor, so I went down the line to the sandstone cave. He quickly followed, touching down as the rain picked up, and we all huddled behind the large flake of rock to avoid the storm. Without warning and within seconds of our arrival a blast of thunder rocked the sandstone walls as a white flash lit up the cave. The resonance was so deep and loud that I felt it in my chest, the sound waves rolling through my body like an electrical current. We all looked at each other in the realization that rather than simply being under the blast of thunder, we had actually been inside it.

"You guys get off of there," Eddy's voice crackled over the walkie-talkie. "That blast hit less than a hundred feet from the east face, down below you. The safety of the team is more important than anything else now."

"I didn't know he cared," Volker quipped. It was a moment aching for comic relief, and Scott laughed so hard he almost fell over. "We shouldn't go down," he continued. "We are fairly safe behind this flake, but out there we could be hit."

"He's right," Scott agreed.

We waited a couple minutes, then gave into our eagerness to be safely back at the compound and descended during a slight lull, leaving the ropes and equipment behind. Volker was right about the protection the flake gave us, but there was no telling whether the storm would last twenty minutes or twenty days, and fleeing the giant lightning rod at first chance seemed prudent. We slid down the ropes in a slight rain, the darkest part of the cloud hovering slightly off to the south. As it happened, the storm eased in intensity after a half hour or so, just as we reached the base of the spire.

"Guys, there is something else I have to do," I said as we huddled there, dripping, and the clouds began to brighten as the thunder faded off into the distance.

"Yeah, I know," Dave said.

"If we can, we'll get the equipment down," Scott offered as Volker threw some gear into a backpack. "You guys go do what you have to do."

Everyone understood that something had drawn me to the Highlands long before any of them had ever heard of Batu Lawi. Scott and Dave started back up the ropes to remove the last of the anchors as Volker and I started down from the stone ridge toward the saddle. For me, the adventure on Batu Lawi wouldn't be complete until I'd had a meeting, of sorts, with Maj. Tom Harrisson.

CHAPTER 14

October 1945

B Y EARLY OCTOBER, Maj. Tom Harrisson had been in the Highlands of Borneo for half a year. Although certain events had directly involved his divisional commanders at Morotai and Darwin, for the most part Tom had fought the war in a manner in keeping with the lives of the locals. Tom had adopted their ways, was speaking their language and essentially living the life of a Kelabit. His day-to-day decision-making was as much for the Kelabit as it was for the Allies, and his commanders had all but given him carte blanche in leading his troops. For the commanders, safe in their dry offices on the coast, the peculiarities of running a tribal army were impossible to understand, and the job itself was anything but desirable. Tom Harrisson had proved to be exactly the man they needed to achieve their goals.

Following the dropping of the atomic bombs and subsequent surrender of the Japanese, the century's most devastating war finally came to an end. On Borneo, however, time was moving a bit slower. It would be another month before the surrender was accepted by the Japanese commanders in Kuching, leaving many allied POWs and surviving members of the Brooke government to lament life in the concentration camps well into the month of September. A reluctance to accept defeat had been somewhat expected, but some of the actions of the Japanese, including those toward POWs who had survived the entire war and were now in a camp in North Borneo, were reprehensible. Of the twenty-five hundred Australian men taken captive defending the oil fields in 1941, only twenty-eight had survived the labor camps and long marches forced on them by the Imperial Army. Sick with disease, malnourished, and clearly posing no threat to their captors, these last twenty-eight men ought to have been released when the hostilities ceased. Instead, on August 22, 1945, about a week before the signing of the armistice, and a couple of weeks after the fighting had ended, they were gunned down by imperial soldiers. The incident appeared to be nothing more than a statement of defiance.

This mentality was what Tom Harrisson and his tribal army faced immediately after the war, but it quickly became apparent that the divisional commanders were in denial about the ongoing situation. Tom's Australian field commanders were called out of the jungle to be sent home, but all forty-two of them voiced a wish to stay with their comrades in arms. The Miri contingent of Japanese, led by the ruthless Captain Kamimura, was still in full force and had been raiding longhouses and killing livestock along the Trusan River. They had moved up the Trusan drainage and were now less than thirty miles from the Highlands. These Japanese were heavily armed, had no way of knowing that the emperor had surrendered, and had shown no interest in surrendering of their own accord.

As he had been getting nowhere with his radio reports and requests to division HQ, Harrisson flew from Bario to Labuan to explain the situation to General Wooten. He was deeply troubled by HQ's attempt to remove the SRD men from the island, and by HQ's refusal to acknowledge the devastating effect Kamimura's troops continued to have on interior peoples. When he arrived at the base he was in no mood for pleasantries. Unfortunately, the divisional commander was in no mood to discuss a war that was supposed to be over.

"General Wooten, sir," Tom said, sitting in the cool office at the new air base and coming right to the point. "We cannot stand down. The Japanese are still fighting in the interior."

"You have been radioing us about this for weeks," the general replied, "but we will not be drawn into battle again for this swamp of an island. Let the Japs fade away, Major. They can't live out there forever."

"I beg your pardon, sir," Harrisson replied. "But they can be there long enough to do a great deal of damage, and I worry that . . ."

"Major," the general interrupted. "I'm not even sure who you're working for anymore." He signaled to his aide, who then handed him a few pages of typed text. Tom could see the words *Borneo is Indivisible by Tom Harrisson* set across the top of the first page. "This little essay you've written is not something army officers should have time to work on, and it is giving me a headache," the general continued angrily. The report had been Tom's written request for the Allies to allow the people of Borneo to decide their own fate and become a sovereign nation rather than be divided as Western colonies.

"Sir," Tom began. "These tribes entered the war getting along no better than the British and the Soviets did when they joined forces, and they have come out of it as Allies. They have proven they can survive as a nation, so we should give them a chance."

"Major, you're not hearing me," the general stormed. "Our only concern, *your* only concern, is the end of this war. We aren't going to waste a moment of time propping up a new country of primitive tribesmen." Tom was furious but he held his tongue. "I have already spoken with the Dutch leaders and they will be in charge of Dutch Borneo just as they were prior to the war. The fate of Sarawak is still to be determined."

"Sir, we *cannot* do that," Tom persisted. The weight of the whole war seemed to be pressing down on him and tears began to well up in his eyes. "They have fought for us knowing they are their own people. To just—"

"We *are* doing it, Major," the general snapped. "This is not open for discussion. I suggest you fly back to the Highlands and prepare yourself to leave. You've been here too long."

Harrisson was led out of the room by the aide. He was soon at the main hangar, lining up a pilot and plane to return to Bario. After a bumpy flight he was back in the Highlands, where Long and Illerich were still receiving reports on the movement of the Japanese. Many of his recruits had come back to the Highlands for their new assignment. The idea that the war had ended seemed absurd to them, and it was obvious that Rajah Harrisson would formulate a new plan to wipe out this last force of Japanese.

The longhouses raided most recently had been warned of the Japanese approach by Tom's scouts and thus had removed many of their valuables, food stores, and livestock before the Japanese came rampaging through. The people had fled and hid in the forest, but this could not go on forever. Only a few days after his return to the Highlands the report of another longhouse raid came in, and Harrisson's lack of action was bothering the Kelabit. The headmen called a meeting with Tom in the long room of the Bawang longhouse to discuss the situation. Penghulu Miri, the most prominent of the chiefs, opened the dialogue.

"If the men at Labuan say the Japanese are not a problem, it is because they are not seeing what is happening," said Miri gravely. "To the Kelabit, Murut, Kenyah, and Iban, this is the biggest and most important war we have ever fought. We cannot allow these men to go on destroying our homes for the rest of time."

"I understand," Tom said. "But the war is over. For most of the world peace has been declared. My commanders will not allow us to fight."

"Do they expect us to just live as nomads, running from these men?" wondered Penghulu Badak.

"I am sorry," Tom said. "My hands have been tied on this matter and I fear that my leaders will react badly to you fighting the Japanese. My leaders have a lot of power."

"We must do something, Tuan Major," Miri pressed Tom. "This cannot continue."

Tom responded with a sigh. He was caught in the middle of two forces, one concerned with its global position and the other just trying to get through the day. He had to do something for these people, but any action would be perceived as subversive and could bring down the wrath of whatever government would soon be in charge.

Tom went to the radio room and again called Labuan, but ran into the same filibustering he'd seen in the previous weeks. After a few hours of discussion, however, division command relented a bit—they decided that the best course of action, so as to avoid confrontation and get Harrisson off their back, was to simply inform the Miri contingent of Japanese that the war was over. They felt that the Kelabit reports of hundreds of armed soldiers were gross exaggerations, and one officer had even gone so far as to question whether the Kelabit actually knew how to count. They assumed that with only a few men in the field, the Japanese would be more than willing to call it quits if someone just notified them of the war's end. They ordered Tom to send in envoys to explain that hostilities had ceased and the emperor had surrendered.

Tom knew that the Japanese force was still being closely watched, and that a large group of Kelabit and Murut guerrillas were within striking range. He radioed Allied Command's orders to the Bornean soldiers in the field, and an envoy of four Kelabit and Iban volunteers was sent to notify the Japanese commander of the armistice. They walked into the Japanese camp carrying a white flag and were shown to Captain Kamimura, but at that point events took an unfortunate turn. Captain Kamimura, like most Japanese soldiers, refused to believe that his emperor would ever surrender. To him this was nothing more than a trick, or a way to gather information on the strength of his force. Within minutes of arriving the four messengers were executed.

The news made its way back to Tom almost immediately, and he regretfully informed Penghulu Miri and the other leaders. The Kelabit responded by calling for discussions with the headmen of the nearby tribes, asking Tom to explain the situation to everyone. He did so, and then listened as they discussed the problem. In the past year the Kelabit, Murut, Kenyah, and Iban had been shown the worst the Japanese Empire could muster, with longhouses burned, crops destroyed, and men, women, and children killed in cold blood.

For them, the fact that the Japanese government had surrendered unconditionally was a distant and all but meaningless fact. There was no reason to pretend the war was over when the Japanese on Borneo refused to surrender and had brutally murdered their messengers. It was clear they were ready to take matters into their own hands, with or without anyone else's support. Tom sympathized, but knowing what the long-term repercussions could be, he was determined to get Allied Command involved. The following morning he again set out to Labuan to discuss the matter with Major General Wooten.

Tom went straight to the general's office, where he was offered drinks and food. He wasn't interested, but noted that it was a civility that hadn't been offered on his previous trip. He was shown into the office only to find that General Wooten was no longer in command.

"Good morning, Major Harrisson." The man stood up and offered his hand. "I'm General Windeyer. I replaced General Wooten a couple days ago." He sat down and beckoned Tom to take a seat on the opposite side of the desk. "I understand we still have a problem with a rogue Japanese contingent, Major Harrisson."

"Yes sir, two days ago my envoy was executed by the Japanese commander," Harrisson said. "I see no reason to believe that this man wants to surrender, or even any sign that he will entertain discussion of the matter." As Tom spoke the general nodded in affirmation.

"Let me explain our position," the general began evenly. "If Allied troops, for any reason, were to kill any Japanese and word of it got out, it could be perceived as murder to any other Japanese troops in the Pacific Theater. We could restart the war."

The kind demeanor and seemingly open-minded approach of General Windeyer was not what Tom had expected, but it lightened his mood a bit and he pressed forward. "Allied soldiers are being killed, sir," he replied, "as are the families of Allied soldiers. The tribes of Borneo became part of the alliance when we induced them to fight in our war. As I see it, we are shirking a responsibility we have to these people. They risked and gave their lives for us. It could be said that the Allies duped an innocent group of people into fighting for them, and then left these people to die."

"You're right, Major," the general said solemnly, then stared at Tom for a moment, obviously in deep thought. "You're right, Major. This problem needs to be put to rest." He turned to his aide and said, "Have we brought General Baba up from Kuching yet?"

"Yes, sir," said the aide. "He was brought in this morning."

"What if we were to send him into the Highlands with Major Harrisson to find these Japanese?" the general queried. "We can get him to do that, can't we?"

"He's not really in that kind of shape, sir," said the aide. "I don't think he spent that much time in the field."

"Well, according to Major Harrisson, General Baba's men are killing Allied soldiers. Get him in here so I can have a word with him." The aide quickly exited the room. "All right, Major Harrisson," said the general as he adjusted himself in his teak chair. "You can have this your way, but done by the book. I want you to personally find this Captain Kamimura. General Baba was the head of all Japanese Imperial forces on Borneo, so if anyone can shut these guys down, it's him. We'll find a radioman for you so I can get a report on your whereabouts *at least* twice a day. If I don't hear from you twice a day, your permission is revoked." Tom nodded as the general spoke. "If you can find another volunteer on this base, take him along, but I don't want any Australian soldiers who were drafted going up there. The last thing I want to do at this stage of the game is write another letter to another mother." He paused, then leaned forward in his chair. "In any event, I can't find any reason for a single shot to be fired. Do you understand?"

"Yes, sir," Harrisson agreed.

The arrangements were made, including where to meet and at what time on the following morning, and Tom went to the officers club for a drink. While there he met an Australian major who had been through some of the worst arenas the war had offered on Borneo. Major Rex Blow had been taken captive in British North Borneo by the Japanese, but had escaped to the Philippines in 1943.

Since then he had been waging a guerrilla campaign against the Japanese, but was now thankfully relieved of his duties. Tom had a couple drinks with Rex and asked him if he'd join in the mission. The major had no intention of going back into the jungle to fight an enemy that had already surrendered and refused Tom's pressing for quite some time. But finally, after a full bottle of whiskey, Tom had broken him down. They met the next morning with Corporal Nibbs, the general's assigned radioman, and were then presented with one of General Baba's aides, Captain Maru. The captain was well educated and had served in the Borneo headquarters under General Baba for most of the war. He carried a sealed packet with orders, signed by the general, stating that Kamimura was to surrender immediately.

They set off across Brunei Bay in a small boat just after sunrise. The four men made their way to the mouth of the Trusan River, brown and swollen with the October rains, then followed it into the jungle. A monsoonal downpour continued for much of the first day, and dark clouds gave the jungle a somber and sobering feeling. The river was wide but much of it was shrouded in huge, vine-choked trees, and the boat had to weave back and forth to avoid the logs and branches floating down with the current. After four continuous days on the river they arrived at Long Semado, site of the most recent raid by Kamimura's men. Unexpectedly, they met up with a few of the Kelabit recruits from Bario.

The recruits reported how the rogue force had raided Long Semado a few days earlier, then moved up the Trusan a bit farther and crossed over to one of its tributaries, the Kalalan. That put them within twenty miles of Bawang, a distance that could be covered in one day by any fit army.

In speaking with the Kelabit men, Tom came to the realization that the number of Kelabit, Kenyan, and Murut soldiers following the Japanese had grown substantially since he'd flown out to Labuan. The Kelabit leaders, angry at the lack of support from their supposed allies, had let as many men as wanted go to challenge the Japanese before they entered the Kelabit Highlands. He couldn't blame them, but sensed the mounting tension and desperately wanted to get to his men and stop them before all hell broke loose.

"We have to get a move on," Tom said to Rex. "We're supposed to be unarmed, but talking with these men gives me the impression that you and I have a very ready and motivated army at our disposal. I have a feeling that if we don't get to Kamimura soon, my troops will attack the Japanese or, worse, the Japanese will reach our head-quarters in the Highlands."

"I always say," ventured Rex, "that it's better to have an army and not need it, than not have one and wish you did. I only hope we can catch up with them."

They trekked until dark, eating cold rice for dinner and flicking leeches from their bodies throughout the night. The next morning they continued on in a cool drizzle. Sometime in mid-afternoon they stopped for water and heard, not far to the north, the sound of gun-fire. All four of them dropped their water bottles and began running up the streambed toward the gunfire. After a mile or so they crossed the eastern slopes of Gunung Murud, then broke out of the forest to an astonishing sight. A wide-open plain of paddies and grassy fields was spread out around his troops, the varying greens of the grasses and rice shoots illuminated in the midday sun. To the southwest rose Gunung Murud, its dark summit shrouded in a heavy, gray cloud. But out near the middle of the open field was a small longhouse on a knoll, perhaps no more than a half mile away, and Tom could clearly see the khaki-brown uniforms of Japanese troops moving around it. The Kelabit and Murut were lined up along the plain's perimeter, their backs to the forest and their rifles leveled at the longhouse. He could see that they had just been shooting, but with his arrival everyone quit firing.

"What the hell is happening here?" Tom called out.

For a moment none of the Kelabit spoke, then one of the men from Bario stood up and tried to explain. The Japanese had been tracked and then caught by the large contingent of Borneans just as they began raiding the deserted longhouse. No one seemed to know who fired first, but both sides had begun taking shots at each other. The Kelabit and Murut had been preparing to charge the longhouse, and the Japanese had dug in around it.

Tom listened, then went to each group of Kelabit and Murut soldiers huddled around the perimeter of the field to explain the situation. They willfully set down their rifles at Tom's request and agreed to wait for Captain Maru to try and diffuse the situation. A large, white sheet was placed on a bamboo pole and Captain Maru, in full imperial military uniform, started across the shallow pools of rice shoots. The white sheet fluttered across the sky of broken clouds as small birds, feeding on the rice, flew up just in front of his footsteps. Harrisson and his men watched as Maru reached the longhouse. They could see that he was talking to the men on the veranda, then he stepped up the stairs and looked in the door. Disappearing inside, he went about explaining that the war had ended and that Japan was now an occupied country. After about an hour, Captain Maru walked out and down the steps. Captain Kamimura and his officers followed, all with their heads bowed, and Maru began waving for Tom's men to come over.

Tom shouted in Kelabit that there was to be no shooting under any circumstances unless they were fired on first. He made sure this was repeated in Iban, then he and his men began wading toward the longhouse. By the time they reached the dry knoll, all of the Japanese troops along with a line of conscripts and support personnel, including two nurses, had emerged from the building and were standing in columns. On Tom's word a few Kelabit men ran through the lines of Japanese soldiers, taking their rifles and piling them in front of the longhouse. Tom stood nearby with a Sten gun, watching over the proceedings to make sure his men behaved themselves and that the Japanese soldiers didn't have second thoughts. After dropping some rifles in a pile, a young Kelabit man was summoned by a few of the elders. He conversed with them for a moment, then ran up the hill to deliver a message to Tom.

"Rajah Tom," he said in Kelabit, "these men need salt very much. Their necks have swollen and we can see that their eyes look shallow."

"Thank you, Agan," Tom replied. "We will get it to them as soon as they have been disarmed." He smiled as the young Kelabit ran back into the files of Japanese soldiers to gather more weapons. One of the most amazing traits Tom had discovered about the Kelabit was their ability to accept change. An hour before they'd been exchanging gunshots with these men, but now they were concerned that the men didn't have enough salt. It was a striking testament to the character of these people, of their willingness to avail themselves to their fellow man regardless of the history that had come before.

After everyone had been disarmed, the Kelabit ran off to the sides of the column and gathered behind Harrisson, waiting to see what would come next. The clouds had parted and the sun was beating down and Tom could see a few of the Japanese soldiers, thin with malnutrition and weary from months in the jungle, waver a bit in the stifling heat. Captain Maru yelled something to the soldiers, then everyone watched as Captain Kamimura stepped forward. Nodding to Maru, he carefully unhooked his sword from his belt and handed it to Rajah Tom Harrisson. On a remote plain in central Borneo, on October 28, 1945, nearly two months after Emperor Hirohito had signed the armistice in Tokyo Bay, the last major Japanese force surrendered to the Allies. The war was truly over.

CHAPTER 15

March 12, 1999

FOLLOWING WORLD WAR II, Vyner Brooke gave control of Sarawak over to the British and they administered it just as they did every other colony. The Brookes had held the rights and culture of the inland people to be above all else, but the British hardly noticed them. The boundaries between Sarawak, Dutch Borneo, Sabah, and Brunei were all reinforced without thought for the tribal layout of the inland people. Trade was promoted with the outside world, with the rivers opened up and airstrips scoured out of the forest. Laws were established with little consideration for the rules that had existed for generations before, and missionaries were allowed into the island's interior to promote their faith.

Tom Harrisson had remained in Bario for a year after the war and in Kuching, the capital of Sarawak, for much of the remaining thirty years of his life. He had watched as many of these changes took place. He married a Kelabit woman and dedicated himself to studying the Kelabit's lives. More than anything, he tried to help them with the transition from being a remote Highland tribe to being a part of the larger world. He helped set up schools across the Highlands and promoted the establishment of a government medical clinic. His airstrip was widened and made more durable, and he taught the Kelabit how to use air transport to sell their highly prized rice at markets on the coast.

Volker and I talked about the history of Sarawak as we worked our way toward the south summit of Batu Lawi. The rainwater blew from the bushes in sheets, soaking us through our Gore-Tex and filling our packs with water. We traversed along the base of the spire, then descended the white slabs to the saddle. Water ran down the rock faces and up our sleeves as we tried to grip the coarse stone, shivering in the cold wind blowing over the ridge. We reached the saddle, then continued along the ridge toward the south summit. The main peak where we had stood just hours before had all but disappeared, the storm clouds providing us with little more than glimpses and vague silhouettes of the dark tower. The south summit, much lower and hardly a true spire, was still visible, though the swirling mist and rain obscured it at times.

"Where are we going?" Volker asked as we passed the porters. They were huddled under a boulder, snuggled together in an attempt to stay warm while they waited out the storm. They cheered and gave us a thumbs-up as we passed, but wisely made no effort to come out into the heavy weather.

"Just follow me," I said.

We climbed a small tree that leaned against the ridge, then up over a few boulders and through a groove of mossy blocks. Cresting another boulder we found Eddy, his camera and tripod wrapped in a North Face jacket and aimed at the main peak from a slight alcove in the rock. The steep wall of the boulder, bleached white and lacking the moss that covered so much of Batu Lawi's sandstone, curved away from the camera towards the spire. In the middle of this boulder, a brass plaque, aqua-green with corrosion, hung from three rusting steel bolts. A rotting and frail chunk of log, dusty brown like an old chunk of driftwood, rested on top of the plaque.

"This is why we're here," I said as we stepped up to the small tablet.

"What is a brass plaque doing in the middle of the rainforest?"

Volker asked me. A double blast of lightning and thunder pelted the main peak behind us and we ducked instinctively. Volker looked to the spire, then leaned in close to the wall and read the green-and-brown lettering aloud.

> *. . . of Flight 200 . . .*
> *They successfully dropped us at Bareo 25/3/45*
> *But they never got back to Morotai. By Batu Lawi*
> *We steered on this and four previous attempts.*
> *The RAAF called it Mount 200*
> *I pledged my word to climb it for them in their memory.*
> *Here, in loneliness, I remember my friends.*
>
> *Nagalewan Rajah*

A sentence or two under the main inscription pointed out that the quote had been taken from what was left of an original plaque, carved in wood and now rotting atop the new brass one. The brass version had been placed on the mountain by the Australian Army in 1988 in memory of Harrisson.

"Who is Nagalewan Rajah?" Volker wondered.

"I believe it's Harrisson," I said. "The original plaque, the wood one, was carved and placed here by Harrisson in 1946. The plane that dropped him in here never made it back to the base. It was shot down while strafing a Japanese boat, and Harrisson came to climb the mountain in their memory. 'Nagalewan' means headman in Kelabit, and the rajahs, as you know, were the rulers of Sarawak. Harrisson had been named rajah by the Kelabit just after he landed, so this could be him using his Kelabit name, or it could be the signature of someone who came here with him. I'm not sure, but the plaque is his."

"He came right to this spot?" Volker asked, glancing across the ridge. The rain was beginning to lighten a bit and the main peak was now visible between the parting clouds. Off in the distance I could see Gunung Murud, the place where Tom Harrisson's war had ended.

"Yes," I replied, glancing back at Batu Lawi. "He vowed to climb the mountain but couldn't get up the main spire because it was too difficult. He climbed to here instead."

Eddy had been filming us for a moment, and Chris had come up from behind and was taking photos of the peak as the storm parted around it. I had been reading about this peak, this region, and these people for months, and a lot was running through my head. Volker hadn't been as engrossed with the mystique and history of Batu Lawi, but I could see that he now wanted to know everything. We stood in the chilly drizzle for a while and, from memory, I told him as much as I could remember.

"The whole story is a bit ironic," Volker said. "He was sent here on an almost suicidal mission, but the guys who delivered him died and he escaped without a scratch."

"And to add to that irony," I said, "he devoted much of his life to helping the Kelabit adjust to life in the twentieth century, but his arrival was the first big dose of the modern world that these people got."

We stood there a few more minutes, then made our way back to the base of the main peak to retrieve the gear. It was soaked and very heavy, and it seemed that we had far more gear now than when we first arrived at the mountain. A few of the porters had managed to outlast the storm, and they came up to help us carry the equipment down.

The trek back to camp was mostly silent, all of us deep in our own thoughts. We entered the camp to find the rest of the porters lining the trail, all of them excited about our reaching the summit and wanting to shake our hands in congratulations. I reminded them that the successful ascent of the mountain was not just rooted in our skills—it had been a team effort, and we would not have been able to pull it off without their help. "You helped to carry our ropes and equipment, made the camp comfortable, and fed us at night and in the morning," I said. "This climb is as much your success as it is ours." Shyly, they each came forward and thanked me again for noting their contribution. Each of them seemed as genuine and sincere in their thanks as anyone I'd ever known. It felt odd when I remembered that I'd met them only a couple weeks earlier.

We ate a dinner of rice and beans and I immediately went to my tent, making notes in my diary and listening to the low-key celebration taking place inside the hut. It seemed that the Kelabit were truly happy with our accomplishment, and I fell asleep that night listening not only to the now familiar sounds of forest but the soft melodies of hymns and traditional songs being sung just a few feet away.

The walk out of the jungle was as beautiful as the walk in, and drier to boot. Eddy and Dave talked about climbs they had done, climbs they planned to do, and a few filming projects each of them had coming up. Chris mostly walked on his own, though he stopped us at times to take a few photos. Scott kept pace with the film guys, completely engrossed in their climbing stories, and Volker and I trailed along with Jacob, learning more about the forest and the intricacies of Malaysian politics.

Our arrival back at the longhouse was met with another celebration. All the people of Pa Ukat wanted to see the men who had climbed Batu Lawi, the sentinel of the Kelabit Highlands. While waiting for the Skyvan to return, I got to meet a man who had actually fought alongside Tom Harrisson. He was old and much slower than he would have been in those days, but his eyes lit up brightly when I asked him about Major Harrisson and fighting the Japanese. He told me a few things that conflicted with Harrisson's own accounts of the war, including a point on the business of trophy taking. Harrisson rarely alluded to it in *World Within*, but when I asked this man if Japanese heads had rolled after a battle, his reply with a smile was, "Only when no one was looking."

I found that little bit of history to be a revered and glorious time for the Kelabit, and that when I'd mention Tom Harrisson to anyone in the Highlands they'd smile and open up with warm stories. Harrisson had known that there was no preventing the outside world from coming to Bario, so he built schools to help get the Kelabit a step ahead of the other tribes in the region. On his arrival, no Kelabit could read or speak English and only a handful could speak Malay. Now there are lawyers, architects, and, as we found, even airplane mechanics from the Kelabit Highlands. Tom Harrisson was one of the first men to bring the world into Bario, and fortunately for the Kelabit he cared about what would happen when it came. He and his men have been immortalized to some degree by the disproportionate number of Kelabit who are named Tom and after the other men who fought in the Highlands. Harrisson has been dead now for more than twenty years but he has become, as much as anyone can, a folk hero to the Kelabit.

Almost everyone in the Highlands today is a member of the Borneo Evangelical Mission, a fundamental Christian Church that has a large following all over the island. Today only the old men have elongated earlobes decorated with brass rings or leopard's teeth. Tattooing as well as all-night parties with gallons of borak passed around are rare, and exposed breasts while working in the fields are unheard of. The Kelabit and all the people of Borneo's interior have seen many changes since World War II, but some things remain the same. They still grow rice and care for water buffalo. They still harvest vegetables from the forest and enjoy hunting more than any other endeavor. They still swing their parangs and compete over who is stronger or who can carry a bigger pack.

And, occasionally, a few foreigners will drop out of the clouds and the Kelabit will trek to the upper reaches of the Limbang, carrying heavy loads and helping the outsiders succeed on an odd and unlikely mission.

Author's Other Note

A FEW LAST POINTS need to be made about the climbing of Batu Lawi. To begin with, we were not the first people to climb the mountain. The first ascent was made in 1986 by a British military group. One account says they climbed partway up the route we ascended, but were forced down by some of the more difficult climbing and opted to take very "jungly" route on the north side. I was told by the Kelabit that one of them could not get off the summit and was thus plucked off by a helicopter. In 1996 an Australian group climbed the spire as well, taking a route that criss-crossed over ours. We appear to be the first group that put a serious effort into climbing the east face of the mountain. Someday it will be a great crag, and when climbers have lots of time to spend on Batu Lawi there will be some classic routes there. Sadly, the approaching logging roads may have already given this peak a drive-in access.

Guide to Climbing Terms

AID CLIMBING VS. FREE CLIMBING

Aid climbing requires the use of equipment to move over the rock. Free climbing means to use only your hands and feet on natural holds on the rock to move over the rock. In free climbing the equipment is used only to protect the climber in the event of a fall, while in aid climbing the equipment is actually utilized as a means of ascent. While free climbing, if you pull on a single piece of gear or rest by letting the rope hold your weight, you are using aid and thus are instantly "aid climbing."

BELAY

The word belay is both a noun and a verb. To belay is to hold the rope in such a way that you can safely arrest your partner if he/she falls. The word belay also is used to describe the spot where the act of belaying has happened, as in, "He set up the belay on the ledge."

BOLT

Bolts are the safest form of protection. A small hole, usually 3/8 of an inch in diameter, is drilled and the bolt is placed in the hole. Bolts are semipermanent forms of protection, so all subsequent climbers can utilize them. The first ascentionist decides where and when a bolt can be used.

CARABINER

A snap link of aluminum used to attach various pieces of equipment while climbing. Some carabiners have gates that lock closed, giving the climber an added degree of safety.

CHIMNEY

A chimney is a crack in the wall wide enough to get your body into.

CRACK

A split in the rock face that can be utilized as a hold for climbers.

FRIEND

Made by Wild Country Equipment, a friend is a camming device that can be wedged in a crack and used as protection gear.

HOLD

A hold is any feature on the rock which can be held onto and used for upward movement.

HOOK

A hook is a bent piece of steel that can be used to snag onto the smallest of holds and thus aid the climber in ascent.

PITON

Pitons come in many shapes and sizes. They are pegs that can be nailed into cracks and then hung on for aid.

RAPPEL

To rappel is to slide down the rope using various friction devices to control your descent. This is also known as abseiling.

SLING

A section of strong nylon cord and webbing that can link together pieces of equipment.

WALL-NUT

Made by DMM Equipment, a Wall-nut is a wedge of aluminum on a steel cable that can be wedged into cracks as protection gear.

ZIPPER

The act of falling and pulling out a series of pieces of protection gear.

Bibliography

World Within: A Borneo Story, by Tom Harrisson, Cresset, 1958.

A Scientific Journey through Bario: The Kelabit Highlands of Sarawak, by the University of Malaysia, Pelanduk Publications, 1998.

The White Rajahs of Sarawak, by Robert Payne, Oxford University Press (Kuala Lumpur), 1997.

The Most Offending Soul Alive: Tom Harrisson and his Remarkable Life, by Judith M. Heimann, University of Hawaii Press, 1998.

Borneo: Australia's Proud but Tragic Heritage, by Kevin Smith, published by Kevin Smith, 2000.

Mountains of Malaysia—A Practical Guide and Manual, by John Briggs, Longman, 1988.

Borneo Log: The Struggle for Sarawak's Forests, by William W. Bevis, University of Washington Press, 1995.

The Oxford Companion to World War II, by I. C. B. Dear and M. R. D. Foot, Oxford University Press, 1995.

Rajah Brooke's Borneo, by D. J. M. Tate, Falcon Press, 1987.

A World Only Lit By Fire, by William Manchester, Back Bay Books, 1992.

The Prize: The Epic Quest for Oil, Money, and Power, by Daniel Yergin, Simon and Schuster, 1991.

American Caesar: Douglas MacArthur, 1880–1964, by William Manchester, Dell Publishing, 1978.

Reefs To Rainforests: Mangroves To Mountains, by Thom Henley, Dawn of Happiness Resort Company.

Tropical Rain Forest in South-East Asia: A Pictorial Journey, by Ken Rubeli, Tropical Press, 1986.

Stranger in the Forest: On Foot across Borneo, by Eric Hansen, Houghton Mifflin, 1988.

Sarawak Style, by Luca Invernizzi Tettoni and Edric Ong, Times Editions, 1996.

Tales From a Headhunter, by Kris Jitab, Times Books International, 1991.

Nine Dayak Nights, by W. R. Geddes, Oxford University Press, 1957.

The Oxford Handbook for Clinical Medicine, by Hope-Longmore-McManus-Wood-Allum, Oxford University Press, 1998.

Action Asia, December/January 1998, Edition 6, Vol. 6, "The Eagle Flies over Batu Lawi."

National Geographic, September 1998, Vol. 194, No. 3, "Borneo's White Mountain."

Australian Geographic, July/September 1995, No. 39, "Blade Runners."

Encarta, Microsoft, 1999.

Malaysia, Singapore, and Brunei: A Travel Survival Kit, by Geoff Crowther and Tony Wheeler, Lonely Planet, 1988.

Malaysia, by Insight Guides, APA Publications, 1994.

Borneo: Malaysia, Indonesia, and Brunei, by Robert Young Pelton, Fielding's Worldwide, 1995.

Sabah and Sarawak with Brunei Darussalam, by Wendy Hutton, Periplus Travel Guides, 1993.

Acknowledgments

Unless you have written a book of this nature, it would be hard to understand just how many people need to be thanked for their contributions. I have to thank so many acquaintances who casually mentioned a bit of information that then led me to another source, and so many people in the literary industry who offered their advice, not to mention friends who supported me when my mind was blocking out Borneo and I just couldn't write. If your name isn't here, I apologize. I owe virtually everyone I know a little something for this book.

Just getting a book published, regardless of its quality, is a desperate act and far more difficult than climbing Batu Lawi. I owe a great deal to my agent, Carolyn French, who managed to find the perfect editor. That editor, Ann Campbell, along with Amanda Gross and Catherine Pollock, who work with her at Broadway Books, has done an amazing job of working with me on this project. Ann needs to be singled out, as she truly understood how to get more out of me as a writer and how to make this manuscript into a book. She recognized some of the subtle points I was trying to make, and was able to pull more from me with just the right questions. I can't tell you how hard it is to find a good editor, and how good it is to have found the right one.

All the people at the production company and at The North Face, both of whom backed us with little background information on our adventure. I also need to thank Rob Haggart at *Outside Magazine*, who put me in contact with those two organizations, and helped make it possible for us to complete the trip. The Book Trader, my local used-book store, helped me track down some of the manuscripts I needed to reconstruct the historical narrative. Jaqui Cole and her mother, Monica, helped me get in touch with Sergeant Barrie, who in turn gave me his memoirs of the war. Kim and Kyle Mills helped me with the flow of the story and general editing, as did Deanne Musolf Crouch, Jeremy Schmidt, Gerd Schoeffl, Jim Woodmencey, Forest Dramis, and Martha Faegin. Also, the final edit done under the usual haste and stress, could not have been done without the help of Michelle Garbert.

I would also like to thank everyone who went with me to Batu Lawi, but special kudos go to Volker, Jacob, and our Kelabit porters. Volker has stood by me through thick and thin on many a climbing trip, and my appreciation for his support on this one, as well as when I was putting the manuscript together, is beyond words. Jacob Melai was caught between numerous groups during the trip and did a great job of steering all in one direction. Finally, I have to thank the Kelabit of Pa Ukat and the Bario Highlands. Without them, neither of these stories would have taken place.

SAM LIGHTNER, JR., is an internationally renowned rock climber who is credited with the first ascent of more than one hundred routes around the world, and has traveled to more than forty-five countries. He has appeared on the cover of *Outside* magazine, and his 1999 ascent of Batu Lawi was the subject of a documentary. He divides his time between Jackson Hole, Wyoming, and Thailand. He can be reached at climbborneo@hotmail.com

Made in the USA
San Bernardino, CA
28 October 2015